Who Should Read This Book?

"**R**ead" may be the wrong word. "Engage" would be better, because this is not so much a book as it is a classic text, and Jewish classics are not read so much as they are engaged. Included here are a classic text of Jewish prayer, spanning 2,000 years of Jewish experience with the world and with God; and thoughtful commentaries on that text, each one reaching back in a different way, again through 2,000 years of time. The question ought to be, "Who should engage this book in personal dialogue?"

If you like to pray, or find prayer services baffling: Whether you are Orthodox, Conservative, Reconstructionist, or Reform, you will find that *My People's Prayer Book* tells you what you need to know to pray.

- The Hebrew text here is the most authentic one we have, and the variations among the Jewish movements are described and explained. They are all treated as equally authentic.

- The translation is honest, altogether unique, and outfitted with notes comparing it to others' translations.

- Of special interest is a full description of the Halakhah (the "how-to") of prayer and the philosophy behind it.

If you are a spiritual seeker or Jewishly curious: If you have wondered what Judaism is all about, the prayer book is the place to begin. It is the one and only book that Jews read each and every day. The commentaries explain how the prayers were born and synopsize insights of founding Rabbis, medieval authorities, Chasidic masters, and modern theologians. The layout replicates the look of Jewish classics: a text surrounded by many marginal commentaries, allowing you to skip back and forth across centuries of insight.

If you are a teacher or student: This is a perfect book for adult studies, or for youth groups, teenagers, and camps. Any single page provides comparative insight from the length and breadth of Jewish tradition, about the texts that have mattered most in the daily life of the Jewish people.

If you are a scholar: Though written in friendly prose, this book is composed by scholars: professors of Bible, Rabbinics, Medieval Studies, Liturgy, Theology, Linguistics, Jewish Law, Mysticism, and Modern Jewish Thought. No other work summarizes current wisdom on Jewish prayer, drawn from so many disciplines.

If you are not Jewish: You need not be Jewish to understand this book. It provides access for everyone to the Jewish wisdom tradition. It chronicles the ongoing Jewish-Christian dialogue and the roots of Christian prayer in Christianity's Jewish origins.

The *My People's Prayer Book: Traditional Prayers, Modern Commentaries* series

My People's Passover Haggadah: Traditional Texts, Modern Commentaries

My People's Prayer Book

TRADITIONAL PRAYERS, MODERN COMMENTARIES

Vol. 10—Shabbat Morning: *Shacharit* and *Musaf* (Morning and Additional Services)

EDITED BY RABBI LAWRENCE A. HOFFMAN

CONTRIBUTORS

MARC BRETTLER

ELLIOT N. DORFF

DAVID ELLENSON

ELLEN FRANKEL

ALYSSA GRAY

JOEL M. HOFFMAN

LAWRENCE A. HOFFMAN

LAWRENCE KUSHNER

DANIEL LANDES

IVAN G. MARCUS

NEHEMIA POLEN

GORDON TUCKER

Jewish Lights Publishing

My People's Prayer Book: Traditional Prayers, Modern Commentaries
Vol. 10—Shabbat Morning: Shacharit *and* Musaf *(Morning and Additional Services)*

2011 Hardcover Edition, Second Printing

For information regarding permission to reprint material from this book, please mail or fax your request in writing to Jewish Lights Publishing, Permission Department, at the address/fax number listed below, or e-mail your request to permissions@jewishlights.com.

The excerpts on pp. 54 and 101 are reprinted from *Seyder Tkhines*, © 2005, by Devra Kay, published by The Jewish Publication Society with the permission of the publisher, The Jewish Publication Society.

© 2007 by Lawrence A. Hoffman

Library of Congress Cataloging-in-Publication Data
My people's prayer book : traditional prayers, modern commentaries / edited and with introductions by Lawrence A. Hoffman.
p.   cm.
Includes the traditional text of the siddur, English translation, and commentaries.
Contents: vol. 10. Shabbat Morning: *Shacharit* and *Musaf* (Morning and Additional Services).
ISBN: 978-1-58023-240-1 (hc)
ISBN: 978-1-68336-207-4 (pbk.)
1. Siddur. 2. Siddurim—Texts. 3. Judaism—Liturgy—Texts.
I. Hoffman, Lawrence A., 1942– . II. Siddur. English & Hebrew.
BM674.39.M96 1997
296.4'5—dc21   97-26836

CIP
First Edition

Manufactured in the United States of America
www.jewishlights.com
Published by Jewish Lights Publishing

Contents

CONTRIBUTORS

MARC BRETTLER . . . . *Our Biblical Heritage*

ELLIOT N. DORFF . . . . *Theological Reflections*

DAVID ELLENSON . . . . *How the Modern Prayer Book Evolved*

ELLEN FRANKEL . . . . *A Woman's Voice*

ALYSSA GRAY . . . . *Our Talmudic Heritage*

JOEL M. HOFFMAN . . . . *What the Prayers Really Say*

LAWRENCE A. HOFFMAN . . . . *History of the Liturgy*

LAWRENCE KUSHNER AND NEHEMIA POLEN . . *Chasidic and Mystical Perspectives*

DANIEL LANDES . . . . *The Halakhah of Prayer*

IVAN G. MARCUS . . . . *Medieval Piety*

GORDON TUCKER . . . . *Sacred Calendar*

About My People's Prayer Book

My People's Prayer Book is designed to look like a traditional Jewish book. Ever since the dawn of modern printing, Jews have arranged their books so that instead of reading in a linear fashion from the first line of the first page to the last line of the last one, readers were encouraged to linger on a single page and to consult commentaries across the gamut of Jewish thought, all at one and the same time. Every page thus contained a cross-cut of the totality of Jewish tradition.

That intellectual leap across many minds and through the centuries was accomplished by printing a text in the middle of the page and surrounding it with commentaries. Readers could scan the first line or two of the various commentaries and then choose to continue the ones that interested them most, by turning the page— more or less the way newspaper readers get a sense of everything happening on a single day by glancing at all the headlines on page one, then following select stories as they are continued on separate pages further on.

Each new rubric (or liturgical section) is, therefore, introduced in traditional style: the Hebrew prayer with translation in the middle of the page, and the beginning lines of all the commentaries in the margins. Commentaries are continued on the next page or a few pages later (the page number is provided). Readers may dwell for a while on all the comments, deciding which ones to pursue at any given sitting. They may want to compare comments, reading first one and then another. Or having decided, after a while, that a particular commentator is of special interest, they may instinctively search out the opening lines of that commentator's work, as they appear in each introductory page, and then read them through to arrive at a summary understanding of what that particular person has to say.

Introduction to the Liturgy

Shabbat Morning

Lawrence A. Hoffman

We see our landscapes differently depending on whether we travel by ship, plane, or car; or if we are just going for a walk. "One if by land; two if by sea," goes the old American tale about Paul Revere, a lasting remnant of Henry Wadsworth Longfellow's poem *Paul Revere's Ride*. We can only imagine the different view of the American colonies that British troops occasioned because they arrived one way rather than another.

Everyone knows how important it is to plot journeys according to just the right route through space, but the time of our approach is no less consequential. Nights are magical, a time for romance, or, perhaps, as Shakespeare tells us, a "witching" time "when churchyards yawn and hell itself breathes out Contagion." Mornings, by contrast, dawn bright with promise. "In the morning of the world," says Robert Browning, "Earth was nigher heaven than now." Job too recalls mornings as the time when "stars sang together, and all the sons of God shouted for joy." Especially for Jews, the route through time is what matters.

Abraham Joshua Heschel famously noted that Judaism actually prefers carving out meaning in time rather than in space. Jewish ritual becomes our "architecture in time," where Shabbat is our great "cathedral." Think of Shabbat, then, as the destination of a weekly pilgrimage that will be seen differently, depending on our approach. To be sure, once in a while we are pilgrims in space, gifted with an opportunity to visit Eretz Yisrael, the spatial epicenter of our history and our People. But every week, here at home, wherever "home" may be, we revisit our Shabbat cathedral, and the timing of our approach matters deeply. As Gordon Tucker explains in "From *Amidah* to *Amidah*: The Flow of Shabbat Time" (pp. 12–15), the view from Friday night is not the same as the approach from Saturday morning and afternoon. The sacred architecture of Shabbat allows for many vantage points.

This volume of *My People's Prayer Book* analyzes Shabbat by day, the liturgical blueprint for the historic observance of Shabbat morning. Jews who arrived here from central Europe in the nineteenth century very largely made their living as merchants—many cities still bear mostly Jewish names over faded downtown storefronts. Blue laws forced the closing of their shops on Sunday, so Saturday became a shopping day they felt they could not abandon. Friday night became their most significant approach to Shabbat's sanctuary in time. This Friday night innovation was true for almost all Jews, regardless of denomination, and still remains the case, especially for Reform synagogues that trace their heritage to that central European migration. But Orthodox, Reconstructionist, and Conservative Jews have largely reverted to the centrality of Saturday morning, and increasingly, Reform Jews too, nowadays, underscore the celebration of Shabbat by day. If Shabbat is a cathedral "in time," its liturgical architecture "by day" is especially striking.

If you wonder why the landmarks of time are liturgical, consider that time, all time, is punctuated with ritual. Time is analogic—like old-fashioned temperature thermometers, where mercury expands and time gets measured by arbitrary markings on the glass, or like clocks with sweep hands that never stop moving. But human beings like certainty; we are uneasy with neither here nor there, a little of this and that, or somewhere in between points A and B. That is why we do, in fact, inscribe numbers on thermometers and clocks. Nowadays we don't even have to do that because everything comes digitalized—temperatures and times appear magically on a screen, as if they really do proceed in fits and starts, jumping from 10:01 to 10:02 without passing through the space in between. We like digitalized precision—never mind that time doesn't really work that way.

What is true of temperatures and hours is true also of the daily and yearly cycles of human life. We stop it in its tracks, from time to time, to celebrate or mourn what would otherwise be just an uncatchable and unarrestable flow of "forever."

That is where ritual comes in. Daily meals, for example, are more than a feeding schedule. They are occasions to join others in looking forward to or back upon a day. Birthdays and anniversaries are checkpoints for our trip through life. And holidays, whether civic or religious, have their own intrinsic feel that we learn to anticipate, live through, and think about after they are gone. In American life, the ambience of July 4 is unlike that of Thanksgiving Day. For Christians, Christmas is a far cry from Easter. Canadians have Canada Day and celebrate the day after Christmas as Boxing Day; the British too keep Boxing Day, but also Guy Fawkes Day.

So, too, Jews mark time by stopping along the way. The High Holy Days do not feel like Passover; Purim is the polar opposite of Tisha B'av. And Shabbat is the queen of days, a time for rest and for joy, a remembrance of creation and Exodus. Shabbat liturgy has a shape of its own, designed to help us focus on all the spectacle of our cathedral in time.

To appreciate the architecture of Shabbat, we need to return briefly to the shape of time that the weekday liturgy provides—a topic discussed more fully in the introductions to earlier volumes of this series but easily summarized here.

2

Most worshipers know the frustration of arriving for services and being handed a prayer book that looks nothing like any other book they have ever seen. With no map of its design, its contents are confusing, more like a shapeless mass of verbiage than a carefully constructed whole; a jumble of noise, not a symphony; a blotch of random colors, hardly a masterpiece of art. But prayer *is* an art form, and like the other arts, the first step toward appreciating it is to recognize its structure.

Structure is everything. Novels don't look like poetry, but both are literary genres; someone familiar with one might at least make some sense of the other. Waltzes differ from marches, but both are examples of music. A person who knows only literature, however, would have no idea what to make of musical scores; and vice versa. So what is liturgy? Its written contents look like literature, but people "act it out," so it is really a subdivision of drama. That makes the prayer book into a kind of dramatic script. Only liturgical experts buy a prayer book to "read it," and when they do, they are like drama critics, imagining how the play will be "staged," at which time it becomes the act of prayer. To differentiate the act of prayer from the contents of the act (also called "the prayers"), we call the former just "prayer"—in the singular, without the article "a" or "the." (Another word for it is "worship.")

But prayer is a particular kind of drama. When the actress playing Lady Macbeth leaves a performance, she becomes her regular "real" self again. She is not allowed, that is, to murder someone on the way home and plead "not guilty" on the grounds that she is Lady Macbeth, and murder is just what Lady Macbeth ordinarily does. In prayer, however, we play ourselves; we are expected to internalize the lines of the script as really our own and play them out in life itself—taking the prophets seriously, for instance, and therefore committing to the worship of God and to God's will.

There is another difference too. The script of a Shakespearean drama never changes. No one changes the ending, making Romeo and Juliet rise from the dead and get married after all; no one adds a new monologue for Hamlet. But the Jewish script of prayer has changed regularly through the ages. That is where structure comes in. Despite the many changes that have entered our prayer script through the centuries, the structural integrity of Jewish prayer remains intact. Regardless of alterations that, over time, have crept into a prayer's wording, or even of a new prayer that is added somewhere, we know how to pray it by its placement in the overall liturgical structure called "a Jewish service." What, then, is the ever-present structure of a Jewish service?

The liturgy as a whole is organized by "services," which, in turn, are divided into discrete subunits called "rubrics" (the way a street is divided into blocks, some short and some long, but all part of the same street). Praying through a service entails making our way through each consecutive rubric—the way walking down a street requires going from one block to the next. Blocks differ in appearance and function— a shopping mall, for example, as opposed to the road through an apartment complex. The path through our liturgy, then, is made up of services, each one containing different "blocks" of material called rubrics, each one shaped differently from the others.

What gives each rubric its special shape is the components within it called prayers. Like city blocks, each with its own distinctive character determined by the local landscape, rubrics have character based on the kinds of prayers they contain.

In sum, the liturgy has services, the services have rubrics, and rubrics have prayers. Unfortunately, it is common also to call an entire rubric a "prayer," in which case, we should think of the liturgy as having long prayers (the rubrics) that divide into several shorter ones (a rubric's internal set of "prayers").

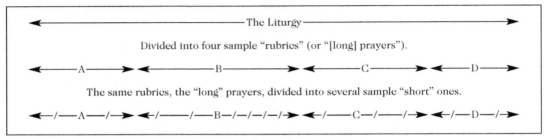

Services, Rubrics, and Prayers

Ordinary weekdays feature three services, named after the time of day when they are said: morning *(Shacharit)*, afternoon *(Minchah)*, and evening *(Ma'ariv or Arvit)*. For convenience sake, the latter two are usually recited in tandem, one just before the sun sets, and the other immediately afterward. All three follow the same basic structure, but the morning service is the longest (it has the most rubrics, seven in all); it is the only relevant one for this volume, which addresses the liturgy of Shabbat morning specifically.

The mornings of Shabbat and holy days (sometimes shortened to "holiday")—like Rosh Hashanah, Yom Kippur, Sukkot, and Passover—actually have two services within them: not just the morning service *(Shacharit)*, but an additional one following, called *Musaf* (pronounced moo-SAHF, but popularly, MOO-sahf; *Musaf* means "additional"). It was added because our various services to some extent parallel the timing of sacrifices in the Temple of old, which featured an additional offering on such sacred occasions. (For details, see L. Hoffman, "*Musaf*," p. 123, 128–129.) The standard daily and Shabbat prayer book is called a *Siddur* (pronounced see-DOOR); the holiday prayer book is a *machzor* (pronounced mahkh-ZOHR).

The Siddur, then, is made up of services; each service consists of rubrics; each rubric has prayers; and sometimes rubrics are called prayers, in which case their components are prayers as well. We said above that the character of rubrics depends on the kinds of prayers they contain. Not all prayers are alike, that is. Some are biblical quotations, ranging in size from a single line to entire chapters, usually psalms. There are citations from rabbinic literature also, chunks of Mishnah or Talmud that serve as a sort of Torah study within the service. Medieval poetry is found here too, familiar things like *Adon Olam* or older staples (called *piyyutim* [pronounced pee-yoo-TEEM]; sing., *piyyut* [pee-YOOT]) marked less by rhyme and rhythm than by clever word plays and alphabetic acrostics. And there are long passages of prose, the work (again) of medieval spiritual masters but couched in standard rabbinic style without regard for poetic rules.

Most of these prose passages are what we call blessings, a uniquely rabbinic vehicle for addressing God, and the primary liturgical expression of Jewish spirituality. Blessings (known also as "benedictions" or, in Hebrew, *b'rakhot* [pronounced b'-rah-KHOT]; sing., *b'rakhah* [b-'rah-KHAH]) are so familiar that Jewish worshipers take them for granted. We are mostly aware of "short blessings," the one-line formulas that are customarily recited over bread and wine, for instance, or prior to performing a commandment (like lighting Shabbat candles). But there are "long blessings" too, whole paragraphs or even sets of paragraphs on a given theme. These are best thought of as small theological essays on such topics as deliverance, the sanctity of time, the rebuilding of Jerusalem, and the like. They sometimes start with the words *Barukh atah Adonai ...* ("Blessed are You, Adonai ..."), and then they are easily spotted. But more often they begin with no particular verbal formula and are hard to identify until their last line, which invariably does say *Barukh atah Adonai ...* ("Blessed are You, Adonai ...") followed by a short synopsis of the blessing's theme ("... who sanctifies the Sabbath," "... who hears prayer," "... who redeems Israel," and so forth). This final summarizing sentence is called a *chatimah* (pronounced khah-tee-MAH), meaning a "seal," like the seal made from a signet ring that seals an envelope.

The bulk of the service, as it was laid down in antiquity, consists of strings of blessings, one after the other, or of biblical quotations bracketed by blessings that introduce and conclude them. By the tenth century the creation of blessings largely ceased, and eventually Jewish law actually opposed the coining of new ones on the grounds that post-talmudic Judaism was too spiritually depleted to emulate the literary work of the giants of the Jewish past. Not all Jews agree with that assessment today, but the traditional liturgy that forms our text here contains no blessings from later than the tenth century.

At the liturgy's core are three rubrics:

1. The *Sh'ma* [pronounced sh'-MAH] and Its Blessings.
2. The *Amidah*—known also as the *T'fillah* (pronounced t'-fee-LAH, or, popularly, t'-FEE-lah). The daily version is also called *Sh'moneh Esreh* (pronounced sh'-moh-NEH ehs-RAY, or, popularly, sh'MOH-neh EHS-ray).
3. The public reading of Torah.

The *Sh'ma* and Its Blessings and the *Amidah* are recited daily—the former twice (morning and night) and the latter at every service. Indeed, theoretically, a service is not technically a service without an *Amidah*, since the *Amidah* is said to be a stand-in for the ancient sacrifices that were the original "services" to God. Torah is read on Monday and Thursday (market days in antiquity, when crowds were likely to gather), and on Shabbat and holy days, of course.

The *Sh'ma* and Its Blessings is essentially a Jewish creed, a statement of what Jews have traditionally affirmed about God, the cosmos, and our human relationship to God and to history. The *Amidah* is largely petitionary (though less so on Shabbat, as we will see later). The Torah reading is a recapitulation of Sinai, an attempt to discover the will of God through sacred scripture. Since the *Sh'ma* and Its Blessings begins the official service, it features a communal Call to Prayer at the beginning: our familiar *Bar'khu* (pronounced bah-r'-KHOO, or, popularly, BAH-r'-khoo).

We come now, finally, to a detailed look at the underlying structure. Rubrics build upon each other in a crescendo-like manner.

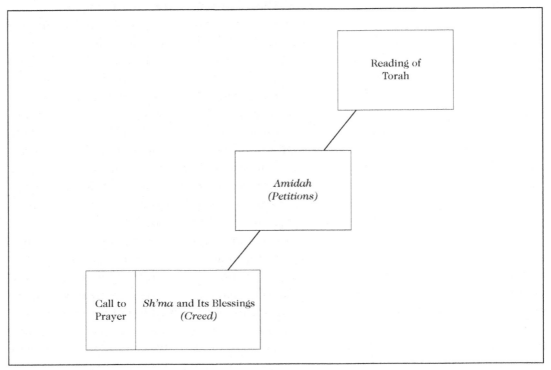

Three Basic Rubrics: Sh'ma, Amidah, *Reading of Torah*

It is, however, hard for individuals who are normally distracted by everyday concerns to constitute a community given over wholeheartedly to prayer. Already in the second century, therefore, we hear of some Rabbis who assembled prior to the actual Call to Prayer in order to sing psalms of praise known as *Hallel* (pronounced hah-LAYL, or, popularly, HAH-layl); and even before that—at home, not the synagogue—it was customary to begin the day immediately upon awakening by reciting a series of daily blessings along with some study texts. By the ninth century, if not earlier, these two units too had become mandatory, and the introductory home ritual for awakening had moved to the synagogue, which is where we have it today. The warm-up section of psalms is called *P'sukei D'zimrah* (pronounced p'soo-KAY d'-zim-RAH, or, popularly, p-SOO-kay d'-ZIM-rah), meaning "Verses of Song"; the prior recital of daily blessings and study texts is called *Birkhot Hashachar* (pronounced beer-KHOT hah-SHAH-khar, or, popularly, BEER-khot hah-SHAH-khar), "Morning Blessings." Since they now precede the main body of the service, gradually building up to it, the larger diagram expands.

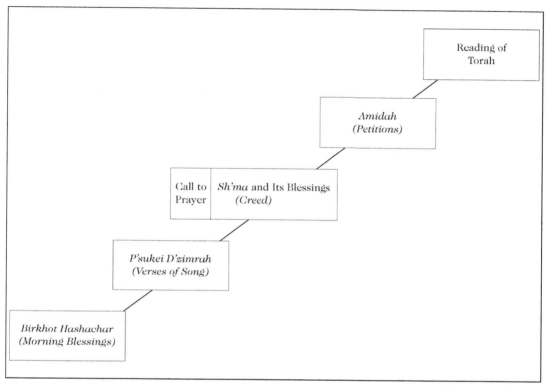

Rubrics Expand from Three to Five

Two other expansions of this basic structure probably occurred in the first two centuries C.E., although our evidence for their being that early is less certain.

First, a conclusion was added. It featured a final prayer called the *Kaddish* (pronounced kah-DEESH, or, popularly, KAH-dish), which eventually became associated with mourning, but began in conjunction with Torah study, and closed the service by looking ahead to the coming of God's ultimate reign of justice. Eventually other prayers were added to the conclusion, including the *Alenu* (pronounced ah-LAY-noo), which had originally been composed as an introduction to the blowing of the shofar on Rosh Hashanah, but was moved here in the Middle Ages.

Second, the Rabbis, who were keenly aware of the limits to human mortality, advised all Jews to come to terms daily with their frailty and ethical imperfection. To do so, they provided an opportunity for a silent confession following the *Amidah* but before the Torah reading. In time, this evolved into silent prayer in general, an opportunity for individuals to assemble their most private thoughts before God. Later still, sometime in the Middle Ages, it expanded on average weekdays into an entire set of supplicatory prayers called the *Tachanun* (pronounced tah-khah-NOON, or, popularly, TAH-khah-noon).

The daily service was thus passed down to us with shape and design. Beginning with daily blessings that celebrate the new day and emphasize the study of sacred texts *(Birkhot Hashachar)*, it continues with songs and psalms *(P'sukei D'zimrah)* that create the environment for prayer. There then follows the core of the liturgy: an official Call to Prayer *(Bar'khu)*, the recital of Jewish belief (the *Sh'ma* and Its Blessings), and communal petitions (the *Amidah*). Individuals pause next to speak privately to God in silent prayer (later expanded into the *Tachanun*), and then, on select days, they read from Torah. The whole concludes with a final *Kaddish*, to which other prayers were added eventually, most notably the *Alenu*.

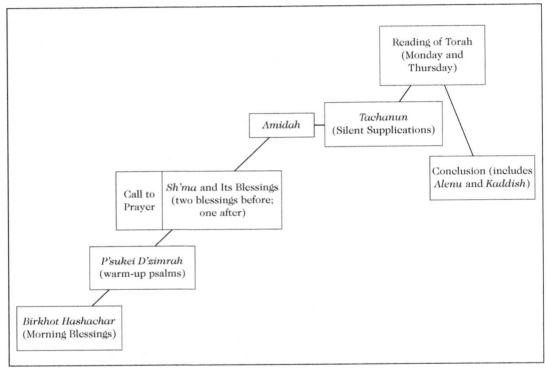

Morning Service as a Whole

SHABBAT MORNING SERVICES: WHAT TO LOOK FOR

On Shabbat and holidays, this basic structure expands to admit special material relevant to the day in question and contracts to omit prayers that are inappropriate for the occasion. Though a place for private prayer remains, its crystallization as a formal set of petitions called *Tachanun* is omitted, since these specially sacred days are felt to be so perfect in themselves as to make petitioning unnecessary. So, too, the middle thirteen petitions of the *Amidah* are excluded, as they are considered especially petitionary in nature. In place of these intermediary blessings, we find a single blessing called *K'dushat Hayom* (pronounced k'-doo-SHAHT hah-YOHM, or, popularly, k'-DOO-shaht hah-

YOHM), meaning "The Sanctification of the Day"—a blessing that declares the holiness of the day in question.

But an entire service is added, a service called *Musaf* (literally, "Addition"), said to correspond to the extra sacrifice that once characterized Shabbat worship in the Temple. Similarly, a prophetic reading called the *Haftarah* (pronounced hahf-tah-RAH, or, popularly, hahf-TOH-rah) joins the Torah reading; and extra psalms and readings for the Sabbath are inserted here and there. The same is true for holidays, when, in addition, numerous *piyyutim* are said, especially for the High Holy Days, when the sheer size of the liturgy seems to get out of hand. But even there, the basic structure remains intact, so that those who know its intrinsic shape can get beyond what looks like random verbiage to find the genius behind the liturgy's design.

We can replicate the diagram on page 8—the final shape of the daily morning service—and chart the major differences for Shabbat with dotted lines that culminate in arrows. See "Morning Service with Shabbat Changes," p. 10.

Each change (at the end of the arrows) represents a Shabbat change that is detailed in the pages of this volume. To be precise, they are as follows:

A. *SHACHARIT* (THE MORNING SERVICE)

1. *P'sukei D'zimrah*

   a. Additional psalms (we include just Psalm 136—the "Great *Hallel*"—as representative of them all).

   b. An extension of the final blessing, called the "Blessing of Song" (*Birkat Hashir* [pronounced beer-KAHT hah-SHEER, or, popularly, BEER-kaht hah-SHEER]).

2. The *Sh'ma* and Its Blessings: An extension of the first blessing, the *Yotser* (pronounced yoh-TSAYR, or, popularly, YOH-tsayr), meaning "who creates," and alluding to the blessing's theme, God's creation of the universe.

3. The *Amidah*

   a. Unique Shabbat wording for the third blessing, the *K'dushat Hashem* (pronounced k'-doo-SHAHT hah-SHEM, or, popularly, k'DOO-shaht hah-SHEM), the "Sanctification of God's Name"—a celebration of God's unique sanctity.

   b. The replacement of the middle petitionary blessings with a *K'dushat Hayom*, a single blessing announcing the "Sanctification of the Day."

4. Torah reading: On weekdays, Torah is read publicly only on Mondays and Thursdays; its reading on Shabbat is longer, as is the set of prayers accompanying it. (These are omitted here, since they are discussed in Volume 4, *Seder K'riat Hatorah: The Torah Service.*)

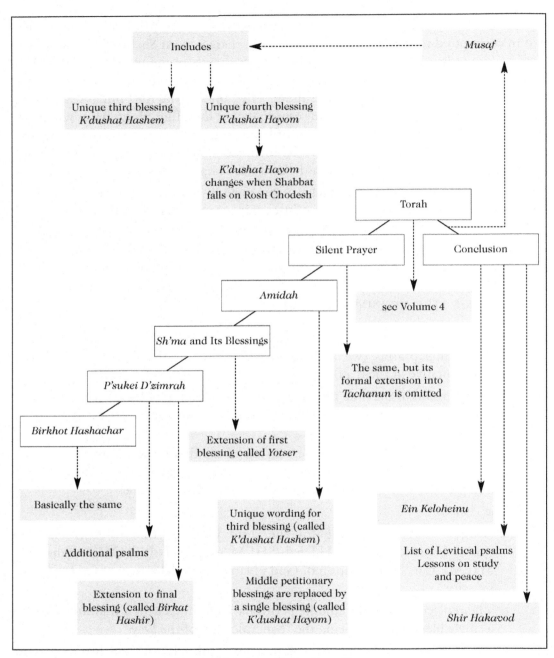

Morning Service with Shabbat Changes

B. *MUSAF* (THE ADDITIONAL SERVICE FOR SHABBAT)

1. The third blessing of the *Amidah*, *K'dushat Hashem*.
2. The fourth (or middle) blessing of the *Amidah*, *K'dushat Hayom*.
3. The fourth blessing *(K'dushat Hayom)* when Shabbat falls on the new moon, Rosh Chodesh (pronounced rohsh KHOH-desh).

C. CONCLUSION (NOW CONCLUDES *MUSAF*, NOT, AS ON WEEKDAYS, *SHACHARIT*)

1. A concluding song, *Ein Keloheinu* (pronounced AYN kay-loh-HAY-noo), meaning "There is none like our God."
2. A final hymn, *Shir Hakavod* (pronounced SHEER hah-kah-VOHD), meaning "Song of Glory."

There are, of course, other, smaller changes incurred by Shabbat, but these are the major ones, as found in a traditional Siddur. Various movements treat them differently, but regardless of denomination or prayer book, all Jews follow the same service structure, and all of us replicate these highlights one way or another. Consider this a guidebook to the architecture of the Jewish cathedral in time. Carry it with you, at least in your mind, the next time you attend services on Shabbat morning. Let this book guide you to a new understanding of what is easily among the greatest Jewish contributions to civilization: the Shabbat, a day of rest, of joy, and of memory.

From Amidah *to* Amidah

The Flow of Shabbat Time

Gordon Tucker

No Jew whose life is marked by regular daily worship can avoid the challenge of repetitiveness in the liturgy. Three times each day an *Amidah* (standing prayer with nineteen *b'rakhot* [blessings]) is recited, all three essentially identical to one another. What's more, given the long-standing Jewish practice to hold the afternoon and evening (*Minchah* and *Ma'ariv* [*Arvit*]) services back-to-back around sunset, two identical *Amidot* are likely to be recited within a few minutes of each other. Fulfilling the rabbinic ideal of experiencing something new in every prayer can thus be difficult.

On Shabbat, however, the challenge is not to find freshness in the midst of *repetition*, but rather to experience the meaning of a liturgical *journey*.

Let's backtrack for a moment. In the usual daily *Amidah*, the middle thirteen of the nineteen blessings address God with a range of physical, political, and spiritual needs. On Shabbat and holy days, these thirteen petitionary *b'rakhot* are replaced by a single *b'rakhah*, which takes note of the sanctity of the day. There are thus a total of seven *b'rakhot* in each *Amidah* for Shabbat and Festivals, and it is the fourth, or middle, one that carries the message of the day. That middle blessing varies with each Shabbat service, thereby providing a guide through the Shabbat experience that begins with sunset Friday night and ends as the sun goes down again late Saturday afternoon.

There are actually four prayer services on Shabbat, since *Musaf* (the "additional" service) is added to the standard three daily ones. We shall not focus on *Musaf* here, because its purpose is clear: to commemorate the additional sacrifice on Shabbat and holy days in the ancient Temple. As such, its middle *b'rakhah* specifically recalls the Temple service. It is rather the three standard prayer services *(Ma'ariv, Shacharit,* and *Minchah)* that interest us. Let us begin in the middle, neither Friday evening (when Shabbat starts) nor late Saturday afternoon (when it ends), but with the *Amidah* for Shabbat morning *(Shacharit)*. What do we find when we look at the fourth *b'rakhah* there?

The general theme of the fourth blessing in all three instances is the sanctity of the Sabbath day, but here we find much greater specificity. The blessing begins rather abruptly with a description of Moses's feeling of pride "with what he received as his portion." Several times in this *b'rakhah*, the Hebrew root *n.t.n* ("to give") appears, as does the word *b'rit* ("covenant"). The blessing is a mini-essay about the *giving* of Torah at Mount Sinai, a *gift* that (1) established the covenant between God and Israel and (2) confirmed Moses's standing as the greatest of the prophets (hence his pride).

The middle *Amidah* blessing for both Friday night (*Ma'ariv*) and Saturday morning (*Shacharit*) features an extended biblical citation on the subject of Shabbat. The biblical passage for *Shacharit* comes from Exodus 31, a chapter whose setting is the foot of Mount Sinai, with the people anxiously awaiting Moses's return. Why is this standing at Mount Sinai the specific theme for Shabbat morning? It is true, of course, that the commandment to observe Shabbat is on the tablets that Moses brought down from Sinai. But Shabbat is only one-tenth of that revelation, and in any case, what is Sinai's special significance to Shabbat *morning*?

The answer becomes clear only when the other two *Amidot* for Shabbat are similarly examined.

We move then from Saturday morning back to the beginning of Shabbat, Friday night. Looking at the middle *b'rakhah* in this liturgical composition, we find Moses missing: God is the *only* character here. God creates Shabbat as the "exclamation point" on all of creation, and God sanctifies it. The root for "sanctify," *k.d.sh*, appears exactly *seven* times in this *b'rakhah*, an allusion to its being the seventh day, perhaps, but in any case underscoring the primeval nature of Sabbath sanctity—which was bestowed on this day of days even before people were, or could be, involved in celebrating it. Created only sometime during the sixth day (Friday), human beings were only hours old when the first Shabbat dawned as God's sacred moment in time. The Friday evening *Amidah*, in other words, takes us back to the beginning, before human history began—to creation itself, when everything was "very good." As we might expect, the extended biblical passage cited here is from Genesis 2, "Heaven and earth and everything associated with them were completed ..."—a description of the very first Shabbat when "God blessed the seventh day and *sanctified* it," at the end of the week of creation.

Last, we come to the *Amidah* for *Minchah*, Saturday afternoon. Once again, the stylistic repetition of verbal roots displays the preferred topics of the middle blessing. In this case two prominent themes become apparent: "unity" (*achdut*) and "rest" (*m'nuchah*). This is a vision of a world at rest, because ever since the Sabbath's creation (Friday night), and its entering human history at Sinai (Saturday morning), it is a world perfected and whole. Unlike the night before, God is not alone anymore; but unlike the morning *Shacharit* service, it is not Moses who is featured, but the patriarchs, Abraham, Isaac, and Jacob, symbols of a world inhabited by human beings who play out God's plans in the universe. Strikingly, however, they appear not just as finite historical characters, but also as timeless symbols of godly devotion who *delight* in what we might call the "Sabbath of the future"—or, more accurately, the "timeless Sabbath."

The *Amidah* of Shabbat *Minchah* therefore presents the fulfillment of history, painted for us in the darkening hours of Shabbat afternoon.

The distinctive versions of the *Amidah* for the three Shabbat services present us with the triad made famous much later by Franz Rosenzweig (1886–1929): creation, revelation, and redemption.

On Friday evening we recall the world's coming into being, brimming with all of its unrealized potential.

On Saturday morning we relive the revelation at Sinai, which covenanted us to a way of life that prominently includes Shabbat itself and that enables us to fulfill the world's, and our, potential.

And on Saturday afternoon, as the new cycle of the workweek looms more immediately before us, we strengthen ourselves with a renewed vision of a world redeemed, a world that we will actualize through the work we do in the coming week, in accord with our covenantal responsibility. The Friday night moment of creation was "very good," but Saturday afternoon's vision is even better—it is of a world redeemed, a world made perfect as the consummation of unity and peace.

But there is only one way for us to bridge the world created as "very good" and the world perfected as "the world redeemed." It is for us, as God's partners in creation, to become God's agents of redemption by committing ourselves to the teaching of Torah, to Moses's legacy, from Saturday morning. In the romantic dusks of Friday and Saturday evenings, we may dream idyllically of past and future. But in the bright light of Shabbat morning, we are to recognize that only through human actions, only by becoming disciples of the greatest of our teachers, only through the gift that God gave Moses, can God's purposes be fulfilled. Torah is the bridge from creation to redemption, the only way to get from a world "very good" to a world redeemed as perfect.

This is the liturgical journey that we are guided through by the Shabbat services. We had no hand in creation. But through revelation of Torah, we may acquire a saving role in redemption. That is our weekly curriculum.

Finally, there is a paradox here of great significance. We began with the thrice-daily repetitiveness of the daily *Amidah*. In fact, even the Festival days display this repetitiveness. But for very minor variations, the *Amidot* for *Ma'ariv*, *Shacharit*, and *Minchah* on the Pilgrimage Festivals, on Rosh Hashanah, and even on Yom Kippur are indistinguishable from one another. It is on the weekly Shabbat, and only then, that we are taken on a liturgical journey through the day and are confronted with a challenge of progress. Now herein lies the paradox. Shabbat presents itself to us as the day that stands outside of time, the day on which our quotidian tasks and endeavors cease, and we rest. How is it that on the days on which we feverishly work, frantically trying to achieve the goals we have set, we have no sense of progression in our prayers, and yet on the day of rest, a significant cosmic journey is enacted? Perhaps it is precisely that the life's journeys we define for ourselves are not always the true journeys, and the liturgical journeys are there to correct that. On the workdays on which we labor to make progress in our private spheres, we so often add precious little to the world, and to an outside observer, we would in effect be running in place. The sometimes experienced monotony of the daily prayers may serve to remind us of that. And suddenly, on the day on which we may furtively lament that our all-important private efforts must be curtailed, on the day on which we may feel as if those not observing Shabbat may be getting ahead of us, we are taught that this process of reflection and prayer may be the only way to learn for the coming week the secret of the progress of which God wants us to be part.

Introduction to the Commentaries

How to Look for Meaning in the Prayers

Lawrence A. Hoffman

THE ART OF JEWISH READING

I remember the day I looked at a manuscript of a prayer book that no one could identify. It had been smuggled out of Russia (then the Soviet Union), and was obviously the liturgy for Rosh Hashanah, but who had written it? And when? It was handwritten, so the style told us much, but in addition, someone had written marginal notes in another handwriting, and yet a third person had written comments to the comments— a third unknown scholar of years gone by whose name we wanted to rescue from oblivion.

Standing before the massive volume, I reflected on the sheer joy of studying a traditional Jewish text. I had seen printed versions before, but never a handwritten instance. What a wonderful habit we Jews developed once upon a time: writing a text in the middle of the page and then filling up the margins with commentaries. Every page becomes a crosscut through Jewish history. Jewish Bibles come that way; so do the Talmud, the Mishnah, and the codes. We never read just the text. We always read it through the prism of the way other people have read it.

To be a Jewish reader, then, is to join the ranks of the millions of readers who came before us, leaving their comments in the margins, the way animals leave tracks in the woods. Go deep into the forest and you will come across deer runs, for example: paths to water sources carved out by hundreds of thousands of deer over time. The deer do not just inhabit the forest; they are part of the forest—they change the forest's contours as they live there, just as the forest changes them, by offering shelter, food, and water. There is no virgin forest, really; it is an ecosystem, a balance between the vegetation and the animals who live there.

So, too, there are no virgin texts. They are also ecosystems, sustaining millions of readers over time. When we read our classic texts, we tread the paths of prior readers, in search of spiritual nourishment. *My People's Prayer Book* is therefore not just

16

the Siddur text; it is the text as read by prominent readers from among the people. You are invited to share our path, and even to break new ground yourself, passing on to others your own marginal notes, should you wish.

THE LITURGICAL TEXT WE USE

This volume completes the liturgy for weekdays and Shabbat. The daily liturgy is discussed in the first seven volumes; Volumes 8 and 9 provide the prayers of Sabbath eve. With Volume 10, *Shabbat Morning*, we supply the alterations and additions that convert the daily morning service into its Shabbat equivalent.

As with prior volumes, our version depends primarily on the Siddur as provided by Philip Birnbaum. Back in 1949 Birnbaum labored over a Siddur that would contain the traditional liturgy in a modern scientific format. He combined the standard Ashkenazi rite with some modifications that had crept in and become popular in America. More than any other text, it is Birnbaum's that has met the test of time and that best represents the traditional liturgy most North Americans know best.

The final text was then translated by Joel M. Hoffman, in consultation with Marc Brettler. The translation strives to reproduce not only the content of the original Hebrew, but also its tone, register, and style, so as to bring to modern readers the same experience (to the greatest extent possible) that the original authors would have conveyed with their words. In terms of content, we assume that, by and large, words have meaning only to the extent that they contribute to sentences and concepts—as, for example, "by and large," which has nothing to do with "by" or "large."

We try to reproduce a tone and register similar to the original text: formal, but not archaic; prose or poetry, depending on the Hebrew. Where the Hebrew uses obscure words, we try to do the same, and where it uses common idiom, we try to use equally common idiom. Parallel structure and other similar literary devices found in the Hebrew are replicated as much as possible in the English translation. Our translations are best appreciated if they are read in conjunction with the running commentary by Joel M. Hoffman that describes why one set of words was chosen rather than another.

We have not doctored the translation of the text to make it more palatable to modern consciousness. Blatant sexisms are retained, for instance, wherever we think the author intended them. We depend upon our commentaries to bridge the gap between the translation of the original and our modern sensibilities.

Some readers have asked why the translation in prior volumes (and this one too) refers so frequently to the Septuagint, called also the LXX. The Septuagint (which means "seventy"—hence the Roman numerals LXX to refer to it) is an ancient Greek translation from the third century B.C.E. As such, it often provides alternative understandings of the biblical text that allow us to get closer to the meaning of the original Hebrew.

The Septuagint covers only biblical passages, of course; there is no such parallel for the Siddur. To begin with, the Siddur is not that old, but more important, its prayers were never canonized the way the Bible was. We have no single translation that provides the "right" prayer book wording from antiquity. Reliable attempts at scientifically accurate translation go back only to the nineteenth century. David Ellenson surveys them (and more recent works as well), not for purposes of our own translation, but to see what the translations (and emendations) of others tell us about the Jewish journey through modernity. As to our translation, however, it became evident that we do not have room to compare and cross-reference all the fine prayerbook translations available today, not even those in general use at the moment. But it seemed a good idea to refer at least to one of them with some frequency, providing interesting alternatives to our own choices. Having chosen the Hebrew text of Philip Birnbaum, we decided to use also the Birnbaum English as the normative "standard" to which our own translation should be compared.

THE COMMENTARIES AND THEIR SOURCES

The heart and soul of *Minhag Ami* is its choice of commentaries that surround the prayerbook text. Translator Joel M. Hoffman explains his choice of words, provides alternatives, and compares his own translation with others. Marc Brettler comments on the way the Bible is embedded in the Siddur. Ellen Frankel ("A Woman's Voice") and Elliot N. Dorff provide theological reflections on what the prayers might mean, should mean, could mean, cannot mean, or have to mean (even if we wish they didn't). Alyssa Gray presents talmudic commentary, and Daniel Landes gives us the Halakhah of prayer, the rules and traditions by which this sacred liturgical drama has traditionally been carried out. Lawrence Kushner and Nehemia Polen supply a kabbalistic commentary, adding wisdom from the world of Chasidic masters, and David Ellenson (to whom we referred above) surveys liberal prayer books of the last two hundred years to see how their writers agonized over attempts to update this book of Jewish books for modern times.

My own historical commentary had to deal with the fact that we used the Birnbaum Siddur intended only for Ashkenazi Jews—more specifically, the Ashkenazi version common in Eastern Europe, often under the influence of Elijah ben Solomon of Vilna, known as the *Gra*, or Vilna Gaon (1720–1797). To balance the picture, I sometimes cite Sefardi practice also. But the word "Sefardi" has two distinct meanings.

Nowadays it usually describes Jews whose liturgy was influenced by Chasidism and the specific brand of Kabbalah initiated by Isaac Luria (the *Ari*) in sixteenth-century Palestine. Master liturgist and scholar of texts E. Daniel Goldschmidt compiled a scientific edition of this variant, and I used that to represent "Sefardi practice." But "Sefardi" can also mean the old Spanish-Portuguese custom carried by Jews from Spain in 1492 and then brought to the Netherlands, whence it moved to

England (among other places) and eventually to America as well. When I want to draw attention to this Spanish-Portuguese custom, I call it that, using as my guide the standard work published in England at the turn of the twentieth century by Moses Gaster, *The Book of Prayer and Order of Service According to the Custom of the Spanish and Portuguese Jews*; and David de Sola Pool's more recent 1983 edition of *Book of Prayer According to the Custom of the Spanish and Portuguese Jews*. At times I cite *Seder Rav Amram* and *Siddur Saadiah*, the first two Jewish prayer books of which we are aware, from ninth- and tenth-century Babylon. At times I also use the Genizah fragments, manuscripts that tell us how Jews prayed in the Land of Israel prior to the Crusades.

Two additions to this volume make it stand out as especially unique. The first is by Ivan G. Marcus, a renowned expert in a medieval school of mystics known as *Chasidei Ashkenaz*. Our Shabbat *Musaf* service concludes with a poem traced to one of this group's founders, Rabbi Judah the Pietist (Yehudah Hechasid; d. 1217). As a poem with esoteric meaning, however, a simple translation misses much of the underlying point. The commentary that Marcus provides gives us insight into the mystical doctrines to which the poem alludes.

As with all other volumes in this series, I provide an introduction ("Shabbat Morning," pp. 1–11) that examines the organization of the liturgy, so that readers can see the logic and aesthetics of its structure. Gordon Tucker provides a second introduction, "From *Amidah* to *Amidah*: The Flow of Shabbat Time" (pp. 12–15), which traces the progression of themes in the three Shabbat services that differ from their weekday version (*Ma'ariv* of Friday night; *Shacharit* of Saturday afternoon; and *Minchah* of Saturday afternoon).

As in previous volumes, our commentators are likely to refer to Halakhah (Jewish law), a topic that deserves its own introduction here, since it is so essential to Judaism, but is not easily accessible to Western readers. Frequently misunderstood as mere legalism, it is actually more akin to Jewish poetry in that it is the height of Jewish writing, the pinnacle of Jewish concern, sheer joy to create or to ponder. It describes, explains, and debates Jewish responsibility, yet is saturated with spiritual importance. Jewish movements can be differentiated by their approach to Halakhah, but Halakhah matters to them all.

The topic of Halakhah is the proper performance of the commandments, said to number 613 and divided into positive and negative ones, numbering 248 and 365 respectively. Strictly speaking, commandments derived directly from Torah (*d'ora'ita*) are of a higher order than those rooted only in rabbinic ordinance (called *d'rabbanan*), but all are binding.

The earliest stratum of Halakhah is found primarily in the Mishnah, a code of Jewish practice promulgated around 200 C.E. The Mishnah is the foundation for further rabbinic discussion in Palestine and Babylonia, which culminated in the two Talmuds, one from each center, called the Palestinian Talmud (or the Yerushalmi) and the Babylonian Talmud (or the Bavli). While dates for both are uncertain, the former is customarily dated to about 400 C.E., and the latter between 550 and 650.

With the canonization of the Bavli, Jewish law developed largely by means of commentary to the Talmuds; and of responsa, applications of talmudic and other precedents to actual cases. These are still the norm today, but they were initiated by authorities in Babylonia called Geonim (sing., Gaon) from about 750 to shortly after 1000. By the turn of the millennium, other schools had developed in North Africa and western Europe. Authorities in these centers are usually called *Rishonim* ("first" or "early" [ones]) until the sixteenth century, when they become known as *Acharonim* ("last" or "later" [ones]).

The first law code is geonic (from about 750), but it was the *Rishonim* who really inaugurated the trend toward codifying, giving us many works, including three major ones that are widely cited here: the *Mishneh Torah*, by Maimonides (Moses ben Maimon, also known as *Rambam*, 1135–1204), born in Spain, but active most of his life in Egypt; the *Tur*, by Jacob ben Asher (1275–1340), son of another giant, Asher ben Yechiel, who had moved to Spain from Germany, allowing Ashkenazi and Sefardi practices to intertwine in his son's magnum opus; and the *Shulchan Arukh*, by Joseph Caro (1488–1575), who also wrote influential commentaries on both the *Mishneh Torah* and the *Tur* before composing what would become the most widely used Jewish legal corpus ever.

Several commentaries here draw centrally on these sources, and not just for halakhic guidance, but for historical information as well. Most of what Jews have written through the ages has been halakhic in nature, so reconstructions of Jewish ritual at any stage of its development, and even the theological assumptions that underlie it, must often be reconstructed from legal sources that purport only to tell us what to do, but end up telling us why as well.

There is no way to convey the richness of even one of these works, let alone the legion of other sources in Jewish tradition on which *My People's Prayer Book* draws. Suffice it to say that the commentaries that follow access many of the greatest works of our people.

The authors of the commentaries represent a panoply of contemporary scholars, all students of the prayerbook text, and all committed to a life of prayer, but representative of left, right, and center in the Jewish world. As editor, I could not ask for a more scholarly and helpful group of colleagues; I am indebted to every one of them, who have together made the editing of this series a joy. Deserving of mention also is medievalist Sharon Koren, who advised me on my own depiction of the *Chasidei Ashkenaz*.

These wonderful colleagues are matched by the many people at Jewish Lights who have supported this volume energetically. Emily Wichland handles all publication details with the kind of love and care that is rare. Stuart M. Matlins, founder of Jewish Lights Publishing, takes personal pride in this series—as well he should. He helped conceptualize it from the start and remains its most ardent supporter. I am grateful for the privilege of working with a publisher as astute and spiritually committed as Stuart. Finally, my thanks are due to Debra Corman, who so arduously and lovingly read and corrected the final manuscript.

The people mentioned here represent all of us, all of *Am Yisrael*, all of those God had in mind when God said to Ezekiel (34:30), "They shall know that I, Adonai their God, am with them, and they, the House of Israel, are my people." Unabashedly scholarly and religious at one and the same time, *Minhag Ami*, "A Way of Prayer for My People," will be deemed a success if it provides the spiritual insight required to fulfill yet another prophecy (Isa. 52:6), that through our prayers,

> My people [*ami*] may know my name
> That they may know, therefore, in that day,
> That I, the One who speaks,
> Behold! Here I am.

1 | Shacharit ("Morning Service")

A. *P'SUKEI D'ZIMRAH* ("VERSES OF SONG"): MORNING "WARM-UP" PRAYERS

I. PSALM 136

1 Give thanks to Adonai for He is good. For his love is everlasting.

2 Give thanks to the God of gods. For his love is everlasting.

3 Give thanks to the Lord of lords. For his love is everlasting.

4 To the One who alone does great wonders. For his love is everlasting.

5 To the One who wisely created the sky. For his love is everlasting.

6 To the One who spread out the earth on the water. For his love is everlasting.

7 To the One who created the great lights. For his love is everlasting.

8 The sun to be ruler by day. For his love is everlasting.

9 The moon and stars to be rulers by night. For his love is everlasting.

10 To the One who struck Egypt through their first-born. For his love is everlasting.

11 And who brought Israel out from their midst. For his love is everlasting.

12 With a strong hand and an outstretched arm. For his love is everlasting.

1 הוֹדוּ לַיָי כִּי טוֹב. כִּי לְעוֹלָם חַסְדּוֹ.

2 הוֹדוּ לֵאלֹהֵי הָאֱלֹהִים. כִּי לְעוֹלָם חַסְדּוֹ.

3 הוֹדוּ לַאֲדֹנֵי הָאֲדֹנִים. כִּי לְעוֹלָם חַסְדּוֹ.

4 לְעֹשֵׂה נִפְלָאוֹת גְּדֹלוֹת לְבַדּוֹ. כִּי לְעוֹלָם חַסְדּוֹ.

5 לְעֹשֵׂה הַשָּׁמַיִם בִּתְבוּנָה. כִּי לְעוֹלָם חַסְדּוֹ.

6 לְרוֹקַע הָאָרֶץ עַל הַמָּיִם. כִּי לְעוֹלָם חַסְדּוֹ.

7 לְעֹשֵׂה אוֹרִים גְּדֹלִים. כִּי לְעוֹלָם חַסְדּוֹ.

8 אֶת הַשֶּׁמֶשׁ לְמֶמְשֶׁלֶת בַּיּוֹם. כִּי לְעוֹלָם חַסְדּוֹ.

9 אֶת הַיָּרֵחַ וְכוֹכָבִים לְמֶמְשְׁלוֹת בַּלָּיְלָה. כִּי לְעוֹלָם חַסְדּוֹ.

10 לְמַכֵּה מִצְרַיִם בִּבְכוֹרֵיהֶם. כִּי לְעוֹלָם חַסְדּוֹ.

¹³ To the One who split the Red Sea. For his love is everlasting.

¹⁴ And brought Israel through it. For his love is everlasting.

¹⁵ And shook Pharaoh and his army in the Red Sea. For his love is everlasting.

¹⁶ To the One who led his people through the desert. For his love is everlasting.

¹⁷ To the One who struck great kings. For his love is everlasting.

¹⁸ And killed mighty kings. For his love is everlasting.

¹⁹ Sichon, king of the Amorites. For his love is everlasting.

²⁰Og, king of Bashan. For his love is everlasting.

²¹ And gave their land as a heritage. For his love is everlasting.

²² A heritage to Israel his servant. For his love is everlasting.

²³ Who remembered us when we were low. For his love is everlasting.

²⁴ And set us free from our enemies. For his love is everlasting.

²⁵ Who gives food to all creatures. For his love is everlasting.

²⁶ Give thanks to the God of heaven. For his love is everlasting.

¹¹וַיּוֹצֵא יִשְׂרָאֵל מִתּוֹכָם. כִּי לְעוֹלָם חַסְדּוֹ.

¹²בְּיָד חֲזָקָה וּבִזְרוֹעַ נְטוּיָה. כִּי לְעוֹלָם חַסְדּוֹ.

¹³לְגֹזֵר יַם סוּף לִגְזָרִים. כִּי לְעוֹלָם חַסְדּוֹ.

¹⁴וְהֶעֱבִיר יִשְׂרָאֵל בְּתוֹכוֹ. כִּי לְעוֹלָם חַסְדּוֹ.

¹⁵וְנִעֵר פַּרְעֹה וְחֵילוֹ בְיַם סוּף. כִּי לְעוֹלָם חַסְדּוֹ.

¹⁶לְמוֹלִיךְ עַמּוֹ בַּמִּדְבָּר. כִּי לְעוֹלָם חַסְדּוֹ.

¹⁷לְמַכֵּה מְלָכִים גְּדֹלִים. כִּי לְעוֹלָם חַסְדּוֹ.

¹⁸וַיַּהֲרֹג מְלָכִים אַדִּירִים. כִּי לְעוֹלָם חַסְדּוֹ.

¹⁹לְסִיחוֹן מֶלֶךְ הָאֱמֹרִי. כִּי לְעוֹלָם חַסְדּוֹ.

²⁰וּלְעוֹג מֶלֶךְ הַבָּשָׁן. כִּי לְעוֹלָם חַסְדּוֹ.

²¹וְנָתַן אַרְצָם לְנַחֲלָה. כִּי לְעוֹלָם חַסְדּוֹ.

²²נַחֲלָה לְיִשְׂרָאֵל עַבְדּוֹ. כִּי לְעוֹלָם חַסְדּוֹ.

²³שֶׁבְּשִׁפְלֵנוּ זָכַר לָנוּ. כִּי לְעוֹלָם חַסְדּוֹ.

²⁴וַיִּפְרְקֵנוּ מִצָּרֵינוּ. כִּי לְעוֹלָם חַסְדּוֹ.

²⁵נֹתֵן לֶחֶם לְכָל בָּשָׂר. כִּי לְעוֹלָם חַסְדּוֹ.

²⁶הוֹדוּ לְאֵל הַשָּׁמָיִם. כִּי לְעוֹלָם חַסְדּוֹ.

BRETTLER (BIBLE)

[1] *"His love is everlasting* [ki l'olam chasdo]*"* Psalm 136 is artfully structured: the consistent refrain *ki l'olam chasdo* concludes each verse. Its opening and closing verses offer grateful acknowledgment to God *(hodu l'Adonai …)*, framing a long description of God's actions in history (vv. 5–24). Surprisingly, its reprise of Israel's past omits the giving of Torah on Sinai, as in Deuteronomy 26:5–9, Joshua 24:3–13, and Psalm 78 (contrast Neh. 9:13: "You came down on Mount Sinai *(p. 27)*

FRANKEL (A WOMAN'S VOICE)

[1] *"His love is everlasting"* Of the twenty-six lines in this psalm, each praising a different divine attribute, all but three refer to God's transcendent power manifested to human beings (especially to God's servant, Israel), through supernatural or, at the very least, superhuman acts. In the beginning, God wrested a world from chaotic darkness by creating heaven and earth and the "great lights." God then wrested a nation—a chosen people—out of the darkness of slavery, *(p. 32)*

DORFF (THEOLOGY)

[1] *"Give thanks to Adonai for He is good* [ki tov]*"* We surely experience tragedy: illness (sometimes painful or even lethal); natural disaster (earthquakes, tornadoes); human evil (injustice, prejudice); and genetic disposition (defects of birth). The psalmist must have known these, *(p. 30)*

I. PSALM 136

[1] Give thanks to Adonai for He is good. For his love is everlasting.

[2] Give thanks to the God of gods. For his love is everlasting.

[3] Give thanks to the Lord of lords. For his love is everlasting.

[4] To the One who alone does great wonders. For his love is everlasting.

ELLENSON (MODERN LITURGIES)

[1] *"Give thanks to Adonai for He is good* [ki tov]*" (opening to Psalm 136)* While the pioneering 1819 Hamburg Siddur omitted this psalm altogether, its 1845 revision included it in its entirety. In the case of the two prayer books of Abraham Geiger, the opposite was the case. His first 1854 prayer book printed the psalm in whole, while his 1870 *Gebetbuch* excluded it.

The contrasting treatments that Hamburg authors and Geiger *(p. 31)*

GRAY (OUR TALMUDIC HERITAGE)

[25] *"Who gives food to all creatures"* The Gemara identifies this psalm as the Great (!) *Hallel.* According to Rabbi Yochanan, this flows from the psalm's depiction of God sitting at the top of the world distributing food to every created being" (Pes. 118a; Mid. T'hillim 136:1). *Rashi* (France, c. 1040–1105) and his grandson *Rashbam* (France, c. 1085–1174) tie Rabbi Yochanan's point directly to this verse, explaining that feeding the world is indeed a "great thing." *(p. 33)*

KUSHNER & POLEN (CHASIDISM)

[4] *"To the One who alone does great wonders"* Yehuda Aryeh Lieb Alter of Ger (d. 1905) finds in Psalm 136:4 an allusion to the core meaning of Shabbat. He suggests in his *Sefat Emet* (s.v. *Bereshit* 5662, para. 2) that Shabbat enables us to comprehend how God guides creation without the mediating laws of nature—in the words of the psalm, "To the One who *alone* does great wonders." Certainly all creation is a great wonder, but when the psalmist adds the word "alone," *(p. 34)*

L. HOFFMAN (HISTORY)

KNOWN IN THE TALMUD AS "THE GREAT HALLEL," PSALM 136 IS SAID IN SOME COMMUNITIES EVERY DAY OF THE WEEK. IN THE RITUAL FOLLOWED HERE, HOWEVER, IT IS ADDED ON SHABBAT AND TYPIFIES THE SHABBAT EXPANSION OF PSALMS IN THE MORNING "WARM-UP" SECTION OF PRAYER, CALLED P'SUKEI D'ZIMRAH *("VERSES OF SONG").*

———◆———

J. HOFFMAN (TRANSLATION)

[1] *"Give thanks to Adonai"* We have translated this line elsewhere as "acknowledge Adonai with thanks." Here we specifically want to retain the phrase "to Adonai" because the rest of the poem consists of lines that continue "to ...," for example, "to the One who alone does great wonders" (see below). We therefore need a verb like "give" that works with "to."

[1] *"For He is good"* Or, "because it is good to do so."

[1] *"For his"* Others, just "his...." The Hebrew repeats *ki* ("for"), connecting this line poetically with the preceding one. In spite of the poetic connection, however, the "For his love is everlasting" lines are insertions into running text and were perhaps even originally intended to be group responses. The poetry of Psalm 136 is best understood by reading *(p. 37)*

הוֹדוּ לַיְיָ כִּי טוֹב. כִּי לְעוֹלָם חַסְדּוֹ.[1]

הוֹדוּ לֵאלֹהֵי הָאֱלֹהִים. כִּי לְעוֹלָם חַסְדּוֹ.[2]

הוֹדוּ לַאֲדֹנֵי הָאֲדֹנִים. כִּי לְעוֹלָם חַסְדּוֹ.[3]

לְעֹשֵׂה נִפְלָאוֹת גְּדֹלוֹת לְבַדּוֹ. כִּי לְעוֹלָם חַסְדּוֹ.[4]

לְעֹשֵׂה הַשָּׁמַיִם בִּתְבוּנָה. כִּי לְעוֹלָם חַסְדּוֹ.[5]

לְרוֹקַע הָאָרֶץ עַל הַמָּיִם. כִּי לְעוֹלָם חַסְדּוֹ.[6]

LANDES (HALAKHAH)

P'sukei D'zimrah Four factors distinguish *P'sukei D'zimrah* of Shabbat from weekdays:

1. It is greatly augmented in the number of psalms [*Ed. Note:* exemplifying them all, we include here only, Psalm 136 (the Great *Hallel*)—see p. 22].
2. The *Birkat Hashir* ("Blessing of Song") that ends the unit is enlarged with *Nishmat kol cha'i.*
3. The prayer service itself begins later, this being the day of *(p. 34)*

⁵ To the One who wisely created the sky. For his love is everlasting.

⁶ To the One who spread out the earth on the water. For his love is everlasting.

⁷ To the One who created the great lights. For his love is everlasting.

⁸ The sun to be ruler by day. For his love is everlasting.

⁹ The moon and stars to be rulers by night. For his love is everlasting.

¹⁰ To the One who struck Egypt through their first-born. For his love is everlasting.

¹¹ And who brought Israel out from their midst. For his love is everlasting.

¹² With a strong hand and an outstretched arm. For his love is everlasting.

¹³ To the One who split the Red Sea. For his love is everlasting.

¹⁴ And brought Israel through it. For his love is everlasting.

¹⁵ And shook Pharaoh and his army in the Red Sea. For his love is everlasting.

¹⁶ To the One who led his people through the desert. For his love is everlasting.

¹⁷ To the One who struck great kings. For his love is everlasting.

¹⁸ And killed mighty kings. For his love is everlasting.

¹⁹ Sichon, king of the Amorites. For his

⁷לְעֹשֵׂה אוֹרִים גְּדֹלִים. כִּי לְעוֹלָם חַסְדּוֹ.

⁸אֶת הַשֶּׁמֶשׁ לְמֶמְשֶׁלֶת בַּיּוֹם. כִּי לְעוֹלָם חַסְדּוֹ.

⁹אֶת הַיָּרֵחַ וְכוֹכָבִים לְמֶמְשְׁלוֹת בַּלָּיְלָה. כִּי לְעוֹלָם חַסְדּוֹ.

¹⁰לְמַכֵּה מִצְרַיִם בִּבְכוֹרֵיהֶם. כִּי לְעוֹלָם חַסְדּוֹ.

¹¹וַיּוֹצֵא יִשְׂרָאֵל מִתּוֹכָם. כִּי לְעוֹלָם חַסְדּוֹ.

¹²בְּיָד חֲזָקָה וּבִזְרוֹעַ נְטוּיָה. כִּי לְעוֹלָם חַסְדּוֹ.

¹³לְגֹזֵר יַם סוּף לִגְזָרִים. כִּי לְעוֹלָם חַסְדּוֹ.

¹⁴וְהֶעֱבִיר יִשְׂרָאֵל בְּתוֹכוֹ. כִּי לְעוֹלָם חַסְדּוֹ.

¹⁵וְנִעֵר פַּרְעֹה וְחֵילוֹ בְיַם סוּף. כִּי לְעוֹלָם חַסְדּוֹ.

¹⁶לְמוֹלִיךְ עַמּוֹ בַּמִּדְבָּר. כִּי לְעוֹלָם חַסְדּוֹ.

¹⁷לְמַכֵּה מְלָכִים גְּדֹלִים. כִּי לְעוֹלָם חַסְדּוֹ.

¹⁸וַיַּהֲרֹג מְלָכִים אַדִּירִים. כִּי לְעוֹלָם חַסְדּוֹ.

¹⁹לְסִיחוֹן מֶלֶךְ הָאֱמֹרִי. כִּי לְעוֹלָם חַסְדּוֹ.

²⁰וּלְעוֹג מֶלֶךְ הַבָּשָׁן. כִּי לְעוֹלָם חַסְדּוֹ.

²¹וְנָתַן אַרְצָם לְנַחֲלָה. כִּי לְעוֹלָם חַסְדּוֹ.

love is everlasting.

²⁰ Og, king of Bashan. For his love is everlasting.

²¹ And gave their land as a heritage. For his love is everlasting.

²² A heritage to Israel his servant. For his love is everlasting.

²³ Who remembered us when we were low. For his love is everlasting.

²⁴ And set us free from our enemies. For his love is everlasting.

²⁵ Who gives food to all creatures. For his love is everlasting.

²⁶ Give thanks to the God of heaven. For his love is everlasting.

22נַחֲלָה לְיִשְׂרָאֵל עַבְדּוֹ. כִּי לְעוֹלָם חַסְדּוֹ.

23שֶׁבְּשִׁפְלֵנוּ זָכַר לָנוּ. כִּי לְעוֹלָם חַסְדּוֹ.

24וַיִּפְרְקֵנוּ מִצָּרֵינוּ. כִּי לְעוֹלָם חַסְדּוֹ.

25נֹתֵן לֶחֶם לְכָל בָּשָׂר. כִּי לְעוֹלָם חַסְדּוֹ.

26הוֹדוּ לְאֵל הַשָּׁמָיִם. כִּי לְעוֹלָם חַסְדּוֹ.

BRETTLER (BIBLE)

and spoke to them from heaven; You gave them right rules and true teachings, good laws and commandments"). Perhaps Sinai is missing here because this psalm emphasizes God's military power.

The formula, *ki l'olam chasdo*, is found in other psalms (106, 107, 118) and, most significantly, in several clearly post-exilic texts, such as Ezra 3:11 ("They sang songs extolling and praising Adonai, *ki l'olam chasdo*") and 1 Chronicles 16:41 ("With them were Heman and Jeduthun and the other selected men designated by name to give praise to Adonai, *ki l'olam chasdo*").

Citing God's favors followed by *ki l'olam chasdo* was probably a common formula used in the Second Temple services, the period to which this psalm should be dated. It might have been sung antiphonally, one group singing the first half of each verse and another responding *ki l'olam chasdo*.

¹ *"Give thanks to Adonai for He is good. For his love is everlasting"* This particular verse is found in a variety of late biblical texts (e.g., 2 Chron. 5:13), often as an opening formula (see Psalms 106, 107, 118). It is unclear if it originates here or if the psalmist has taken a stock phrase from elsewhere. The verse is ambiguous—"good" may refer to God's goodness, as in Psalm 145:9, "Adonai is good to all," or may suggest that it is

good to praise God, as in Psalm 92:2, "It is good to give grateful praise to God."

²⁻³ *"God of gods … Lord of lords* [elohei ha'elohim … adonai ha'adonim]" The superlatives introducing these two verses are likely a reworking of Deuteronomy 10:17, where God is also described as *elohei ha'elohim* and *Adonei ha'adonim*. That context, however, emphasizes God's greatness in terms of his judicial impartiality and care for the underclass, as opposed to highlighting his great actions in history.

⁴ *"Who alone does great wonders* [nifla'ot]" This too is formulaic—see Psalm 72:18, "Blessed is Adonai God, God of Israel, who alone does wondrous things" and Psalm 86:10, "For You are great and perform wonders; You alone are God." If *nifla'ot* is a general term for "wonder," it introduces the rest of the psalm, but it may refer specifically to wonders connected to creation (see Job 9:10), in which case it introduces just the following verses that deal with creation.

⁵⁻⁹ *"To the One who wisely created the sky …"* There are several creation accounts in the Bible. Genesis 1:1–2:4a is fundamentally different than Genesis 2:4b–3:24. Other biblical books rework a well-known Canaanite story, where creation involves control over a rebellious water deity (see, e.g., Ps. 74:13–15, "It was You who drove back the sea with your might, who smashed the heads of the monsters in the waters; it was You who crushed the heads of Leviathan, who left him as food for the denizens of the desert; it was You who released springs and torrents, who made mighty rivers run dry"). Both the order of the elements created and the vocabulary used to describe the process make it clear that this psalm reflects the version of Genesis 1:1–2:4a, composed by the priestly class following the Babylonian exile. The psalmist, however, does not follow this text slavishly: he emphasizes the creation of *shamayim* ("the sky") through *t'vunah* ("wisely") in verse 5, an understanding missing from Genesis (but see Jer. 10:12, 51:15; and Prov. 3:19); he uses the word *roka* ("earth") in reference to the land (v. 6), not the waters (Gen. 1:6–7); and, most significantly, he selects very few details from this creation story, excluding, for example, the creation of animals and humanity.

¹⁰ *"To the One who struck Egypt through their first-born"* This line opens a five-verse (10–15) celebration of the Exodus. The entire earlier history of Israel, including the ancestral period, is omitted, perhaps because it was considered irrelevant in a psalm focused on God's power. Even what is narrated is recalled very selectively; for example, only the final plague, the smiting of the first-born, is recounted (v. 10—Ps. 135:8 is similar, but v. 9 there at least mentions other plagues).

¹² *"With a strong hand and an outstretched arm"* Only in Deuteronomy is this phrase found in reference to the Exodus, suggesting that the sources of this psalm draw not only on the post-exilic priestly author (the final author of Torah, who gave us also the first creation story above—see above, v. 4, "Who alone does great wonders [*nifla'ot*]"), but Deuteronomy too (which came before), and, therefore, the earlier strata of Torah too. Overall, in his drawing on sources, the author is both conservative and creative. The phrase "And shook Pharaoh and his army in the Red Sea" (v. 15) is based on

Exodus 14:27, while the idea that the Red Sea was "split" ("*gazar*"ed into "splittings"[*g'zarim*]) is found only here.

[16] *"Who led his people through the desert"* We now begin a five-verse (16–20) description of God's guiding Israel through the wilderness. It emphasizes God's beneficence, not Israel's rebellions, a common theme elsewhere (e.g., Ps. 78:40, "How often did they defy Him in the wilderness, did they grieve Him in the wasteland!"). Verses 17–18 and 19–20 are a pair of couplets in synonymous parallelism; it is unclear if these "great kings" and "mighty kings" refer only to the kings explicitly mentioned here (Sichon and Og, who resided east of the Jordan—see Numbers 21; Deuteronomy 2–3) or include also the many kings vanquished during the conquest of the land according to the Book of Joshua.

[21–22] *"Heritage* [nachalah]" Here again we find two synonymous verses arranged as a couplet to emphasize the Land of Israel as the "heritage" of the people of Israel. Often, *nachalah* refers to a hereditary portion; here, no one actually hands it down, but Israel is nonetheless portrayed as the legitimate, unquestioned owners of the land (as a deed from God).

[23] *"Low"* This verse begins another couplet. Verse 23 highlights God's concern for those who are "low" *(shafel)*, a common theme of biblical wisdom literature (e.g., Job 5:11, "Who raises the lowly up high, so that the dejected are secure in victory"). It is Israel's "lowliness" ("*shafel*-ness") that led God to deliver them. But both verses stress deliverance from Egypt, akin to earlier verses that emphasize similar deliverance from "mighty kings."

[25] *"Who gives food to all creatures"* It is unclear how this verse fits in a psalm that deals with God's might, not God's mercy. It may reflect a secondary use of the psalm at a time of famine. The theme of God as provider of food is well attested elsewhere, of course (see, e.g., Pss. 146:7, 147:9), but if this was meant to be the climactic conclusion, some mention of feeding the Israelites manna in the desert (see, e.g., Ps. 78:24) would have been expected earlier.

[26] *"Give thanks to the God of heaven"* By reiterating the idea of acknowledging Adonai, the psalm returns to verses 1–3, forming what is called an *inclusio*. The Hebrew phrase *el hashamayim* ("God of heaven") is unique here (although the longer *elohei hashamayim* is found elsewhere, again in mostly late contexts); perhaps the author meant to recall verse 5, "Who wisely created the sky," and the phrase *el hashamayim* is coined for this context for metrical reasons that escape us.

——◆——

DORFF (THEOLOGY)

yet he bids us to thank God anyway for the goodness in our lives.

We tend to dwell on negativity while taking good things for granted. By proclaiming God's goodness, the psalmist illustrates the Jewish principle of *hakarat hatov* (hah-kah-RAHT hah-TOHV), "acknowledging the good," in our lives.

[2] *"The God of gods"* This verse replicates the issue in the more familiar *Mi Khamokha* (see Volume 1, *The Sh'ma and Its Blessings*, p. 119), where we ask rhetorically, "Who is like You among the gods, Adonai!" (Exod. 15:11). In both places, the intent is either *henotheistic* or *monotheistic*. That is, the biblical authors may be saying (henotheistically) that our God is supreme over other gods that exist, or (monotheistically) that the God we worship is supreme over all the gods that other people *think* exist but actually do not. A henotheistic interpretation would mark these texts as very early articulations of Israelite theology, antedating the time when Judaism became unambiguously monotheistic. (On henotheism versus monotheism and on the import of monotheism for morality and justice, see Volume 3, *P'sukei D'zimrah [Morning Psalms]*, p. 169 [Brettler, v. 20], and Volume 8, *Kabbalat Shabbat [Welcoming Shabbat in the Synagogue]*, pp. 70–71.)

[2] *"For his love* [chasdo] *is everlasting"* In addition to meaning "love," *chasdo* denotes God's "faithfulness" or "loyalty." The point is that God can be trusted. No wonder this exclamation is the psalm's recurring refrain, punctuating example after example of God's beneficence.

The Greeks laid the foundation for science by insisting that nature works mechanically, without the willful intervention of gods. The Rabbis, however, took monotheism to mean that the world *is* under the will of God, even though God does not normally intervene—generally, "the world operates according to its custom [*olam k'minhago noheg v'holekh*]" (A.Z. 54b).

[5] *"Who wisely* [bit'vunah] *created the sky"* Had the psalmist used the word *chokhmah* ("knowledge"), he would have called our attention to knowledge learned from experience, presumably from God's creating other worlds. But *t'vunah*, "wisdom, understanding," implies the innate "engineering" capacity that underlies creation. This intricacy of nature has been seen by some philosophers as proof of the existence of God ("the Argument from Design"). That argument ultimately falls short of being absolute *proof*, but (like our psalm here) it does provide *evidence* for why we might believe in God. (For the Argument from Design, otherwise known as the teleological argument, see *Encyclopedia of Philosophy* 8:84–88 and Supplement 564–568.)

[6] *"Who spread out the earth on the water"* From the experience of digging wells and finding water, the ancients believed that the surface of the earth lies across water. (See Volume 9, *Welcoming the Night: Minchah and Ma'ariv [Afternoon and Evening Prayer]*, pp. 48–52.)

[7] *"Who created the great lights"* By first saying, generally, "great lights" and only afterward (vv. 8, 9) specifying the sun and the moon, the poet magnifies our sense of awe. The same technique occurs in verses 17–20, where he first praises God for striking down great and mighty kings (in general) and then spells out the specific kings he has in mind.

[10] *"Who struck Egypt through their first-born"* Similar to Psalm 19, Psalm 136 moves directly from describing God's miraculous wonders in creation to God's redemptive power in history. God is a God of nature and of human affairs. Thus most Jewish thinkers (with the significant exceptions of Spinoza and Mordecai Kaplan) are *theists*, not *deists*. *Deism* affirms God solely as the creative force of nature (the American Founding Fathers were mostly deists who affirmed a "Creator" who endows rights but then retreats from history and lets us handle our own affairs.) *Theism* posits a God who also acts in history. (For the Jewish theistic emphasis on a God of history, evidenced best by the Exodus, see Volume 1, *The Sh'ma and Its Blessings*, pp. 126–127.)

[21–22] *"And gave their land as a heritage ... to Israel his servant"* Here (see also, e.g., Gen. 15:7ff., 17:8, 26:3–4, 28:13–15; Deut. 7:13, 8:1, 8:7–10), the Land of Israel is said to belong to the Israelites not because they took it by force, but because God deeded it to them. As creator (and, therefore, owner) of the entire world (see, e.g., Deut. 10:14), God has the right to parcel it out to whomever God pleases. *Rashi* makes this point to explain why the Torah begins with the creation narrative. Thus Israel owns the Land of Israel not by might, but by moral right. (For how God's creating the world means that God owns it, see Volume 8, *Kabbalat Shabbat [Welcoming Shabbat in the Synagogue]*, p. 54.)

[25] *"Who gives food to all creatures"* This is not literally true, as the psalmist surely knew. He must have meant that all creatures who *do* have food owe it to God, without whom no food would exist. That must be the intent also of the first blessing of *Birkat Hamazon* (Grace after Meals), which affirms God "who sustains *everything*."

———◆———

ELLENSON (MODERN LITURGIES)

accorded this psalm probably had less to do with theological problems regarding its content than with the desire to create an abbreviated service. In 1854, Geiger was intent on attracting a broad swath of followers. He lived in a city where he was by law unable to establish his own independent synagogue. Instead, he was just one officially appointed rabbi of two in the community, the other being strictly Orthodox. As Geiger contended for support, it became politic to suppress many personal views on reform while writing liturgy that would appeal across the Jewish spectrum. He may have felt that the absence of this popular psalm would cost him dearly in terms of his overall religious appeal. By 1870 that consideration was no longer the case, and he was able to omit it. Orthodoxy was losing ground, to the extent that by 1876 it would convince the secular authorities to allow it to establish independent communities. No longer needing to fight as much for support in 1870, Geiger could be more thoroughgoing in his reforms, even though he never reverted to the radicalism that his personal views alone might have dictated.

By contrast, from the very beginning Hamburg was an independent trading city, and a cosmopolitan one at that. The authors of the 1819 Hamburg book also wanted to avoid too strict a Reform stance, but were able (more than Geiger) to appeal to the broad-based desire for a shorter service. By 1845 they must have noted objection to their omitting such a popular piece.

The omission of this psalm in virtually all subsequent Reform Siddurim reflects a consensus among their authors that other psalms or vernacular readings were even better suited, by content or by brevity, than this one. They were looking for psalms that were spiritually and morally uplifting, and in that regard, Psalm 136, no matter how well-known, came up short.

A suggestion as to how Psalm 136 proved lacking as a morally uplifting offering may be found in the explanation that the 1996 Reconstructionist *Kol Haneshamah* provides. Its commentary there explains:

> [While] an abridged version [of Psalm 136 is included because the psalm praises God for a] broad variety of redeeming acts, verses 10–22 have been omitted. These verses narrate the killing of the Egyptian firstborn and Israel's exodus from Egypt, the crossing of the Sea of Reeds and the death of Pharaoh's army, the victorious battles in the wilderness against foreign people, and Israel's inheritance (by conquest) of the land of Canaan. [All these passages are problematic to] contemporary religious sensibilities [that] preclude our rejoicing over the deaths of Israel's enemies.

———◆———

FRANKEL (A WOMAN'S VOICE)

crushing their oppressors in Egypt and mighty kings who later blocked their entry to the Promised Land.

This psalm portrays God as majestic and awesome: the master of life and death. As we chant the hypnotic refrain, *ki l'olam chasdo* ("His love is everlasting"), however, we feel anything but mercy emanating from God's "outstretched arm." For although the world began with wondrous gifts—a stable material universe illumined by the sun, moon, and stars—Israel's beginning as a nation, freed from Egyptian servitude and reassigned to God's service, is marked by violence and destruction: Egypt's first-born are killed, Pharaoh's army drowned, great kings cut down, all in order for Israel to receive its *nachalah*, its heritage. What manner of mercy is this?

Perhaps the key to unlocking this theological paradox can be found in the closing verses of the psalm, when God descends from the heights in order to tend to the earth's inhabitants with *chesed*—"lovingkindness," as the *King James* Version renders it—in order to denote God's special solicitude shown in caring for earthly creatures. This is the *maternal* side of God, who tends to the sick, raises up those who are bent over, clothes the naked, and hears the cry of the bereft.

One of the final verses of this psalm portrays God as the One who "remembered us when we were low [*b'shiflenu*]," literally, in a state of depression. This verse represents an abrupt shift in the psalm's narrative sequence. Having just praised God for redeeming us from Egypt and bringing us successfully into Canaan, why should we be low? And then the psalm veers off on yet another tangent, praising God "Who gives food to all creatures." Why speak of God's maternal nurturing quality in this otherwise grand spectacle of cosmic creation and divine potency?

Only this intimate, mindful God takes notice of our moods, shows sensitivity to our hunger and thirst, and responds to our call for mercy. We can expect no such attention from the "God of gods" *(elohei ha'elohim)* or "Lord of lords" *(Adonei ha'adonim)*, whom we acknowledged at the beginning of the psalm. As we repeat the refrain, "His love is everlasting," we move in our imagination from the love shown Israel in the past—at the dawn of the world, at the dawn of the nation—to the loving-kindness we ask for now, when we feel vulnerable, or when we hunger for faith and sustenance.

◆

GRAY (OUR TALMUDIC HERITAGE)

David Abudarham (Spain, fourteenth century) offers an original explanation of why this psalm is so "great": it consists of twenty-six verses, the numerical value of the tetragrammaton, God's ineffable name (YHVH). It deserves to be called the "Great *Hallel*," in keeping with Psalm 96:4: *ki gadol YHVH um'hulal m'od*, "For *great* is YHVH, and much praised"; the Hebrew for "praised" is *m'hulal*, from the same root as *hallel*.

Rabbi Yehoshua ben Levi links these twenty-six occurrences of *ki l'olam chasdo* to the twenty-six generations that elapsed between the creation of the world and the revelation of Torah at Mount Sinai. Because humanity did not have the merit of Torah observance to earn sustenance, it must have been sustained through God's love *(chasdo)* (Mid. T'hillim 136:1; see also Pes. 118a and Abudarham, who report Rabbi Yehoshua ben Levi's tradition in connection with the word *hodu*, which is puzzling because there are only three mentions of *hodu*). Only the Jewish people ultimately accepted Torah, but Abudarham points out (using Shab. 88a) that God's provision of food to sustain the whole world is predicated on our continuing acceptance of the Torah.

The conceptual connection between the Great *Hallel* and the "*great* thing" that God does by providing food explains why the Jews of Lod (in the Land of Israel) recited this *Hallel* when they were rewarded with rain after a public fast in a time of drought (M. Ta'an. 3:9). Especially in agricultural societies, rain is crucial; its arrival after an unseasonable delay was sufficient reason to evoke the Great *Hallel*.

Rabbi Yochanan characterizes the search for daily sustenance as twice as difficult as the pains of childbirth, and more difficult even than the travails connected with messianic redemption (Pes. 118a). Rabbi Samuel (or Shimon, in another version) bar Nachmani points to Genesis 48:15–16: In verse 15, Jacob calls God his lifelong shepherd; in verse 16, he refers to "the angel who has redeemed me." Jacob thus attributes his daily sustenance—analogous to a shepherd's care for his sheep—directly to God the shepherd, while explaining ultimate redemption only with the appearance of an angel. Angels may bring redemption, but daily sustenance requires the direct intervention of God (Mid. T'hillim 136:9).

KUSHNER & POLEN (CHASIDISM)

it implies a dimension transcending the natural laws of cause and effect.

The unique status of Shabbat is further hinted at in those consecutive verses that reflect the creation sequence of Genesis—heavens (verse 5), earth (verse 6), heavenly lights (verses 7 and following). Our attention is thereby drawn to Shabbat, created last, and, therefore, transcending the creation of the world with all its wondrous natural laws. Like God, Shabbat is utterly unique and alone. The *Sefat Emet* cites Genesis Rabbah 16, which links Adam's placement in the Garden of Eden with the repose of the Sabbath day. So Shabbat, Eden, and God's guiding presence beyond the laws of nature become dimensions of the same reality.

Closer observation reveals even more direct parallels between Shabbat and the Garden of Eden (*eiden* in Hebrew). *Eiden* begins with the Hebrew letter *ayin;* the *nahar,* or "river," that flows from it (Gen. 2:10) starts with a *nun;* and the first word of *gan* ("garden") is *gimel.* The acronym of *ayin, nun,* and *gimel* spells *oneg,* "delight" (or "joy"), as in *oneg Shabbat.*

We find also that God planted shoots in the Garden of Eden—and in the messianic promise of Isaiah 60:21, Israel is called "shoots" planted by God. Thus Eden (which parallels Shabbat) and Israel as messianic promise come together as a single reality beyond time. So on Shabbat, we experience the world-to-come, planted, as it were, by God within the garden; we are *of* it. On Shabbat everything is transparent: comprehending what it is to be saplings planted by the master gardener, we realize our true nature.

LANDES (HALAKHAH)

rest, on which joy (*oneg*) is expressed in sleeping later (*BaCh* [*Bayit Chadash*], Rabbi Joel Sirkes [Poland, 1561–1640]; O. Ch. 281). Halakhic support for starting later comes also from the description of the daily *tamid* (the perpetual sacrifice) on which *Shacharit* is based. Regarding the weekday *tamid,* Numbers 28:4

states, "You shall offer one lamb in the *morning* [*boker*]," while according to Numbers 28:9, the Shabbat *tamid* is to be offered "on Shabbat day [*yom*]." *Boker* implies "early," while *yom* allows for a delay (*R'ma* [Rabbi Moses Isserles], 1530–1572, Cracow; O. Ch. 281:1).

4. The general tempo of the service is more relaxed, making *P'sukei D'zimrah* even longer in duration.

Thus this "warm-up" section of the service starts late and ends significantly later than it does on weekdays. Waiting so long to start services obviously may have an impact upon the prohibition of eating before prayer.

The prohibition of eating is derived from Berachot 10b:

> Rabbi Yose son of Rabbi Chaninah also said in the name of Rabbi Eliezer bar Ya'akov: What is the meaning of the verse, "You shall not eat anything with its blood" (Lev. 19:26)? [It means] do not eat before you have prayed for your blood [i.e., your life]. Rabbi Yitzchak said in the name of Rabbi Yochanan in the name of Rabbi Eliezer bar Ya'akov: Of one who eats and drinks and [only] then says his prayers, Scripture says, "You have cast Me [God] behind your back" (1 Kings 14:9). Read not *gavekha* ["your back"] but *ge'ekha* ["your arrogance"]. Says the holy One blessed be He: First this person exalts himself [by eating], and [only] then he comes to accept the kingdom of heaven [through reciting the *Sh'ma*]?!

It is an act of egocentric pride to take care of your own needs before God's. God cannot come second. Implied here is the notion that the well-being born of eating will dull the urgency of prayer.

The proof text used here, "You shall not eat anything with its blood," is listed by *Sefer Hachinukh* as a biblical prohibition with a wide range of applications, including just tasting anything prior to prayer *(lav sheb'klalot)*. *Minchat Chinukh* 248 (Joseph ben Moses Babad, 1800–1875, Turkey, Safed) therefore observes that the author of *Sefer Hachinukh* must have seen the prohibition against eating prior to prayer not just as rabbinic *(mid'rabbanan)* but as biblical *(mid'ora'ita)*. Of course, as he notes, according to the majority of *Rishonim* (early authorities, prior to the *Shulchan Arukh*, sixteenth century), prayer is only a rabbinic invention, so without the verse, the prohibition can only be rabbinic; but the verse is added as an *asmachta* (literary support) for emphasis. We cannot conclusively determine Maimonides' (1135–1204, Spain, Egypt) position, for even though he famously understands prayer as having biblical status and prohibits eating before it (Laws of Prayer 6:4), he includes the prohibition amongst others that are rabbinic. Nonetheless the *R'ah* (Rabbi Aharon HaLevi, b. 1235, Gerona, Spain), commenting on the talmudic discussion, clearly states that the prohibition stems from the status of prayer as given by Torah.

Regardless of whether the prohibition is of a Torah or a rabbinic nature, it is binding.

Still, halakhic authorities have found some strategies to ease the prohibition:

1. According to the *Kesef Mishneh* (a commentary to Maimonides' *Mishneh Torah* by Joseph Caro, 1488–1575, Bulgaria, Safed), water is not included in the prohibition, for it constitutes no *ga'avah* ("arrogance"; pronounced gah-ah-VAH or,

commonly, GAH-ah-vah), as opposed to eating, which does. Indeed, the *Pri Chadash* (commentary to the *Shulchan Arukh* [O. Ch. 89] by Rabbi Chizkiya Ben David Disilo, b. 1659, Livorno, Italy) even permits drinking coffee to enhance concentration in prayer. It is widely accepted now that all beverages, as long as they are not intoxicating, are permitted before prayer.

2. One may eat for health reasons (even if one is only slightly ill) or as an aid in taking medicine (*Be'ur Hahalakhah*, Israel Meir Hakohen Kagan, 1838–1933, Radom, Poland, O. Ch. 89:3). This exception includes anyone too hungry to concentrate on prayer without eating something first.

3. On Shabbat especially (since prayer starts later than usual) it is more reasonable to fear that weakness will impede proper prayer. In such a case, even pastry may be eaten as long as it is less than the amount that would *kove'a s'udah* ("establish an actual meal"; pronounced, koh-VAY-ah s'-oo-DAH). Eating an actual meal would require saying the *Kiddush* for Shabbat day (see Volume 7, *Shabbat at Home*, p. 162), which should not precede the Shabbat morning service. (See discussion of HaRav Moshe Feinstein [1895–1986, Luban, Russia, and New York], *Igrot Mosheh*, O. Ch. II:2a.)

[25] *"Who gives food to all creatures"* This is the most significant of all the Shabbat (and holy day) additions to *P'sukei D'zimrah*. It is referred to as *Hallel Hagadol*, the "Great *Hallel*" (*Tosefta* Ta'an. 2 and Pes. 137a). This is because of this all-important verse, "who gives food to all creatures," evoking the image of God in heaven sustaining every individual creature—"a great matter" according to *Rashi* (Rabbi Shlomo Yitzchaki, 1040–1105, Troyes, France) and *Rashbam* (Rabbi Samuel ben Meir, 1085–1174, France). Some *Rishonim* (early authorities prior to the *Shulchan Arukh*, sixteenth century) attribute its name to the fact that it has twenty-six verses, the numerical equivalent of the four-letter name of God. Others include the fact that it states, "For his love is everlasting." (See *Sefer Abudarham* [R. David Abudarham, thirteenth to fourteenth century, Seville], "Prayers for Shabbat.")

Hallel Hagadol (Psalm 136) is recited not just here but on two other occasions (according to some authorities, with other psalms too, most notably Psalm 23, which the Talmud cites also as a *Hallel Hagadol*). The most well-known is the Passover Seder. It is associated by many with a fifth (!) cup of wine (see, e.g., the *Ran* [Rabbi Nissim ben Reuven, Spain, early fourteenth century], commentary to Pes. 118a). As recorded by the *Tur* (O. Ch. 481), however, quoting *Rashbam*, it accompanies the *fourth* cup. This Great *Hallel* fits Passover night in that the theme of the evening is total thanksgiving to God. Appropriately, it comes at the penultimate end, next to *Nirtsah* (pronounced neer-TSAH), the final paragraph that expresses satisfaction at completing the Seder properly.

The other recitation of *Hallel Hagadol* is during a fast to ask God to send rain: "They once enacted a fast in Lod [beseeching God for rain], and the rain fell before midday. Rabbi Tarfon instructed them, 'Go eat and drink; make this a festive day.' So they went, ate and drank, and made a festive day, returning at twilight to recite *Hallel*

Hagadol" (M. Ta'an. 19a and parallel Tosefta). This has become the accepted Halakhah: interrupting the fast if rain falls before midday, completing the fast if after. But here too, no less than at the Seder, *Hallel Hagadol* is recited only with a "physically satiated soul and on a full belly" (Maimonides, Laws of Fasts 1:14), fulfilling the verse of *Hallel Hagadol*, "He gives bread to all flesh" (see *Rashi* on Ta'an. 25b).

The liturgical recitation of *Hallel Hagadol* in *P'sukei D'zimrah* of Shabbat and holy days is first mentioned by the *Rishonim*. Tosafot (collection of mini-essays on the Talmud, page by page, written by Franco-German scholars of the *Rashi* school, twelfth to fourteenth centuries) points out (Ta'an. 26a) that *Hallel Hagadol* on Shabbat must come during *P'sukei D'zimrah* because *P'sukei D'zimrah* is technically "pre-prayer" (formal "prayer" is defined as the central sections of [1] the *Sh'ma* and its Blessings and [2] the *Amidah*). Were *Hallel Hagadol* to be recited during a technically "real" prayer section, it would necessitate "the physically satiated soul," as when it is said for the coming of rain and, for that matter, when it is added to the Passover Seder after the meal. This is confirmed by the *Magen Avraham* (Avraham Gombiner, Kalish, 1633–1683, O. Ch. 575:11).

———◆———

J. HOFFMAN (TRANSLATION)

just the first halves of the lines.

[1] *"Love"* Frequently, "mercy." *JPS* gives us "steadfast love," though "steadfast love" lasting "forever" seems redundant. At issue are the nuances of the Hebrew word *chesed*. We know it refers to something good, but specific details are difficult to confirm.

[1] *"Everlasting"* That is, it lasts from now until eternity. Hebrew distinguishes between "forever" in the sense of "in the past up to now" and "from now and evermore." Here we have the latter.

[2] *"God of gods"* Here we assume that the language is to be taken literally, that is, that God outranks the other gods. A less likely possibility is that this construction, as with "Song of Songs," is simply a superlative, as in Birnbaum: "supreme God."

[4] *"To the One who alone does"* This elliptical construction assumes "Give thanks …" as in the preceding three verses. In Hebrew, the verbs now begin appearing in staccato parallelism: *oseh* ("doer"), *oseh* (again, but this time in the sense of "maker"), *roka* ("spreader-out"), etc., thus augmenting the poetic nature of the psalm in a way that we cannot capture in English (for detail, see below, "Created").

[5] *"Wisely"* The English, like the Hebrew, is ambiguous. Either God was wise to create or God's creating involved wisdom. We assume that the latter was intended.

[5] *"Created"* Because the Hebrew uses nouns—"doer," "maker," "spreader-out," etc.

(see above, "To the One who alone does")—it is tenseless. In English, however, we are forced to choose a tense for each line. When the English denotation of tenses must change, as here, from "One who does" (v. 4) to "One who created" (v. 5) we are further forced to stray from the poetic grammatical parallelism of the original. Furthermore, the Hebrew for "do" and "create" here is the same word *(oseh)*. All of these small changes conspire to nearly destroy the original poetry. The original Hebrew reads: "to the Lord," "to God," "to the Lord," "to the doer," "to the maker," etc.; while our English now reads: "to Adonai," "to God," "to the Lord," "to the One who does," and "to the One who created."

[6] *"Spread out"* The Hebrew word here, *roka*, is specifically reminiscent of the word *raki'a* (of Gen. 1:6), typically translated "firmament."

[8] *"The sun"* We now have (with "the sun") an elliptical construction (because it omits an opening verb, like "does," "makes," and "spreads out") inside an elliptical construction (beginning in v. 4, the opening "Give thanks to" was dropped—see above, "The One who alone does"). This line and the next assume the governing verb, "[the One who] created."

[8] *"To be ruler"* Or "to rule," but we prefer "to be ruler," because in a subtle bit of cleverness, the next line notes that the moon and stars are "rulers" (plural), as if each one is its own ruler. We want to replicate this extended imagery in our translation.

[9] *"Rulers"* See above, v. 8, "to be ruler."

[10] *"Through their"* Following *JPS* and *NSRV*.

[13] *"Split"* Literally, "split into splits" *(gozer … lig'zarim)*—a common Hebrew construction in which the verb is reinforced by a noun from the same root, along the lines of "dreamed a dream." But "split the sea into a split" is not English. "Parted the sea into parts" might work, but we want to retain the verb "split" because this rare Hebrew word also appears in Genesis 15, which is alluded to in the concluding prayers when we note that God "remembers the covenant of split pieces." See p. 36 of Volume 6, *Tachunun and Concluding Prayers*.

[13] *"Red Sea"* Or, more literally, "Reed Sea," that is, Sea of Reeds. The similarity in English between "Red Sea" and "Reed Sea" is a coincidence. The Septuagint (or LXX, as it is called, dated from the third century B.C.E.) calls it the "red lake/sea," which in ancient Greek does not sound at all like "reed."

[14] *"Brought Israel"* The Hebrew verb is related to *avar*, meaning "pass." We would therefore prefer a compromise between "let Israel pass" and "made Israel pass," but because no such construction is available in English, we resort to rewording the sentence with an altogether different verb.

[16] *"Led"* The Hebrew *(molikh)* means "led," but it sounds like the word for "king"

(melekh), setting the stage for the next lines—which are all about kings—in a way that our English cannot.

[16] *"Desert"* Or "wilderness."

[19] *"Sichon"* The Hebrew actually has "to Sichon" here and "to Og" in verse 20. This may be a poetic device, to continue the "to" construction that we have seen throughout, in several of the prior verses. But it may also reflect a somewhat rare use of the introductory *lamed*, not meaning "to" at all, but to mark the accusative case (usually the object of a verb). Here, because the kings are the ones whom God struck, they are in the accusative case and therefore require either the *lamed (l')* or the more usual marker, *et*. The author may have chosen *l'* over *et* for poetic reasons.

[23] *"When we were low"* The English seems to refer to depression, but the Hebrew is more general. (The same Hebrew word is used in Modern Hebrew to refer to "low tide.")

[24] *"Set us free"* Others, "rescued." The verb is used elsewhere to refer to removing the yoke from an animal, and earrings from the ears.

[25] *"Food to all creatures"* Literally, "gives bread to all flesh/meat." While we have almost certainly understood the point of the line, the original Hebrew alludes more specifically to the two ancient food sources, grain (bread) and meat, in a way that may not be accidental. The contrast between grains and meats seems to have been a prevalent theme in antiquity. To this day, the Hebrew word *lechem* means (by extension) "food," but more specifically "bread," while the cognate Arabic word, which also implies food, more specifically.

◆ ◆ ◆

II. *BIRKAT HASHIR*—("THE BLESSING OF SONG")
CLOSING BLESSING FOR *P'SUKEI D'ZIMRAH*

A. *Nishmat Kol Cha'i* ("The Breath of Every Living Being")

The breath of every living being will praise You, and the spirit of every mortal being will always glorify and extol You, our king. [2] You have always been and will always be God, and other than You we have no king to save us and redeem us, ransom us and rescue us and sustain us, and love us at every time of sorrow and hardship. [3] We have no king other than You! God of the first and the last, God of all creatures, master of all generations, glorified through great praise, He treats his world with love and his creatures with compassion. [4] Adonai neither rests nor sleeps. He awakens those who sleep, and rouses those who slumber, and grants speech to the mute, and frees the captives, and supports the falling, and raises those who are bent over. [5] It is You alone that we gratefully acknowledge.

[6] Even if our mouths were filled with song like the sea, and our tongues with joy like the sea's many roaring waves, and our lips with praise like the wide expanse of the sky, and even if our eyes shone like the sun and the moon, and even if our hands were spread wide like the eagles in the sky, and even if our feet were light like gazelles, we would be unable to properly acknowledge You with thanks, Adonai our God and our ancestors' God, or to praise your name for even one-thousandth of the thousands of thousands upon thousands and millions upon millions of great things You did for our ancestors and for us: [7] You freed us from Egypt, Adonai our God. You redeemed us from the house of bondage. You nourished us in famines and provided for us in abundance. You delivered

נִשְׁמַת כָּל חַי תְּבָרֵךְ אֶת שִׁמְךָ, יְיָ אֱלֹהֵינוּ, וְרוּחַ כָּל בָּשָׂר תְּפָאֵר וּתְרוֹמֵם זִכְרְךָ, מַלְכֵּנוּ, תָּמִיד. [2] מִן הָעוֹלָם וְעַד הָעוֹלָם אַתָּה אֵל, וּמִבַּלְעָדֶיךָ אֵין לָנוּ מֶלֶךְ גּוֹאֵל וּמוֹשִׁיעַ, פּוֹדֶה וּמַצִּיל וּמְפַרְנֵס, וּמְרַחֵם בְּכָל עֵת צָרָה וְצוּקָה; [3] אֵין לָנוּ מֶלֶךְ אֶלָּא אָתָּה. אֱלֹהֵי הָרִאשׁוֹנִים וְהָאַחֲרוֹנִים, אֱלוֹהַּ כָּל בְּרִיּוֹת, אֲדוֹן כָּל תּוֹלָדוֹת, הַמְהֻלָּל בְּרֹב הַתִּשְׁבָּחוֹת, הַמְנַהֵג עוֹלָמוֹ בְּחֶסֶד וּבְרִיּוֹתָיו בְּרַחֲמִים. [4] וַיְיָ לֹא יָנוּם וְלֹא יִישָׁן, הַמְעוֹרֵר יְשֵׁנִים, וְהַמֵּקִיץ נִרְדָּמִים, וְהַמֵּשִׂיחַ אִלְּמִים, וְהַמַּתִּיר אֲסוּרִים, וְהַסּוֹמֵךְ נוֹפְלִים, וְהַזּוֹקֵף כְּפוּפִים. [5] לְךָ לְבַדְּךָ אֲנַחְנוּ מוֹדִים.

[6] אִלּוּ פִינוּ מָלֵא שִׁירָה כַּיָּם, וּלְשׁוֹנֵנוּ רִנָּה כַּהֲמוֹן גַּלָּיו, וְשִׂפְתוֹתֵינוּ שֶׁבַח כְּמֶרְחֲבֵי רָקִיעַ, וְעֵינֵינוּ מְאִירוֹת כַּשֶּׁמֶשׁ וְכַיָּרֵחַ, וְיָדֵינוּ פְרוּשׂוֹת כְּנִשְׁרֵי שָׁמַיִם, וְרַגְלֵינוּ קַלּוֹת כָּאַיָּלוֹת, אֵין אֲנַחְנוּ מַסְפִּיקִים לְהוֹדוֹת לְךָ, יְיָ אֱלֹהֵינוּ וֵאלֹהֵי אֲבוֹתֵינוּ, וּלְבָרֵךְ אֶת שִׁמְךָ עַל אַחַת מֵאָלֶף, אֶלֶף אַלְפֵי אֲלָפִים וְרִבֵּי רְבָבוֹת פְּעָמִים הַטּוֹבוֹת שֶׁעָשִׂיתָ עִם אֲבוֹתֵינוּ וְעִמָּנוּ. [7] מִמִּצְרַיִם גְּאַלְתָּנוּ, יְיָ אֱלֹהֵינוּ, וּמִבֵּית עֲבָדִים פְּדִיתָנוּ;

us from the sword and saved us from the plague. You freed us from severe stubborn diseases. [8] Until now your kindness has helped us and your love has not abandoned us. Never forsake us, Adonai our God. [9] Therefore, the limbs You apportioned us, and the breath and spirit that You breathed into our nostrils, and the tongue that You put into our mouths, it is all of these that will thank, bless, praise, glorify, exalt, adore, sanctify, and extol You, our king. [10] For to You every mouth will offer thanks, and to You every tongue will swear allegiance, and to You every knee will bend, and before You everyone of height will bow, and every heart will revere You, and every lung sing to your name, in accordance with what is written: All my bones will say: Adonai, who is like You! You save the weak from those who are stronger than them, and the poor and needy from those who rob them. [11] Who can compare to You! Who can equal You! And who can match You, great, mighty, and awesome God, God on high, creator of heaven and earth. [12] We will exalt You and laud You and glorify You and praise your holy name. For it is said, "For David: O my soul, praise Adonai, and my very being, his holy name."

[On festivals, the prayer leader begins here:]

[13] God in your tremendous power, great in your glorious name, mighty forever and awe inspiring in your awe, You are king, seated on a high and exalted throne,

[On Shabbat, the prayer leader begins here:]

[14] Abiding forever, his name is exalted and holy. And it is written: Acclaim Adonai all you righteous, for it is fitting for the upright to offer praise.

בְּרָעָב זַנְתָּנוּ וּבְשָׂבָע כִּלְכַּלְתָּנוּ; מֵחֶרֶב הִצַּלְתָּנוּ וּמִדֶּבֶר מִלַּטְתָּנוּ, וּמֵחֳלָיִם רָעִים וְנֶאֱמָנִים דִּלִּיתָנוּ. [8] עַד הֵנָּה עֲזָרוּנוּ רַחֲמֶיךָ וְלֹא עֲזָבוּנוּ חֲסָדֶיךָ; וְאַל תִּטְּשֵׁנוּ, יְיָ אֱלֹהֵינוּ, לָנֶצַח. [9] עַל כֵּן, אֵבָרִים שֶׁפִּלַּגְתָּ בָּנוּ, וְרוּחַ וּנְשָׁמָה שֶׁנָּפַחְתָּ בְּאַפֵּינוּ, וְלָשׁוֹן אֲשֶׁר שַׂמְתָּ בְּפִינוּ הֵן הֵם יוֹדוּ וִיבָרְכוּ, וִישַׁבְּחוּ וִיפָאֲרוּ, וִירוֹמְמוּ וְיַעֲרִיצוּ, וְיַקְדִּישׁוּ וְיַמְלִיכוּ אֶת שִׁמְךָ, מַלְכֵּנוּ. [10] כִּי כָל פֶּה לְךָ יוֹדֶה, וְכָל לָשׁוֹן לְךָ תִשָּׁבַע, וְכָל בֶּרֶךְ לְךָ תִכְרַע, וְכָל קוֹמָה לְפָנֶיךָ תִשְׁתַּחֲוֶה, וְכָל לְבָבוֹת יִירָאוּךָ, וְכָל קֶרֶב וּכְלָיוֹת יְזַמְּרוּ לִשְׁמֶךָ, כַּדָּבָר שֶׁכָּתוּב: כָּל עַצְמוֹתַי תֹּאמַרְנָה, יְיָ מִי כָמוֹךָ, מַצִּיל עָנִי מֵחָזָק מִמֶּנּוּ, וְעָנִי וְאֶבְיוֹן מִגֹּזְלוֹ. [11] מִי יִדְמֶה לָּךְ, וּמִי יִשְׁוֶה לָּךְ, וּמִי יַעֲרָךְ־לָךְ, הָאֵל הַגָּדוֹל, הַגִּבּוֹר וְהַנּוֹרָא, אֵל עֶלְיוֹן, קֹנֵה שָׁמַיִם וָאָרֶץ. [12] נְהַלֶּלְךָ וּנְשַׁבֵּחֲךָ וּנְפָאֶרְךָ, וּנְבָרֵךְ אֶת שֵׁם קָדְשֶׁךָ, כָּאָמוּר: לְדָוִד, בָּרְכִי נַפְשִׁי אֶת יְיָ, וְכָל קְרָבַי אֶת שֵׁם קָדְשׁוֹ.

[On festivals, the prayer leader begins here:]

[13] הָאֵל בְּתַעֲצֻמוֹת עֻזֶּךָ, הַגָּדוֹל בִּכְבוֹד שְׁמֶךָ, הַגִּבּוֹר לָנֶצַח וְהַנּוֹרָא בְּנוֹרְאוֹתֶיךָ, הַמֶּלֶךְ הַיּוֹשֵׁב עַל כִּסֵּא רָם וְנִשָּׂא.

[On Shabbat, the prayer leader begins here:]

[14] שׁוֹכֵן עַד, מָרוֹם וְקָדוֹשׁ שְׁמוֹ, וְכָתוּב: רַנְּנוּ צַדִּיקִים בַּיְיָ, לַיְשָׁרִים נָאוָה תְהִלָּה.

[15] You will be lauded by the mouths of the upright.
You will be praised by the words of the righteous.
You will be exalted by the tongues of the faithful.
You will be sanctified by the lungs of holy creatures.

[16] With songs of joy, our king, your name shall be glorified by the vast multitudes of your people, the house of Israel, in every generation, [17] for it is the obligation of every creature before You, Adonai our God and our ancestors' God, to thank, magnify, laud, glorify, acclaim, exalt, and praise You, even beyond all the words of the songs and hymns of David son of Jesse your anointed servant.

B. *Yishtabach* ("Let [Your Name] Be Praised")

[18] Let your name be forever praised. Our king, great and holy king and God, in the heavens and on earth. [19] For song and praise, veneration and melody, strength and power, eternity, greatness and might, exaltation and glory, holiness and dominion, blessings and thanks befit You, Adonai our God and our ancestors' God, from now and ever more! [20] Blessed are You, Adonai, greatly lauded king and God, God of grateful acknowledgment, Lord of wonders, who chooses melodious songs, our king, our God, eternal life.

בְּפִי יְשָׁרִים תִּתְהַלָּל,[15]

וּבְדִבְרֵי צַדִּיקִים תִּתְבָּרַךְ,

וּבִלְשׁוֹן חֲסִידִים תִּתְרוֹמָם,

וּבְקֶרֶב קְדוֹשִׁים תִּתְקַדָּשׁ.

וּבְמַקְהֲלוֹת רִבְבוֹת עַמְּךָ בֵּית יִשְׂרָאֵל[16] בְּרִנָּה יִתְפָּאַר שִׁמְךָ, מַלְכֵּנוּ, בְּכָל דּוֹר וָדוֹר; [17]שֶׁכֵּן חוֹבַת כָּל הַיְצוּרִים לְפָנֶיךָ, יְיָ אֱלֹהֵינוּ וֵאלֹהֵי אֲבוֹתֵינוּ, לְהוֹדוֹת, לְהַלֵּל, לְשַׁבֵּחַ, לְפָאֵר, לְרוֹמֵם, לְהַדֵּר, לְבָרֵךְ, לְעַלֵּה וּלְקַלֵּס עַל כָּל דִּבְרֵי שִׁירוֹת וְתִשְׁבְּחוֹת דָּוִד בֶּן־יִשַׁי עַבְדְּךָ מְשִׁיחֶךָ.

יִשְׁתַּבַּח שִׁמְךָ לָעַד, מַלְכֵּנוּ, הָאֵל[18] הַמֶּלֶךְ הַגָּדוֹל וְהַקָּדוֹשׁ, בַּשָּׁמַיִם וּבָאָרֶץ. [19]כִּי לְךָ נָאֶה, יְיָ אֱלֹהֵינוּ וֵאלֹהֵי אֲבוֹתֵינוּ, שִׁיר וּשְׁבָחָה, הַלֵּל וְזִמְרָה, עֹז וּמֶמְשָׁלָה, נֶצַח, גְּדֻלָּה וּגְבוּרָה, תְּהִלָּה וְתִפְאֶרֶת, קְדֻשָּׁה וּמַלְכוּת, בְּרָכוֹת וְהוֹדָאוֹת, מֵעַתָּה וְעַד עוֹלָם. [20] בָּרוּךְ אַתָּה, יְיָ, אֵל מֶלֶךְ גָּדוֹל בַּתִּשְׁבָּחוֹת, אֵל הַהוֹדָאוֹת, אֲדוֹן הַנִּפְלָאוֹת, הַבּוֹחֵר בְּשִׁירֵי זִמְרָה, מֶלֶךְ, אֵל, חֵי הָעוֹלָמִים.

BRETTLER (BIBLE)

[1] *"The breath of every living being [Nishmat kol cha'i]"* Overall, this prayer quotes biblical verses, has a large number of references to biblical texts and ideas, and even displays some elements of biblical parallelism. But it is not characterized by *bicola*, the technical word we apply to the specific way that biblical poetry is arranged in parallelism. Also, its central idea—that the gulf between humans and God is so great that any human praise of God is inadequate—is not found in the psalms, which are nothing if not such praise. The concept of human inadequacy does appear elsewhere in the Bible, however, especially in the Book of Job. *(p. 49)*

DORFF (THEOLOGY)

[1] *"The breath of every living being ... our king ..."* This paragraph could be read as a totally universalist description of God, applying to all creation. In that case, "our king" would refer to the sovereign of all creatures, humanity first and foremost, but only as part of *(p. 53)*

ELLENSON (MODERN LITURGIES)

[1] *"The breath of every living being"* Marcia Falk, in her *Book of Blessings*, entitles this prayer "The Breath of Life" and does not specify, as the traditional prayer does, a personal God as the object of praise and blessing. Instead, she begins her prayer with *(p. 54)*

FRANKEL (A WOMAN'S VOICE)

[1] *"The breath [nishmat] of every living being"* Following is an excerpt of a *t'khine* (a women's prayer composed in Yiddish) found in a collection of daily *t'khines*, probably printed in Prague around 1700. The reader is instructed to recite this prayer "every day with *kavone* [devotional intention]." The author explains that "these beautiful *t'khines* were created for pious women and girls" and assures the reader that "this *t'khine* is well worth the money, for it was brought into print by a *(p. 54)*

II. *BIRKAT HASHIR*—("BLESSING OF SONG" CLOSING BLESSING FOR *P'SUKEI D'ZIMRAH*

A. *Nishmat Kol Cha'i* ("The Breath of Every Living Being")

[1] The breath of every living being will praise You, and the spirit of every mortal being will always glorify and extol You, our king. [2] You have always been and will always be God, and other than You we have no king to save us and redeem us, ransom us and rescue us

GRAY (OUR TALMUDIC HERITAGE)

[1] *"The breath of every living being [Nishmat kol cha'i]"* Barukh Halevi Epstein (Russia, 1880–1940) connects *Nishmat kol cha'i* with the verse that appears in the liturgy just prior: "On that day Adonai shall be one and his name shall be one" (Zech. 14:9). At the time of redemption, when God's name is indeed one, the souls of all humans will be uplifted to the extent that "the breath of every living being will praise You."

Rabbi Epstein stipulates *(p. 55)*

KUSHNER & POLEN (CHASIDISM)

[10] *"Before You everyone of height will bow"* Boruch of Mezbizh (d. 1811), grandson of the Baal Shem Tov, creatively misreads the phrase to mean not that everyone who is standing upright will bow down, but that a person may bow down even when apparently standing erect because the main thing is the broken heart (*Y'sod Ha'avodah* 65). And this sacred mystery is a primary distinction between serving an earthly king of flesh and blood and the Holy One of Being. *(p. 57)*

L. HOFFMAN (HISTORY)

*THE WARM-UP SECTION (*P'SUKEI D'ZIMRAH *["VERSES OF SONG"]), WHICH CONSISTS OF PSALMS AND SONGS, APPROPRIATELY ENDS WITH* BIRKAT HASHIR, *A "BLESSING OF SONG." ON WEEKDAYS, WHEN WE HAVE LESS TIME TO PRAY, WE USE THE SHORT FORM, "LET YOUR NAME BE FOREVER PRAISED" (SEE* VOLUME 3, P'SUKEI D'ZIMRAH [MORNING PSALMS], *P. 177). THAT SMALLER FORM OCCURS HERE TOO (PP. 48–49), BUT ONLY AS THE LAST PARAGRAPH TO A LARGER VERSION OF THE BLESSING, BEGINNING, "THE BREATH OF EVERY LIVING BEING WILL PRAISE YOU" (*NISHMAT KOL CHA'I T'VAREIKH*). WITH THIS FINAL BENEDICTION, PRAISING GOD AS "GOD … WHO CHOOSES MELODIOUS SONGS," OUR WARM-UP IS COMPLETE AND WE CAN MOVE ON TO THE OFFICIAL CALL TO PRAYER (THE* BAR'KHU),* *(p. 59)*

[1] נִשְׁמַת כָּל חַי תְּבָרֵךְ אֶת שִׁמְךָ, יְיָ אֱלֹהֵינוּ, וְרוּחַ כָּל בָּשָׂר תְּפָאֵר וּתְרוֹמֵם זִכְרְךָ, מַלְכֵּנוּ, תָּמִיד. [2] מִן הָעוֹלָם וְעַד הָעוֹלָם אַתָּה אֵל, וּמִבַּלְעָדֶיךָ אֵין לָנוּ מֶלֶךְ גּוֹאֵל וּמוֹשִׁיעַ, פּוֹדֶה וּמַצִּיל וּמְפַרְנֵס, וּמְרַחֵם בְּכָל עֵת צָרָה

LANDES (HALAKHAH)

[1] *"The breath of every living being [Nishmat kol cha'i]"* This poetic compilation, added on Shabbat and holy days to introduce the usual introductory prayer here (*Yishtabach*), fulfills no specific halakhic demand but is nonetheless prized by Halakhah. Thus, other than *Ashrei* (which is the heart of *P'sukei D'zimrah*), it alone is allowed to interrupt the recitation of *Yishtabach*: if, that is, one inadvertently skips *Nishmat*, beginning instead with the usual *Yishtabach*, and *(p. 57)*

J. HOFFMAN (TRANSLATION)

[1] *"Breath"* Hebrew, *n'shamah*, frequently translated "soul." Here the word appears in parallel with *ru'ach*. Both words roughly mean "spirit," "soul," "breath," etc. From these basic meanings, the words have taken on additional metaphoric meaning, not just in Hebrew, but in English too. For example, the English sentence, "Not a soul was left in the room," refers to bodies, not to souls.

[1] *"You"* Literally, "your name," in parallel with "your memory," *(p. 63)*

and sustain us, and love us at every time of sorrow and hardship. ³We have no king other than You! God of the first and the last, God of all creatures, master of all generations, glorified through great praise, He treats his world with love and his creatures with compassion. ⁴Adonai neither rests nor sleeps. He awakens those who sleep, and rouses those who slumber, and grants speech to the mute, and frees the captives, and supports the falling, and raises those who are bent over. ⁵It is You alone that we gratefully acknowledge.

⁶Even if our mouths were filled with song like the sea, and our tongues with joy like the sea's many roaring waves, and our lips with praise like the wide expanse of the sky, and even if our eyes shone like the sun and the moon, and even if our hands were spread wide like the eagles in the sky, and even if our feet were light like gazelles, we would be unable to properly acknowledge You with thanks, Adonai our God and our ancestors' God, or to praise your name for even one-thousandth of the thousands of thousands upon thousands and millions upon millions of great things You did for our ancestors and for us: ⁷You freed us from Egypt, Adonai our God. You redeemed us from the house of bondage. You nourished us in famines and provided for us in abundance. You

וְצוּקָה; ³אֵין לָנוּ מֶלֶךְ אֶלָּא אָתָּה. אֱלֹהֵי הָרִאשׁוֹנִים וְהָאַחֲרוֹנִים, אֱלוֹהַּ כָּל בְּרִיּוֹת, אֲדוֹן כָּל תּוֹלָדוֹת, הַמְהֻלָּל בְּרֹב הַתִּשְׁבָּחוֹת, הַמְנַהֵג עוֹלָמוֹ בְּחֶסֶד וּבְרִיּוֹתָיו בְּרַחֲמִים. ⁴וַייָ לֹא יָנוּם וְלֹא יִישָׁן, הַמְעוֹרֵר יְשֵׁנִים, וְהַמֵּקִיץ נִרְדָּמִים, וְהַמֵּשִׂיחַ אִלְּמִים, וְהַמַּתִּיר אֲסוּרִים, וְהַסּוֹמֵךְ נוֹפְלִים, וְהַזּוֹקֵף כְּפוּפִים. ⁵לְךָ לְבַדְּךָ אֲנַחְנוּ מוֹדִים.

⁶אִלּוּ פִינוּ מָלֵא שִׁירָה כַּיָּם, וּלְשׁוֹנֵנוּ רִנָּה כַּהֲמוֹן גַּלָּיו, וְשִׂפְתוֹתֵינוּ שֶׁבַח כְּמֶרְחֲבֵי רָקִיעַ, וְעֵינֵינוּ מְאִירוֹת כַּשֶּׁמֶשׁ וְכַיָּרֵחַ, וְיָדֵינוּ פְרוּשׂוֹת כְּנִשְׁרֵי שָׁמָיִם, וְרַגְלֵינוּ קַלּוֹת כָּאַיָּלוֹת, אֵין אֲנַחְנוּ מַסְפִּיקִים לְהוֹדוֹת לְךָ, יְיָ אֱלֹהֵינוּ וֵאלֹהֵי אֲבוֹתֵינוּ, וּלְבָרֵךְ אֶת שְׁמֶךָ עַל אַחַת מֵאֶלֶף, אֶלֶף אַלְפֵי אֲלָפִים וְרִבֵּי רְבָבוֹת פְּעָמִים הַטּוֹבוֹת שֶׁעָשִׂיתָ עִם אֲבוֹתֵינוּ וְעִמָּנוּ. ⁷מִמִּצְרַיִם גְּאַלְתָּנוּ, יְיָ אֱלֹהֵינוּ, וּמִבֵּית עֲבָדִים פְּדִיתָנוּ; בְּרָעָב זַנְתָּנוּ וּבְשָׂבָע כִּלְכַּלְתָּנוּ; מֵחֶרֶב הִצַּלְתָּנוּ וּמִדֶּבֶר מִלַּטְתָּנוּ, וּמֵחֳלָיִם רָעִים וְנֶאֱמָנִים דִּלִּיתָנוּ. ⁸עַד הֵנָּה עֲזָרוּנוּ רַחֲמֶיךָ וְלֹא עֲזָבוּנוּ חֲסָדֶיךָ; וְאַל תִּטְּשֵׁנוּ, יְיָ אֱלֹהֵינוּ, לָנֶצַח. ⁹עַל כֵּן, אֵבָרִים שֶׁפִּלַּגְתָּ בָּנוּ, וְרוּחַ וּנְשָׁמָה שֶׁנָּפַחְתָּ בְּאַפֵּינוּ, וְלָשׁוֹן אֲשֶׁר שַׂמְתָּ בְּפִינוּ הֵן הֵם יוֹדוּ וִיבָרְכוּ, וִישַׁבְּחוּ

delivered us from the sword and saved us from the plague. You freed us from severe stubborn diseases. 8 Until now your kindness has helped us and your love has not abandoned us. Never forsake us, Adonai our God. 9 Therefore, the limbs You apportioned us, and the breath and spirit that You breathed into our nostrils, and the tongue that You put into our mouths, it is all of these that will thank, bless, praise, glorify, exalt, adore, sanctify, and extol You, our king. 10 For to You every mouth will offer thanks, and to You every tongue will swear allegiance, and to You every knee will bend, and before You everyone of height will bow, and every heart will revere You, and every lung sing to your name, in accordance with what is written: All my bones will say: Adonai, who is like You! You save the weak from those who are stronger than them, and the poor and needy from those who rob them. 11 Who can compare to You! Who can equal You! And who can match You, great, mighty, and awesome God, God on high, creator of heaven and earth. 12 We will exalt You and laud You and glorify You and praise your holy name. For it is said, "For David: O my soul, praise Adonai, and my very being, his holy name."

[On festivals, the prayer leader begins here:]

13 God in your tremendous power, great in your glorious name, mighty

וִיפָאֲרוּ, וִירוֹמְמוּ וְיַעֲרִיצוּ, וְיַקְדִּישׁוּ וְיַמְלִיכוּ אֶת שִׁמְךָ, מַלְכֵּנוּ. 10כִּי כָל פֶּה לְךָ יוֹדֶה, וְכָל לָשׁוֹן לְךָ תִשָּׁבַע, וְכָל בֶּרֶךְ לְךָ תִכְרַע, וְכָל קוֹמָה לְפָנֶיךָ תִשְׁתַּחֲוֶה, וְכָל לְבָבוֹת יִירָאוּךָ, וְכָל קֶרֶב וּכְלָיוֹת יְזַמְּרוּ לִשְׁמֶךָ, כַּדָּבָר שֶׁכָּתוּב: כָּל עַצְמוֹתַי תֹּאמַרְנָה, יְיָ, מִי כָמוֹךָ, מַצִּיל עָנִי מֵחָזָק מִמֶּנּוּ, וְעָנִי וְאֶבְיוֹן מִגֹּזְלוֹ. 11מִי יִדְמֶה לָּךְ, וּמִי יִשְׁוֶה לָּךְ, וּמִי יַעֲרָךְ־לָךְ, הָאֵל הַגָּדוֹל, הַגִּבּוֹר וְהַנּוֹרָא, אֵל עֶלְיוֹן, קֹנֵה שָׁמַיִם וָאָרֶץ. 12נְהַלֶּלְךָ וּנְשַׁבֵּחֲךָ וּנְפָאֶרְךָ, וּנְבָרֵךְ אֶת שֵׁם קָדְשֶׁךָ, כָּאָמוּר: לְדָוִד, בָּרְכִי נַפְשִׁי אֶת יְיָ, וְכָל קְרָבַי אֶת שֵׁם קָדְשׁוֹ.

[On festivals, the prayer leader begins here:]

13הָאֵל בְּתַעֲצֻמוֹת עֻזֶּךָ, הַגָּדוֹל בִּכְבוֹד שְׁמֶךָ, הַגִּבּוֹר לָנֶצַח וְהַנּוֹרָא בְּנוֹרְאוֹתֶיךָ, הַמֶּלֶךְ הַיּוֹשֵׁב עַל כִּסֵּא רָם וְנִשָּׂא.

[On Shabbat, the prayer leader begins here:]

14שׁוֹכֵן עַד, מָרוֹם וְקָדוֹשׁ שְׁמוֹ, וְכָתוּב: רַנְּנוּ צַדִּיקִים בַּיְיָ, לַיְשָׁרִים נָאוָה תְהִלָּה. 15בְּפִי יְשָׁרִים תִּתְהַלָּל, וּבְדִבְרֵי צַדִּיקִים תִּתְבָּרַךְ, וּבִלְשׁוֹן חֲסִידִים תִּתְרוֹמָם, וּבְקֶרֶב קְדוֹשִׁים תִּתְקַדָּשׁ. 16וּבְמַקְהֲלוֹת רִבְבוֹת עַמְּךָ בֵּית יִשְׂרָאֵל בְּרִנָּה יִתְפָּאַר שִׁמְךָ, מַלְכֵּנוּ, בְּכָל דּוֹר וָדוֹר; 17שֶׁכֵּן חוֹבַת כָּל הַיְצוּרִים לְפָנֶיךָ,

forever and awe inspiring in your awe, You are king, seated on a high and exalted throne,

[On Shabbat, the prayer leader begins here:]

14 Abiding forever, his name is exalted and holy. And it is written: Acclaim Adonai all you righteous, for it is fitting for the upright to offer praise.

15 You will be lauded by the mouths of the upright.
You will be praised by the words of the righteous.
You will be exalted by the tongues of the faithful.
You will be sanctified by the lungs of holy creatures.

16 With songs of joy, our king, your name shall be glorified by the vast multitudes of your people, the house of Israel, in every generation, 17 for it is the obligation of every creature before You, Adonai our God and our ancestors' God, to thank, magnify, laud, glorify, acclaim, exalt, and praise You, even beyond all the words of the songs and hymns of David son of Jesse your anointed servant.

B. **Yishtabach** ("Let [Your Name] Be Praised")

18 Let your name be forever praised. Our king, great and holy king and God, in the heavens and on earth. 19 For song and praise, veneration and melody, strength and power, eternity, greatness and might, exaltation and

יְיָ אֱלֹהֵינוּ וֵאלֹהֵי אֲבוֹתֵינוּ, לְהוֹדוֹת, לְהַלֵּל, לְשַׁבֵּחַ, לְפָאֵר, לְרוֹמֵם, לְהַדֵּר, לְבָרֵךְ, לְעַלֵּה וּלְקַלֵּס עַל כָּל דִּבְרֵי שִׁירוֹת וְתִשְׁבְּחוֹת דָּוִד בֶּן־יִשַׁי עַבְדְּךָ מְשִׁיחֶךָ.

18 יִשְׁתַּבַּח שִׁמְךָ לָעַד, מַלְכֵּנוּ, הָאֵל הַמֶּלֶךְ הַגָּדוֹל וְהַקָּדוֹשׁ, בַּשָּׁמַיִם וּבָאָרֶץ. 19 כִּי לְךָ נָאֶה, יְיָ אֱלֹהֵינוּ וֵאלֹהֵי אֲבוֹתֵינוּ, שִׁיר וּשְׁבָחָה, הַלֵּל וְזִמְרָה, עֹז וּמֶמְשָׁלָה, נֶצַח, גְּדֻלָּה וּגְבוּרָה, תְּהִלָּה

glory, holiness and dominion, blessings and thanks befit You, Adonai our God and our ancestors' God, from now and ever more! [20]Blessed are You, Adonai, greatly lauded king and God, God of grateful acknowledgment, Lord of wonders, who chooses melodious songs, our king, our God, eternal life.

וְתִפְאֶרֶת, קְדֻשָּׁה וּמַלְכוּת, בְּרָכוֹת וְהוֹדָאוֹת, מֵעַתָּה וְעַד עוֹלָם. [20]בָּרוּךְ אַתָּה, יְיָ, אֵל מֶלֶךְ גָּדוֹל בַּתִּשְׁבָּחוֹת, אֵל הַהוֹדָאוֹת, אֲדוֹן הַנִּפְלָאוֹת, הַבּוֹחֵר בְּשִׁירֵי זִמְרָה, מֶלֶךְ, אֵל, חֵי הָעוֹלָמִים.

BRETTLER (BIBLE)

[1] *"Breath of every living being … spirit of every mortal being"* Examples of parallelism that typifies biblical poetry. We find these very instances already in the Bible.

[1] *"Will praise You"* [lit. *"your name,"* shimkha]*"* A common biblical idea (e.g., the conclusion of Ps. 145: "My mouth shall utter the praise of Adonai, and all creatures shall bless his holy *name* forever and ever"). To accomplish the blessing of God's name, the Bible uses specific blessing formulae, such as Ruth 4:14, "Blessed is Adonai." These serve as implicit recognitions of God's power.

[2] *"Other than You we have no king"* This section of the prayer typifies the absolute monotheism of later biblical Israel, often using stock biblical phrases: "You have always been and will always be God" *(min ha'olam … ha'olam … atah el)*. Noticeable also is the alliterative *tsarah v'tsukah* ("sorrow and hardship").

[4] *"Neither rests nor sleeps"* Based on Psalm 121:4, "See, the guardian of Israel neither rests nor sleeps!" For the opposite notion, see Psalm 44:24, "Rouse Yourself; why do You sleep, Adonai? Awaken, do not reject us forever!" The next line of our prayer, "awakens those who sleep," follows logically: an always wakeful deity can awaken others.

[4] *"Supports the falling"* Only the final pair of ideas is biblical: in Psalm 145:14 *(Ashre)*, "Adonai supports all who stumble, and makes all who are bent stand straight." The rest of the sentence, however, still copies biblical style.

[6] *"Even … eagles"* Three parallel pairs, continuing the biblical model of parallelism (though many of the phrases and images are not biblical). The first image ("Even if our mouths were filled with song like the sea") may allude to the vastness of the sea, or to verses like Psalm 96:11 (see also 98:7), which depict the sea as rejoicing very loudly: "Let the heavens rejoice and the earth exult; let the sea and all within it thunder."

[6] *"One-thousandth of the thousands of thousands"* A truly superlative number, even greater than what is described in Daniel 7:10, "A river of fire streamed forth before Him; thousands upon thousands served Him; myriads upon myriads attended Him; The court sat and the books were opened."

[7] *"You freed us from Egypt"* We might expect this paradigmatic act of God to reappear as poetic reprise. The beginning words suggest so, but it appears only once and then leads to other, more general acts of God's beneficence and power feeding people, and saving them from the "famines, swords, plague" *(ra'av, cherev, dever),* a triad especially common in Jeremiah and Ezekiel.

[8] *"Until now your kindness"* See similarly Psalm 40:12, "Adonai, You will not withhold from me your compassion; Your steadfast love will protect me always." Like 2 Kings 14:26, the author puns with *azarunu* ("helped us") and *azavunu* ("abandoned us").

[8] *"Never [Al ... lanetsach]"* This conclusion, which has biblical roots (1 Kings 8:57; Ps. 27:9), breaks the style of biblical parallelism that we have seen so far. Quite possibly, the concluding *lanetsach* ("forever"—thus, *al lanetsach,* literally, "not forever = never") harks back to *tamid,* "always," (in verse 1), which begins the description of facts about God that *lanetsach* now concludes. The next verse, beginning "therefore" *(al ken),* draws out the implications of those facts.

[9] *"Limbs ... breath ... spirit ... nostrils ... tongue"* For purposes of praising God, the human body is divided into three parts: "limbs" *(evarim),* "breath and spirit" *(ru'ach un'shamah),* and "tongue" *(lashon).* As to the body, ancient Judaism stipulated many limbs that could express divine devotion, including bowing from the knees (see v. 10) and raising one's hands in worship (see, e.g., Ps. 28:2, "Listen to my plea for mercy when ... I lift my hands toward your inner sanctuary."). The root *n.p.ch* ("breathe") used in reference to the *ru'ach un'shamah* reflects the creation of Adam in the second creation story (Gen. 2:7), but in the Bible the phrase *ru'ach un'shamah* denotes breath or life-force. It is rabbinic culture that changed it to mean a soul, separate from the body. The long list of verbs ("thank, bless, praise ...") is a way of expressing how superlatively all parts of body and soul will praise God. No comparable list of so many consecutive reinforcing verbs is found in the Bible.

[10] *"For to You ... "* This verse is an exposition of Psalm 35:10, which is quoted at the end. The author's point is that the entire body is participating in acknowledging God. The ancients had a quite imprecise sense of anatomy, however: the brain is missing here, its cognitive and emotional functions being fulfilled by the heart and kidneys.

[11] *"Who can compare to You! ... "* A conflation and reworking of Isaiah 40:18, 40:25, from the anonymous prophet we call Deutero-Isaiah, who prophesied during the Babylonian exile and emphasized God's incomparability: "To whom, then, can you liken God, what form compare to Him?" "To whom, then, can you liken Me, to whom can I be compared?—says the Holy One."

[11] *"Great, mighty, and awesome God"* Quoting Deuteronomy 10:17 or Nehemiah 9:32.

[11] *"God on high [elyon], creator of heaven and earth"* This divine name is first used by the Canaanite king Melchizedek, when he blesses Abram (Gen. 14:19), but there, he likely has in mind the old Canaanite creator deity Il or El (hence, El-yon). The God of Israel absorbed many of his characteristics, so that Abram later blesses the king of Sodom in the name of "Adonai, God on high, creator of heaven and earth" (Gen. 14:22).

[12] *"We will exalt You ... For it is said"* Like verse 10, this too begins with a parallel list of verbs that explicate and expand a biblical verse that follows. The verse in question, Psalm 103:1, is thematically similar to our prayer. In fact, all the significant words from Psalm 103:1 are found elsewhere in *Nishmat kol cha'i*, suggesting that the whole thing is an elaboration and extension of that psalm.

[13] *"Great in your glorious name ... inspiring in your awe"* Other than "inspiring in your awe," all other examples of God's greatness here have biblical precedents. The odd "great in your glorious name" is a conflation of Psalm 138:5, "Great is the majesty of Adonai!" and several verses that mention "the glory of the [God's] name" (e.g., Ps. 29:2, "Ascribe to Adonai the glory of his name"). The conclusion ("king, seated on a high and exalted throne") reflects God's appearance to Isaiah, most likely at his dedication as a prophet (Isa. 6:1, "I saw God seated on a high and exalted throne").

[14] *"Abiding forever, his name is exalted and holy"* A reworking of Isaiah 57:15, "For thus said He who high aloft forever dwells, whose name is holy: I dwell on high, in holiness." The end, "fitting for the upright to offer praise," quotes the opening of Psalm 33.

[15] *"Mouths of the upright"* Based on Isaiah 45:23, "By Myself have I sworn, from my mouth has issued truth, a word that shall not turn back: To Me every knee shall bend, every tongue swear loyalty." The "mouth" and "knee" are augmented by "lungs [of holy creatures]" *(kerev)* to integrate Psalm 103:1, cited above (v. 12, "We will exalt [requiring lungs] You.... For it is said").

[15] *"Upright ... righteous ... faithful ... holy creatures [Y'sharim, TSadikim, CHasidim, K'doshim]"* An acrostic YiTSCHaK ("Isaac"). The Bible has alphabetic acrostics, but never spell out specific words or names.

The first two pairs of second and third words *(y'sharim tit'hallal; tsadikim titbarakh)* are common biblical word pairs, while the second two pairs *(chasidim titromam; k'doshim titkadash)* are innovative. In some biblical texts, *chasidim* denotes a specific class of people; here, however, the context suggests just generally righteous individuals.

[17] *"Every creature"* The obligation of "every creature," *kol hay'tsurim,* implying everything created (every *y'tsur,* not just people), to praise God may seem odd to us,

but Jonah 3:8, for example, narrates the obligation of "man and beast" to "cry mightily to God." The logic is faultless: why shouldn't all created beings acknowledge their creator?

[17] *"David son of Jesse [David ben Yishai]"* The reference is to the Book of Psalms, which some rabbinic traditions attribute to David, even though many psalms are anonymous compositions or contain titles or superscriptions attributing authorship to other figures.

[17] *"Your anointed servant* [m'shichekha]*"* Literally, "your anointed one," a reference to pouring oil on the king as part of the enthronement ritual. This title is used frequently of Saul in 1 Samuel, and once of David in 2 Samuel 19:22. In biblical literature, the term *mashi'ach* never refers to the ideal future king (messiah), though this is the likely sense of the term here.

[18] *"Let your name be forever praised"* The concluding prayer of *P'sukei D'zimrah*, which is a post-biblical composition. With the rubric's introduction, "Blessed is the One," it forms an *inclusio* (a rhetorical style whereby the end reiterates the beginning; see Brettler, "Let my mouth speak Adonai's praise, and all creatures praise his holy name for ever and ever," Volume 3, *P'sukei D'zimrah [Morning Psalms]*, p. 117).

[18] *"Our king, great and holy king"* As a summary prayer, it continues the central image of the *P'sukei D'zimrah*, God's kingship, which was stressed in the prayers leading up to it and in Psalms 145–150 before that.

[18] *"In the heavens and on earth"* Returning to the introductory verse of Psalm 150 (see Brettler, "Sanctuary ... heaven of power," Volume 3, *P'sukei D'zimrah [Morning Psalms]*, p. 142).

[19] *"For song and praise ... blessings and thanks"* A string of largely synonymous nouns. This style begins in the late biblical period and develops later (see Brettler, "Greatness and power and glory ... great and strong," Volume 3, *P'sukei D'zimrah [Morning Psalms]*, p. 156).

[20] *"God, greatly lauded king ... God of grateful acknowledgment"* A continuation of the style of the previous section, in this case using short phrases that are very similar in meaning.

[20] *"Who chooses melodious songs"* "Choose" in the sense of "desire." The entire section concludes by justifying itself. The *P'sukei D'zimrah* will work because God likes melodious songs.

[20] *"Our king, our God, eternal life"* An effective summary of many of the attributes of God recited in the earlier hymns; indeed, the final phrase, *chei olamim*, here translated "eternal life," reiterates the extent of God's great power, the main theme of Psalms 145–150.

◆

DORFF (THEOLOGY)

"every living being." It is also possible, however, to interpret this paragraph as switching effortlessly between the universal God of all and the particular God of Israel, where "our king" would refer specifically to the People Israel, as would the "we" in "we have no king other than You" (v. 3). Asserting a universal God who is also specifically Israel's is the point of juxtaposing the first, universalist blessing before the *Sh'ma* to the second (particularist) blessing, in which God is praised for loving the People Israel by providing Torah (see Volume 1, *The Sh'ma and Its Blessings*, p. 71).

⁶ *"Even if our mouths were filled with song ... unable to properly acknowledge You"* What does it mean to be unable to thank God enough? Does that make us so insignificant that we have no worth at all?

Our potentially utter worthlessness is envisioned even more starkly in the early morning prayer that asks, "What are we? What is our life? What is our goodness? ... All the heroes are as nothing before You" (see Volume 5, *Birkhot Hashachar [Morning Blessings]*, pp. 160–169). We learn there that only God's covenant rescues us from our inherent lowliness. Here we get a different answer: "Your kindness has helped us and your love has not abandoned us" (v. 8). It is God's compassion and fidelity that give us worth.

In both cases, God's relationship to us lends our lives value. This notion contrasts sharply with some Christian (Augustinian and Calvinist) conceptions of human beings as being hopelessly depraved from the moment of birth (tainted with original sin), unable to earn salvation through deeds, and unworthy to be saved by God. Only faith in Jesus can save, and (in Calvinism) even that will save just the elect few. For Jews, by contrast, our lack of merit is balanced by our ongoing relationship with God, who values us.

⁶ *"The millions upon millions of great things"* As Philip Birnbaum points out (*Siddur Hashalem*, pp. 331–332), this paragraph from the Talmud (Ber. 59b; Ta'an. 6b) is part of the prayer for rain. "The millions upon millions of great things" probably denotes raindrops, each one a separate favor. More broadly, however, the prayer indicates the extent of our indebtedness to God for absolutely everything we have. It therefore switches without a beat from an allusion to rain to God's redeeming us from Egypt. This leads the Talmud (Pes. 118a) to recommend this psalm for the Seder.

The Hebrew word for Egypt is *mitsrayim*, from the root *metsar*, "strait," probably an allusion to the way the Nile empties into the Mediterranean Sea through a series of straits. But midrashically, redemption from Egypt (*mitsrayim*) may be extended to include all the straits (*metsarim*) of life: hunger, thirst, prejudice, war, disability, illness, etc. We thank God for saving us not just from Egypt but from these other horrors also.

¹⁰ *"You save the weak from those who are stronger than them, and the poor and needy from those who rob them"* God is the mighty ruler of the universe, but also our moral paradigm. "Maker of the heaven and earth, the sea and all that is in them," we say in

our morning prayers, "the grantor of justice to the oppressed, provider of bread to the hungry ... who frees the captives, opens the eyes of the blind, uprights the bent over, and loves the righteous. Adonai guards strangers, and upholds the orphan and widow" (Ps. 146:6–9; see Volume 3, *P'sukei D'zimrah [Morning Psalms]*, pp. 124–127).

———◆———

ELLENSON (MODERN LITURGIES)

the words, "The breath of all life will bless; the body will exclaim," and completes her prayer by drawing upon the traditional liturgy in her own innovative way. She writes:

> Were our mouths filled with song as the sea and our tongues lapping joy like the waves and our lips singing praises broad as the sky and our eyes like the sun and the moon and our arms open wide as the eagle's wings and our feet leaping light as the deer's, it would not be enough to tell the wonder.

[19] *"Adonai our God and our ancestors'* [avoteinu, *'our fathers'*] *God"* In keeping with a contemporary egalitarian sensibility, a number of modern Siddurim, including the Reform *Mishkan T'filah* (2006), the Masorti *Va'ani Tefillati* (1998), and the Reconstructionist *Kol Haneshamah* (1996), add *imoteinu* ("our mothers") to this phrase.

———◆———

FRANKEL (A WOMAN'S VOICE)

pious woman, Rokh'l, daughter of Reb Mord'khe Soyfer, of blessed memory, of the holy community of Fintshuv." The sentiments and many of the phrases of this Yiddish prayer echo those found in *Nishmat*:

> How can I praise Him adequately
> When even a portion of the praise
> That falls from my lips
> Could fill the entire world.
>
> He feeds everyone with His grace
> And with his mercy.
> He is righteous.
> Blessed is the name of His glorious kingdom
> Forever and ever.
>
> He is the eternal King.
> He is the highest,
> And His heart is compassionate
> As are His ways.
>
> He is the first Father,
> And He is the last Father,
> Who is merciful to His beloved children.

(From Devra Kay, Seyder Tkhines: The Forgotten Book of Common Prayer for Jewish Women [Philadelphia: Jewish Publication Society, 2004], pp. 243–244])

[18] *"Let your name be forever praised"* The *P'sukei D'zimrah* section of the morning prayers begins and ends with a call to praise God. We begin with a personal *kavvanah* (a prayer of intention): "With this do I prepare my mouth to thank, praise, and glorify my creator" (see Volume 3, *P'sukei D'zimrah [Morning Psalms]*, p. 49). Then, after having recited many psalms and hymns of praise, we round out this section with a concluding blessing, thanking God for accepting our songs of praise. After all, how dare we assume that our words will be adequate to the task of praising God? For even here, as we pile up a mountain of accolades—"song and praise, veneration and melody, strength and power, eternity, greatness and might, exaltation and glory, holiness and dominion, blessings and thanks befit You"—we fall far short of rendering sufficient homage to the infinite and eternal One. In the end, we can only *aspire* to praise, and hope that *el hahoda'ot*, "the God of greatful acknowledgment," will accept our yearning as its own fulfillment.

———◆———

GRAY (OUR TALMUDIC HERITAGE)

that "the breath of every living being" need not be limited to humans. The Torah refers to all animals as creatures with a "breath of life," as in Genesis 7:22, where the Flood destroys everything with a "breath of life." But how can animals sing praises to God? Epstein cites talmudic stories claiming that animals have done exactly that. At Avodah Zarah 24b, the Talmud says that the cows carrying the ark of the covenant back to the Israelites from its captivity among the Philistines (1 Sam. 6:12) sang praise to God, while according to Hullin 64b, a species of bird sings praise to God when it finds water in its desert habitation. Perhaps when animals behave as they were created to, their behavior is itself a song of praise to God. Could it be that we humans too sing praise to God just by acting morally as we are created to do?

[2-3] *"At every time of sorrow and hardship. We have no king other than You!"* Barukh Halevi Epstein (Russia, 1880–1940) sees this line as an affirmation of the Jewish people's unshakable faith in God. Unlike pagan peoples, who turn on their gods in anger when they suffer reversals (see Isa. 8:21, "And it shall be that when he [a worshiper] is hungry, he will become angry and curse his king and his god"), Jews understand that whatever befalls them, they have no ruler but God. No wonder the Talmud admonishes us (Ber. 54a) to recite blessings to God even when evil befalls us ("Blessed are You ... the true judge"), and not just for the good in our lives (when we say, "Blessed are You ... who is good and does good").

[3] *"Glorified through great praise"* A *sh'liach tsibbur* (a prayer leader) once led prayers in the presence of Rabbi Chaninah, lavishly praising God with adjective upon adjective. When the service ended, Rabbi Chaninah chided him for praising God so verbosely. Since no one can praise God adequately (God being infinite), effusive praise could be seen as an unintended slight—analogous to praising an earthly king for his collection

of silver, when his real wealth is in gold (Ber. 33b). This being so, our prayer, wisely and simply, refers to God as being "glorified through great praise."

[4] *"Adonai neither rests nor sleeps"* The Talmud proposes two different theologically significant ideas of how God, who "neither slumbers nor sleeps," spends time. Yitzchak bar Shmuel says in the name of Rav that at the transitions between the three watches of the night, God sits in sorrow, roaring like a lion over the destruction of the Temple and the consequent exile of Israel: "Woe to the children because of whose sins I destroyed my house, and burned my sanctuary, and exiled them among the nations of the world" (Ber. 3a). Rav Judah in the name of Rav says that God divides the twelve hours of daylight into four parts: studying Torah for the first three hours, judging the world for the second three, feeding all living beings for the third three, and then playing with the giant sea creature Leviathan for the fourth three (A.Z. 3b). In a touching alternative tradition, the Talmud says that God spends the fourth set of three hours teaching Torah to schoolchildren no longer on earth—schoolchildren (we may assume) who died young (A.Z. 3b).

[6] *"Great things You did for our ancestors and for us"* The reference to good things done both for our ancestors and for us is reminiscent of Exodus 15:2, "This is my God and I will enshrine Him; the God of my father, and I will exalt Him." The *Mekhilta D'rabbi Yishmael* (*B'shalach, Shirata* 3) pictures the community of Israel telling God: "Master of the universe! Not [only] for the miracles You did for me do I sing before You, but for those [as well] that You did for my ancestors and will do for me in every generation."

[7] *"Provided for us in abundance [uv'sova kilkaltanu]"* The wording here is challenging: it says that God provided for us *v'sova* ("in [times of] abundance"), but how remarkable is that? More telling would have been God's provision in a time of famine. Both Abudarham (fourteenth-century Spain) and Barukh Halevi Epstein (Russia, 1880–1940) point to the Talmud (B.B. 91b) where Rabbi Yochanan recalls a time when food was abundant but people went hungry because they didn't have money to buy it. So even in a time of plenty, God provides for us—by ensuring the financial means to purchase what we need.

[18] *"Let your name be forever praised"* See Judith Hauptman, Volume 3, *P'sukei D'zimrah (Morning Psalms)*, p. 178 (v. 1 "Let your name be forever praised").

[20] *"Blessed are You, Adonai, God, greatly lauded king"* Siddur Rashi (Franco-Germany, c. twelfth century) points out that this concluding *chatimah* (the final line of the blessing) is not for *Yishtabach* alone, but for all of *P'sukei D'zimrah*.

———◆———

KUSHNER & POLEN (CHASIDISM)

Mendl of Vorki was once asked, what constitutes a true Jew? He replied, "Three things are fitting for us: upright kneeling, silent screaming, and motionless dance" (Martin Buber, *Tales of the Hasidim: The Later Masters*, trans. Olga Marx [New York: Schocken, 1961], p. 302).

[10] *"All my bones will say: Adonai, who is like You!"* The Imre Emet (son of the Sefat Emet), Avraham Mordecai Alter, would awaken at 4:30 A.M., a full three hours before the beginning of morning prayers. When questioned about this he once replied to Rabbi Shammai Ginzburg, "Not all my limbs awaken at the same pace. You must understand that there are parts of my body that need more time than others before they are fully awake."

[20] *"Who chooses melodious songs"* Zev Wolf of Zhitomir, in his *Or HaMeir* (*Yesod HaAvodah*, p. 28), is struck by the pleonasm of "melodious" and "songs" used together. Either word would have sufficed. He solves the problem by suggesting that the consonants that make up *shir*, the word for song *(shin, yod, resh)*, might also be pronounced as *sh'yar*, meaning "leftover" (plural, *sh'yarim*, or, popularly, *shirayim*). Among Chasidim, *shirayim*, or "leftovers," refer to the crumbs remaining from a rebbe's meal. Though it strikes the modern reader as strange, to partake of these remnants—after they had been on the plate of such a holy person—was a great honor, even a gift. Disciples were known to fight with one another over the *shirayim*: the crumbs (or the songs!) from the master's table. It was not uncommon, furthermore, for each rebbe to have his (or her) own, either self-composed or favorite, melody. In this context, "melodious songs" now means "melodious leftovers" or "the remnants of a melody."

What remains when the music stops? Surely there must be more than dumb silence. The silence of the walk to the car after a symphony concert is now silent in a new way. The air is redolent with the remnants of the music. Some things simply cannot be uttered. And this is what God chooses—these remnants of song.

◆

LANDES (HALAKHAH)

then realizes the error before completing *Yishtabach*, one returns, recites *Nishmat kol cha'i*, and says *Yishtabach* all over again from its beginning (*Be'ur Hahalakhah* 281:1). If one has completed *Yishtabach*, but not begun the *Bar'khu* that follows it, then one simply adds *Nishmat* (*Sha'arai T'shuvah* [Rabbi Hayim Mordecai Margoliot, early commentary on *Shulchan Arukh*], O. Ch. 281:1). A tradition stemming from Rabbi Judah the Pietist (Yehudah Hechasid, 1150–1217; author also of *Shir Hakavod* [pronounced SHEER hah-kah-VOHD]—see p. 177) holds that someone saved from disaster should recite *Nishmat* in front of a *minyan*. The Ben Ish Cha'i (R. Yosef Chaim ben Eliyahu, 1835–1904, Baghdad [Toldot 3]) insists that this prayer be recited *bin'imah* (pronounced bih-n'-ee-MAH), "in song."

Rabbi Nehemia Alter was the son of the Rebbe of Gur who authored the *S'fat Emet*, a beloved work of classical Chasidic thought. He served as the halakhic authority in Lodz, Poland during the onset of the Holocaust, where he declared at a public meeting, "One does not have to sanctify the name of God *(kiddush hashem)* specifically with guns [in resistance]. Let everyone sanctify God according to his own abilities. Let us not lower ourselves in front of the gentiles; also let us not fulfill their orders which bring us to death. When Rabbi Alter was deported, he donned his clothes for Shabbat and carried his *tallit* and *t'fillin*. Under his arm was a copy of the *S'fat Emet*. Entering the railroad car he sang *Nishmat kol cha'i* ("The breath of every living being will praise You") with great enthusiasm. He was shoved off the car to his death by an enraged Nazi officer, who cried, "This is surely a Jewish leader. Let him go *there*. Even *there* they need Jewish leaders…." (Daniel Landes, "Spiritual Responses in the Ghettoes," in Alex Grobman, Sybil Milton, and Daniel Landes [ed.] *Critical Issues of the Holocaust* [New York: Rossel Books, 1995], pp. 199–200).

As a universalistic prayer connecting the soul of *every living being (kol cha'i)* to God, *Nishmat* is enshrined by Halakhah as a necessary component of Jewish prayer: asking for the well-being of all the world.

[14] *"Abiding forever* [Shokhen ad]*"* On Shabbat the *sh'liach tsibbur* ("prayer leader") for *Shacharit* begins here, as opposed to weekdays, when he begins with verse 16, "With songs of joy … Your name shall be glorified" *(Yishtabach)*. This paragraph, "Abiding forever" *(Shokhen ad)*, speaks of uplift and holiness fit for Shabbat day.

On festivals, the *sh'liach tsibbur* begins with verse 13, "God" *(ha'el)*. Actually, the *Kol Bo* records the precise custom as follows:

> "God in your tremendous power" *(Ha'el beta'atsumot uzekha)*
> On Shavuot, begin with *ta'atsumot uzekha*, "your tremendous power," for power is associated with Torah which we celebrate on that day. On Sukkot, begin with *hagadol bikh'vod sh'mekha*, "great in your glorious name," for glory is associated with Sukkot, as we see from the "clouds of glory" *(ananei kavod)* that accompanied the Israelites in the desert and which is the precedent for dwelling in booths. And on Passover, begin with *hagibbor lanetsach*, "mighty forever," for God appeared at the splitting of the sea as a *gibbor* ("a mighty warrior"). On Rosh Hashanah and on Yom Kippur, begin with *hamelekh* ("the king"), recited with great awe, for this is the time we crown king over all.

[18] *"Let your name be forever praised"* Some blessings begin and end with *Barukh*, while others just end that way. The general rule is that the first of a series of blessings one after the other starts with the familiar *Barukh* formula, but blessings that follow it do not. Individual blessings that are not part of a string normally have the *Barukh* opening also. We would expect, then, that this, the culminating blessing of the *P'sukei D'zimrah*, would begin with *Barukh*, for it seems to stand alone as the final bracket, so to speak, of the rubric as a whole. However, it is treated halakhically as if it is integrally connected to the opening blessing, "Blessed is the One by whose speech" *(Barukh she'amar)*, with which the rubric began (see Volume 3, *P'sukei D'zimrah* [*Morning Psalms*], p. 49). A worshiper therefore never makes this blessing without the opening one and, since they are intended as brackets for biblical praise, at least the *Ashre* must be recited (Psalm 145, see Volume 3, *P'sukei D'zimrah*, p. 112). If one says it alone, it

is treated as a "blessing said in vain" *(b'rakhah l'vatallah)*, an instance of taking God's name in vain *(Shulchan Arukh*, O. Ch. 536; *Mishnah B'rurah* 3:4).

Because it is a blessing over the singing of praise to God, by which we mean all the psalms and songs that precede it and that constitute the *P'sukei D'zimrah*, it should be sung sweetly *(Kaf Hgachayim* 48).

[19] *"Song and praise ... blessings and thanks"* Fifteen terms of praise, all in all. It is customary to sing all the way through them without any interruption.

❖

L. HOFFMAN (HISTORY)

WHICH MARKS THE OPENING OF OUR NEXT MAJOR SECTION OF THE SERVICE, THE SH'MA AND ITS BLESSINGS.

[1] *"The breath of every living being* [Nishmat kol cha'i]" Early on (before 200 C.E.), the liturgy featured sets of psalms (or sometimes just a single psalm alone) known as *Hallels*. One such *Hallel* (the Daily *Hallel*) forms the bulk of the *P'sukei D'zimrah*, a warm-up set of prayers prior to the morning *Sh'ma* and *Amidah*. Two others (the Egyptian *Hallel* and the Great *Hallel*) conclude the Passover Seder. The latter is said on Shabbat also. See pp. 22–23.

A *Hallel* customarily ends with a "Blessing of Song" *(Birkat Hashir)*, a title that occurs generically (no specific examples are given) in the Mishnah's discussion of the Passover Seder (M. Pes. 10:7). The Talmud (Pes. 118a) identifies two prayers that fit the bill: (1) *Y'hall'lukha* ("They will praise You") and (2) *Nishmat kol cha'i*. Yet a third alternative, probably equally ancient, is (3) *Yishtabach* ("[Let your name] be [forever] praised").

- *Y'hall'lukha* (#1) is still part of our Passover Haggadah; it also sometimes concludes the *P'sukei D'zimrah* of early medieval Eretz Yisrael.
- *Yishtabach* (#3) is how *we* (not the Jews in medieval Eretz Yisrael) end *P'sukei D'zimrah*.
- On Shabbat we preface *Yishtabach* with *Nishmat kol cha'i* (#2).

The Talmud cites *Nishmat kol cha'i* in the name of Rabbi Yochanan, a third-century Palestinian teacher. If the attribution is correct, some form of *Nishmat kol cha'i* must have existed relatively early. I say "some form" because liturgical wording remained fluid for centuries, so other than the first three signature words *(nishmat kol cha'i)*, the rest of the prayer in antiquity may not have corresponded to what we now say. Elsewhere both Yochanan and Bar Kappara, an older contemporary, cite other lines from our version of the prayer, but they are just stock phrases that prayer leaders might have drawn on, the way American politicians might insert snippets from the Declaration of Independence in their stump speeches. In the absence of written texts, prayer leaders cited these stock phrases while composing prayers on the spot, sometimes for that occasion alone. There was no single authentic version yet, just the idea of saying some sort of praise of God that began *Nishmat kol cha'i.*

[1] *"The breath of every living being ... the spirit of every mortal being* [Nishmat kol cha'i ... ru'ach kol basar]*"* Classical Hebrew knows three words that we usually translate as "soul": *n'shamah, ru'ach,* and *nefesh.* Our prayer mentions two of them *(n'shamah* and *ru'ach)* in a way that replicates the parallel structure that is typical of biblical poetry *(nishmat* is the possessive form of *n'shamah).* So *nishmat* [1a] *kol cha'i* [2a] ("the soul of every living being") parallels *ru'ach* [1b] *kol basar* [2b] ("the spirit of every mortal being").

Later authorities looked for deeper meaning in the words for soul. In his biblical commentary to the verse, "The man [Adam] became a living *nefesh,*" for example, *Rashi* (France, d. 1105) observes that animals too have a *nefesh.* What distinguishes human beings, he concludes, is our possession of a *n'shamah,* a higher level of soul from which consciousness and speech derive.

Kabbalistic thinking assigned different levels of soul to the three words. *Nefesh* is the lowest, common to all animals; *ru'ach* soars above that; and *n'shamah* is higher still, most intimately in touch with God. Our prayer includes these two higher souls, but not the lowest one.

Another strain of kabbalistic interpretation, mentioned by the sixteenth-century kabbalist Moses Alsheikh, interprets the *n'shamah* of *Nishmat kol cha'i* as the soul available only to *tsadikim,* those specially righteous persons who are called "the life [*cha'i*] of the universe." The *ru'ach* of *ru'ach kol basar* denotes the *average* human soul, sufficient, however, to know the gift of language and to apply it to its proper end, praise of God.

That is why *Nishmat kol cha'i* praises "your [God's] *name*" (*shimkha*—translated here, however, as just "You"), while *ru'ach kol basar* is content with *zikhr'kha* (literally, "your [God's] *memory*"—translated here also as "You"). Average people with only the lower-level *ru'ach* remain a step removed from God's name; only the *tsadikim,* gifted also with *n'shamah,* may praise God's name directly.

[5] *"It is You alone"* We generally experience being saved by people, not by God—as when a lifeguard saves a drowning swimmer or a doctor saves a patient. But even there (says our prayer) thanks should go to God, the enabling force behind all human activity. Human saviors merely do God's will. So goes the traditional reading—with which I have difficulty.

Should the gratitude of survivors from Hitler's death camps have been directed to the Allies who freed them or God? If the Allies were God's chosen agents, why didn't God arrange for their arrival before so many others were killed?

The only way I make sense of this passage is to remove God as micromanager of human destiny and retain God instead as a creator who established the universe according to various forces (gravity, evolution, free will, and so on), but then gave up the right to interfere with those forces as they operate through time.

We may say that God created a world where the human impulse to do good sometimes succeeds and sometimes fails. When we see humanity at its best, we should remember that however much some people do evil (with God apparently unable to stay their hand), others access the tendency to good that God implants within us. We thank God for establishing the *possibility* of human good that we sometimes employ successfully to deliver those who are enslaved or in despair.

[14] *"Abiding forever* [shokhen ad]"* Medieval Jews, who examined prayers studiously to find textual hints of their authorship, discovered an adroitly hidden reverse acrostic (almost impossible to find in the Hebrew, let alone explain in the English) involving several prayer sentences, the first letters of which spell the name Shimon (Simon). *SHokhen ad* provides the opening *shin*. Assuming that someone named "Simon" was the author, they wondered which Simon it was.

The most incredible speculation comes from *Machzor Vitry* (France, eleventh century), which reports the tradition that Simon Peter wrote the prayer "when he sat upon the rock." The author is shocked at this suggestion, since it evokes the founding myth of the papacy, rooted in Matthew 16:18, where Jesus proclaims, "And I tell you, you are Peter, and on this rock [*petra* in Greek] I will build my church." The myth depends on a midrashic pun—Peter is *Petros*, in Greek, the masculine equivalent of the feminine *petra*, "rock." Peter is a nickname for the disciple Simon (Shimon in Hebrew), known, therefore, as Simon Peter.

The Jewish identification goes back to an enigmatic Jewish text called *Aggad'ta D'shimon Kefa*, *kefa* being the Aramaic word for "rock." (In the Christian Bible, too, Simon Peter is sometimes named Simon Kefa.) We know little about this *Aggad'ta*, but the idea that a disciple of Jesus had composed a Jewish prayer was shocking enough for thirteenth-century rabbis who had read *Machzor Vitry* to propose an alternative Shimon: Shimon ben Shetach, a predecessor of Hillel and Shammai (first century B.C.E.—so even before Jesus, let alone his disciples).

Neither claim has anything to recommend it. Even the acrostic is dubious. In all probability, our prayer is a combination of several fragments of praise, not all of which were originally recited universally. We should picture an oral age when prayer leaders drew liberally on stock phrases, often rooted in biblical language, and strung them together creatively to produce blessings. Most have disappeared. Bur ours was somehow written down and survived long enough to be canonized by rabbis in Babylonia (the Geonim) in the ninth and tenth centuries. (See "The breath of every living being [*Nishmat kol cha'i*]," pp. 59–60.)

[15] *"Y'sharim* ['upright'] *tit'halal* ['You will be lauded']"* From the first of four parallel verses, carrying a double acrostic in the Hebrew. The first acrostic is obvious: combining the first letters of every second word produces *y.ts.ch.k*. Since Hebrew is written purely with consonants, thereby inviting us to supply whatever vowels we like, we can read the word as *YiTSCHaK* ("Isaac"). The second is harder to find. The initial syllable *(tit)*

61

of every third word (like *tit'hallal*) is just the grammatical prefix that converts a verb into the passive voice. If we drop the prefix and concentrate instead on the letters after it, we get *h.v.r.k.* That combination yields nothing significant, but the Spanish savant David Abudarham (fourteenth century) had a text where the relevant words appeared in different order: *titRomam, titBarakh* (the B is a variant form of the Hebrew letter V), *titKadash, titHadar—r.v.k.h,* which can be read as RiVKaH ("Rebekah," Isaac's wife). The Sefardi rite still arranges the words as Abudarham had them.

[18] *"Let your name be forever praised"* The beginning of the closing blessing. We have several instances of a *Hallel* in the liturgy (see "The Daily *Hallel*: The Core of the *P'sukei D'zimrah*," in Volume 3, *P'sukei D'zimrah [Morning Psalms],* p. 7), all of which begin and end with a blessing. Bracketing biblical material with rabbinic blessings was the norm. We have it in the *Sh'ma* too, for instance, and also in the reading of Torah.

The blessing that follows a *Hallel* is called *Birkat Hashir,* "The Blessing of Song," an apt title for the conclusion of a section dedicated to singing God's praise. The Mishnah (Pes. 10:7) already knows about a Blessing of Song said after the *Hallel* that is recited as part of the Passover Seder, but it does not tell us what the prayer actually was. The Talmud's attempt to identify it evokes the citation of two prayers that must have functioned as Blessings of Song. One is *Nishmat kol cha'i,* which indeed is used here on Shabbat. To it is appended *Yishtabach,* the normal weekday version.

There is no way to know who wrote *Yishtabach* or when, but that has not stopped people from trying to deduce its authorship. The fourteenth-century Spanish commentator David Abudarham, for instance, noted that the four words in the middle of the prayer, *shimkha la'ad malkenu ha'el,* begin with *shin, lamed, mem,* and *heh*—the consonants that spell the Hebrew name Shlomo (Solomon), from which he concluded, "Perhaps the sage who wrote this was named Solomon, or he composed it in honor of King Solomon."

The person who is the prayer leader usually changes at this point in the service. Until now, the liturgy has been a "warm-up" to the main prayers, the *Sh'ma* and Its Blessings and the *Amidah.* Traditionally, the role of leading the congregation in prayer becomes more important once the introductory warm-up is completed. The person who acts officially as the cantor, therefore, usually takes over the service only at this point.

Technically, the change should wait until the Blessing of Song is over, since the blessing is still part of the *P'sukei D'zimrah.* But it was considered unlucky to stop for conversation between the end of the *P'sukei D'zimrah* and the beginning of the *Sh'ma* and Its Blessings. Medieval authorities cite the Palestinian Talmud as saying that anyone who talks then commits a sin. Our versions of the Palestinian Talmud lack that line, but we do have a midrash that tells a relevant story in the name of Rabbi Elazar ben Rabbi Yose: "I was out for a walk once, when I ran into Elijah the prophet, may he be remembered for good, and with him were 4,000 camels, each one loaded with a heavy burden. 'What are the camels carrying?' I asked. He answered. 'They are carrying fury and anger, to pay back people who talk between the end of *P'sukei D'zimrah* and the beginning of the *Sh'ma* and Its Blessings.'"

Now we know why the prayer leader for the main prayers does not wait to begin until after the *P'sukei D'zimrah* really concludes. In order to go directly from the one rubric to the other without a pause in which people might converse, the prayer leader for the main sections of the weekday service begins here. On Shabbat, the prayer leader begins with "Abiding forever" *(shokhen ad)*; see p. 42.

Interestingly enough, Amram, the author of our first prayer book, reports the ban on talking, but he modifies it. He permits discussion regarding the needs of the community or on behalf of someone poor who is being fed from the communal *tzedakah* fund and who stops by to receive help.

In their discussion of this prayer, medieval law codes usually include requirements for a prayer leader. These go back to the Mishnah (c. 200) but received considerable interpretation in the years that followed. They are matters of knowledge and of character. According to Joseph Caro (sixteenth century), prayer leaders must be free of sin, with a good reputation, humble, and acceptable to the congregation. They must also be gifted with a "sweet voice that penetrates the heart of those who hear it," and they have to be practiced in reading any passage in the Bible. If no one is available with all these traits, we are to choose "the best person available in terms of wisdom and good deeds."

———◆———

J. HOFFMAN (TRANSLATION)

next, but both "name" *(shem)* and "memory" *(zekher)* are used metaphorically in Hebrew in ways that we cannot capture in English. So rather than resorting to misleading translations of the words, we capture the point of the Hebrew.

[1] *"Mortal being"* More or less following Birnbaum's "all mortals." We add "being" because we added it above ("living being") and we want to preserve the parallel structure.

[2] *"Ransom us and rescue us"* The imagery here may be that we are condemned to some miserable afterlife, but we can be ransomed from its keeper and thereby rescued from it.

[2] *"Love* [m'rachem]*"* Or "show mercy." Once again, we do not know the exact nuance of the Hebrew, and in any event, no one English word captures it.

[2] *"Sorrow and hardship"* Hebrew, *tsarah* and *tsukah*. We cannot capture the alliteration in our English.

[3] *"God of the first and the last"* Probably an idiom, perhaps similar to our "young and old." This may be a merism used to represent one of the accompanying phrases following, "master of all generations." (A merism is the expression of a gamut by referring to its extremes.)

³*"God"* Hebrew, *elo'ah*, which is different than the more common word for "God" (*elohim*) that we just saw ("God of the first and the last"). Unfortunately we cannot make this distinction in English.

Elo'ah is grammatically the singular of *elohim*, probably a back-formation from the more common *elohim*. That is, first the word *elohim* entered the Hebrew language. Then, because *elohim* appeared to be plural, ending as it does in *-im*, it gave rise to *elo'ah*. We see a similar process in the English word "statistic," which was coined (in its present meaning of "fact about" or "datum") as a back-formation from the previously existing word "statistics." As it happens, while the word *elohim* may be plural, it also may derive from the ancient pagan god *elim*. Either way, the original Hebrew word *elohim* was coined by inserting a *heh* into a previously existing word. (See Joel M. Hoffman, *In the Beginning: A Short History of the Hebrew Language* [New York: NYU Press, 2004], chap. 4.)

³*"Master"* Or "lord," but only as a common noun, not "the Lord," referring specifically to God, as Birnbaum, who capitalizes the word here, would have it.

³*"Generations"* Or just "creatures that were born," not necessarily humans, that is.

⁴*"Rests nor sleeps"* Commonly, "sleeps or slumbers," but we need to reserve "slumber" for below.

⁴*"Raises those who are bent over"* In keeping with our translation in Volume 2 (*The Amidah*), we would prefer (both here and in that volume) a single word for the Hebrew *k'fufim*, but we are forced to resort to the longer phrase, "those who ...," thus interrupting the parallelism of the Hebrew (those who sleep, those who slumber, the mute, the captives, the falling, those who are bent over).

⁶*"Filled with song like the sea"* Birnbaum's emendation to "filled with song as the sea [is with water]" seems to miss the point here, namely, that the great and mighty sea itself is singing! We see similar imagery, for example, in Psalm 98, where the sea makes noise, the rivers clap hands, and the mountains sing, all in praise of God.

⁶*"Joy"* Birnbaum's "ringing praise" is a nicely poetic interpretation.

⁶*"The sea's"* Literally, "its." We substitute "the sea's" because in English the antecedent is unclear—it may be either "the sea" or "joy." In Hebrew, however, we know it must be "the sea" because like the possessive pronoun "its," "the sea" is grammatically masculine, while "joy" is feminine.

⁶*"Many roaring* [hamon]" The Hebrew here is a pun. *Hamon* means both "many" and "roaring." We are forced to spell out the pun in English.

⁶*"Eagles"* Zoologically, *nesher*, "eagle," is probably actually a vulture. We say "eagles," however, to achieve poetic impact. The Hebrew *nesher* denotes a thing of majesty and grace. The same cannot be said for the English "vulture."

⁶ *"Sky"* The Hebrew *shamayim*, "sky," is also used for "heaven." Here it is clearly "sky," so that's how we translate it, but in so doing we lose the subtle symbolism of the Hebrew, which suggests not just breadth but depth as well.

⁶ *"Gazelles"* Or "deer." Again (see "Eagles," above), zoological considerations are less important here than the poetry.

⁶ *"Millions"* More likely, the Hebrew word refers to ten thousand, not one million, but the point here is imagery, not a specific arithmetic count.

⁶ *"Great things"* Birnbaum's "favors" does not find support in the Hebrew.

⁷ *"You freed us from Egypt"* By putting "From Egypt" first, the Hebrew sentence structure emphasizes "Egypt" in a way that our translation does not. We could use "From Egypt you freed us" or "It was from Egypt that you freed us," but we would have to repeat that awkward grammar in the following lines, and the complexity would detract from the poetry of the passage.

⁷ *"House of bondage"* Literally, "house of slaves." Both translations have merit. The metaphoric "house of bondage" is by far the more familiar appellation, while the literal "house of slaves" raises the interesting possibility that the phrase refers to an actual building.

⁷ *"In famines"* "During famines" would be better, but we need "in" to match "in abundance" next. The Hebrew poetically puts "famine" and "abundance" in contrasting parallel.

⁷ *"Stubborn"* "Stubborn" in the sense that they are difficult to cure. Birnbaum's "lasting" is almost the same point. Curiously, the Hebrew word here is *ne'eman*, frequently translated "faithful" as an attribute of God.

⁹ *"Limbs"* Or "pinions," that is, bird feathers as they are used in flight. Alas, that word is more familiar to English readers as the toothed cog that forms part of rack-and-pinion steering. At any rate, the limbs are most certainly still attached to bodies.

⁹ *"Apportioned us* [pilagtanu]" Following Birnbaum. The Hebrew verb (from the root *p.l.g*) is rare, usually used metaphorically in regard to water. "The limbs that you showered on us" comes close, but for the grotesque image of a "limb shower." With no better option, we are stuck using a rare English word to match the rare Hebrew word, even though we miss the point.

⁹ *"Extol"* Literally, "declare you king," but we have no single word to capture that in English, and we do not want to destroy the cadence here.

⁹ *"You"* Again, literally, "your name."

¹⁰ *"Swear allegiance"* We would prefer a single verb here, "swear"; but the resulting

English, "swear to God," is not the point here.

[10] *"Everyone of height"* Again, we would prefer a single word here, but in English, "every tallness" makes no sense at all.

[10] *"Heart ... lung"* We have two parallel references to parts of the human body, *lev* and *kerev ukhlayot*. The Hebrew *k'layot* is frequently used metaphorically in parallel with *lev*. The *k'layot* are the kidneys; metaphorically *lev* means not "heart," but "mind" (see Volume 1, *The Sh'ma and Its Blessings*, pp. 100, 102). English usage governing the verb "revere" demands "heart," however, so we use it here. *Ukhlayot* appears alongside *kerev*, so the phrase must refer to two different internal organs, probably the gut *(kerev)* and the kidneys *(ukhlayot)*. Birnbaum's "inmost being" (for both of them, considered together) allows him to avoid translating the Hebrew literally—perhaps wisely, since the English "kidneys and gut" is hardly positive; and it certainly does not convey the sense of the Hebrew, which implies an internal organ that fits the context of singing— hence, "lung." Another option would be "heart," since we do say, metaphorically, "My heart sings." But we already have "heart" for *lev*.

[10] *"Written"* The quotation (from Psalm 35) extends from "All my bones" to "rob them." But the quotation also contains an internal quotation ("All my bones will say"). It is not clear if the bones are saying just "who is like You" or also the next part, up to "those who rob them." Unable to know for sure, we do not include any quotation marks here.

[11] *"Match"* We need a fourth near synonym for the concept "be like." We already have "is like you," "compare to you," and "equal you." "Match" is pretty close here.

[12] *"Exalt"* Better, "praise," but we will need "praise" immediately below.

[12] *"For David"* Or "David's." The quotation is from Psalm 103:1, which begins, as many psalms do, with an attribution.

[12] *"Praise"* Or "bless."

[12] *"My very being* [kol k'rova'i]" *K'rova'i* is practically the same as *kerev*, which (with *k'layot*) we translated in verse 10 as "lung." The sense here may be "all my innards," which is captured well by the English idiom "my very being."

[13] *"Tremendous power"* Following Birnbaum.

[13] *"Great in your glorious name"* Or, more literally, "the great one" *(hagadol)*. This is the second of a series of phrases that in Hebrew mostly follow the pattern "the X in your Y." The first, immediately prior, reads, literally, "the God in your tremendous power." But in English, "God," not "the God," is called for, so we obey that pattern throughout, avoiding "the" in what follows. That is, we use indefinite nouns throughout—not "the great," but "great," and similarly, "mighty," "awe-inspiring," and "king."

[13] *"Awe inspiring"* Were it not for the colloquial use of "awesome" to mean simply "great" (in an exaggerated sense, since it is applied to just about anything that is "cool"), we would prefer "awesome" here.

[13] *"You are"* We add this both to make the English into a sentence and to facilitate "king" instead of "the king" (see previous page, "Great in your glorious name").

[13] *"Seated on a high and exalted throne"* We would prefer to end this line with the words "high and exalted," as the Hebrew does when it ends, *ram v'nisa*. Though hard to see from the English, these last two words *(ram v'nisa)* actually occur near the beginning of the following phrase. But the second line is reminiscent of Isaiah 6:1: "seated on a throne high and exalted." That was probably what the author intended, but instead we get the beginning of Isaiah 57:15. That *ram v'nisa* appears only once may be due to haplography, that is, mistakenly writing only once *(ram v'nisa)* instead of twice, the second one being Isaiah 6:1—that is *ram v'nisa, ram v'nisa*.

[14] *"Abiding forever"* Or "you abide forever," but we want to allow this line to be read as part of the previous one; see immediately above. It is not clear what it means for God to "abide" forever, but whatever the Hebrew means, our English says the same thing.

[14] *"Exalted and holy"* So reads the Hebrew here. It looks like a slightly awkward paraphrase of Isaiah 57:15, but the original is awkward in another place. This fact combined with considerable textual variation (for example, in the Septuagint) suggests that our canonical version of Isaiah may be corrupt here, and this prayer may reflect not a paraphrase but another tradition.

[14] *"Acclaim Adonai"* Others, "rejoice in Adonai," but "rejoice in" doesn't make much sense. We think this line is in parallel with the next.

[15] *"Faithful"* We would prefer "righteous" here, but we need another synonym. The Hebrew words were chosen not for their specific meanings, but for the acronyms they form. See L. Hoffman, *"Y'sharim,"* v. 15, p. 61.

[15] *"Lungs"* Again, we choose an internal organ that makes sense in context (see above, "Heart … lung"). We disagree with Birnbaum, who identifies the Hebrew here *(b'kerev)* not as "internal organ," but as "inside," giving him the nearly nonsensical, "inside the holy [You are] sanctified." "Sanctified by the lungs," as we have it, implies a joyful shout of acclaim.

[15] *"Holy creatures"* We would prefer "the holy" here, in parallel with "the upright," etc., but unlike "the upright," "the holy" implies a category (like "the beautiful" or "the good"), rather than "holy creatures."

[16] *"Vast multitudes"* Birnbaum's "assemblies of the tens of thousands" seems too literal. While the Hebrew word here may mean "ten thousand," the fact that we have no English equivalent forces us to find another way of expressing what the prayer has

in mind. "Millions" would be another possibility.

[17] *"Beyond all the words of the songs and hymns of David son of Jesse your anointed servant"* Better would be "beyond all of David's words of song ..." but "beyond all of David son of Jesse, your anointed servant's words ..." becomes too confusing to read.

[20] *"Eternal life"* That is, the One who lives forever. ("Eternal liver" is obviously wrong.)

◆ ◆ ◆

B. *Sh'ma Uvirkhoteha* ("The *Sh'ma* and Its Blessings"): Talking about God

I. The *Yotser* ("Blessing on Creation")

A. *Hakol Yodukha* ("All Will Gratefully Acknowledge You")

[1] Blessed are You, Adonai our God, ruler of the world, who forms light and creates darkness, makes peace and creates everything.

[2] All will gratefully acknowledge You and all will praise You, and all will say, "Adonai is the most holy." [3] All will exalt You forever, You who form all, God who unlocks the gates to the east every day, and opens the windows of the sky, who brings the sun out from its place, and the moon from where it abides, illumining the entire world and its inhabitants whom He created in mercy, [4] illumining the earth and those who dwell there in mercy, in his goodness forever renewing daily the work of creation. [5] The exalted ruler ever since, lauded, glorified, and extolled for days immemorial, [6] God immemorial, in your great mercy have mercy on us: lord, acting as our strength; rock, acting as our protector; defender, acting as our salvation; protector, acting on our behalf. [7] None is so valuable as You, and there is none other than You. There is nothing without You. Who is like You! [8] None is so valuable as You, Adonai our God, in this world, and there is none other than You, our king, in the life of the world-to-come. [9] There is nothing without You, our redeemer, in the days of the messiah, and none is like You, our savior, when the dead will be revived.

בָּרוּךְ אַתָּה, יְיָ אֱלֹהֵינוּ, מֶלֶךְ [1]
הָעוֹלָם, יוֹצֵר אוֹר וּבוֹרֵא חֹשֶׁךְ,
עֹשֶׂה שָׁלוֹם, וּבוֹרֵא אֶת הַכֹּל.

הַכֹּל יוֹדוּךָ וְהַכֹּל יְשַׁבְּחוּךָ, וְהַכֹּל [2]
יֹאמְרוּ אֵין קָדוֹשׁ כַּיְיָ. [3] הַכֹּל יְרוֹמְמוּךָ
סֶּלָה, יוֹצֵר הַכֹּל, הָאֵל הַפּוֹתֵחַ בְּכָל יוֹם
דַּלְתוֹת שַׁעֲרֵי מִזְרָח, וּבוֹקֵעַ חַלּוֹנֵי
רָקִיעַ, מוֹצִיא חַמָּה מִמְּקוֹמָהּ, וּלְבָנָה
מִמְּכוֹן שִׁבְתָּהּ, וּמֵאִיר לָעוֹלָם כֻּלּוֹ
וּלְיוֹשְׁבָיו שֶׁבָּרָא בְּמִדַּת רַחֲמִים.
[4] הַמֵּאִיר לָאָרֶץ וְלַדָּרִים עָלֶיהָ בְּרַחֲמִים,
וּבְטוּבוֹ מְחַדֵּשׁ בְּכָל יוֹם תָּמִיד מַעֲשֵׂה
בְרֵאשִׁית. [5] הַמֶּלֶךְ הַמְרוֹמָם לְבַדּוֹ מֵאָז,
הַמְשֻׁבָּח וְהַמְפֹאָר וְהַמִּתְנַשֵּׂא מִימוֹת
עוֹלָם. [6] אֱלֹהֵי עוֹלָם, בְּרַחֲמֶיךָ הָרַבִּים
רַחֵם עָלֵינוּ, אֲדוֹן עֻזֵּנוּ, צוּר מִשְׂגַּבֵּנוּ,
מָגֵן יִשְׁעֵנוּ, מִשְׂגָּב בַּעֲדֵנוּ. [7] אֵין כְּעֶרְכְּךָ
וְאֵין זוּלָתֶךָ; אֶפֶס בִּלְתֶּךָ, וּמִי דּוֹמֶה לָּךְ.
[8] אֵין כְּעֶרְכְּךָ, יְיָ אֱלֹהֵינוּ, בָּעוֹלָם הַזֶּה;
וְאֵין זוּלָתְךָ, מַלְכֵּנוּ, לְחַיֵּי הָעוֹלָם הַבָּא.
[9] אֶפֶס בִּלְתְּךָ, גּוֹאֲלֵנוּ, לִימוֹת הַמָּשִׁיחַ;
וְאֵין דּוֹמֶה לָךְ, מוֹשִׁיעֵנוּ, לִתְחִיַּת
הַמֵּתִים.

69

BRETTLER (BIBLE)

[1] *"Makes peace and creates everything"* Except for the last word, this is a quotation from Isaiah 45:7, which reads *hara*, "trouble," not *hakol*, "everything." The biblical context makes "trouble" a better translation than the usual word, "evil," because it is juxtaposed with *shalom*, "peace" in the sense of "tranquility." The "Isaiah" passage is really by an anonymous prophet whose work is appended to Isaiah, and more properly called Second- or Deutero-Isaiah. He was active in the Babylonian exile (586–538 B.C.E.), when various forms of Persian dualism, including Zoroastrianism, became the norm. Our verse is thus polemical, *(p. 73)*

DORFF (THEOLOGY)

[3] *"Who unlocks the gates to the east every day, and opens the windows of the sky"* More than metaphors, these phrases were originally taken as accurate descriptions of how the sun rises and the rain falls. (See Volume 9, *Welcoming the Night: Minchah and Ma'ariv [Afternoon and Evening Prayer]*, pp. 50–52 .) *(p. 74)*

FRANKEL (A WOMAN'S VOICE)

[3] *"God who unlocks the gates to the east every day"* Today we understand that the rhythm of our days—our regular cycle of waking and sleeping—results from the rotation of the earth. But to the pre-Copernican mind, the daily rising of the sun was seen as an act of divine will and, therefore, unpredictable: even though day had dutifully followed night from time immemorial, God might one day disrupt this orderliness and plunge the world back into primeval chaos—a world without light, without distinctions between day and night. In this prayer we thank God for regularly and reliably "bring[ing] the sun out from its place, and the moon from where it abides."

How does this prayer depict the heavenly alternation of day *(p. 76)*

I. THE *YOTSER* ("BLESSING ON CREATION")

A. *Hakol Yodukha* ("All Will Gratefully Acknowledge You")

[1] Blessed are You, Adonai our God, ruler of the world, who forms light and creates darkness, makes peace and creates everything.

[2] All will gratefully acknowledge You and all will praise You, and all will say, "Adonai is the most holy." [3] All will exalt You forever, You who form all, God who

GRAY (OUR TALMUDIC HERITAGE)

[3] *"Whom He created in mercy [shebara b'midat rachamim]"* According to Genesis Rabbah 12:15, God said, "If I create the world with the attribute of mercy [alone], sins will increase [because the attribute of mercy will prevent God from imposing punishment]), but if I create the world with the attribute of justice [alone], the world could not endure [because each inevitable sin would earn its just punishment without being tempered by mercy]). Rather, I will create it *(p. 76)*

KUSHNER & POLEN (CHASIDISM)

[7] *"None is so valuable as You, and there is none other than You"* Issachar Dov Baer of Zlotchov's *M'vaser Tsedek, Y'sod Ha'avodah* (65, para. 2, bottom) cites a tradition that one cannot begin to pray properly until one has made oneself as nothing (see "Let us declare your awe," p. 123). This sense of nothingness, for the *M'vaser Tsedek*, however, can have two meanings corresponding to the two apparently redundant phrases: "none is so valuable as You" and "there is none other than You." According *(p. 76)*

L. HOFFMAN (HISTORY)

THE SERVICE NOW PROCEEDS TO THE SH'MA AND ITS BLESSINGS, THE FIRST OF THE THREE MAJOR SERVICE RUBRICS (THE OTHER TWO ARE THE AMIDAH AND THE READING OF TORAH). ONLY THE FIRST OF THE SH'MA'S THREE BLESSINGS, THE YOTSER (PRAISING GOD FOR CREATION) IS ALTERED ON SHABBAT—IN THREE WAYS:

1. The first is the prose passage featured here ("All will gratefully acknowledge You" [*Hakol yodukha*]), noting that *(p. 77)*

J. HOFFMAN (TRANSLATION)

[2] *"All"* More accurately, "everyone and everything," which might include angels, animals, etc. We do not have a convenient way of expressing this in English. We use "all" because we will need it immediately below.

[2] *"Adonai is the most holy"* Others, "none is holy as Adonai," but the Hebrew *ein* encompasses both "no one" and "nothing" in a way that "none" does not. Furthermore, in English, "none" is the opposite of "all," but in Hebrew, *ein*, "none," is not the opposite of *kol*, "all." So we reword the sentence.

[3] *"Form"* Or "create," but we used "forms" for this verb immediately above.

[3] *"Unlocks"* Better, "opens," but we need two words for "open," *(p. 78)*

¹בָּרוּךְ אַתָּה, יְיָ אֱלֹהֵינוּ, מֶלֶךְ הָעוֹלָם, יוֹצֵר אוֹר וּבוֹרֵא חֹשֶׁךְ, עֹשֶׂה שָׁלוֹם, וּבוֹרֵא אֶת הַכֹּל.

²הַכֹּל יוֹדוּךָ וְהַכֹּל יְשַׁבְּחוּךָ, וְהַכֹּל יֹאמְרוּ אֵין קָדוֹשׁ כַּיְיָ. ³הַכֹּל יְרוֹמְמוּךָ סֶּלָה, יוֹצֵר הַכֹּל, הָאֵל הַפּוֹתֵחַ בְּכָל יוֹם דַּלְתוֹת שַׁעֲרֵי מִזְרָח, וּבוֹקֵעַ חַלּוֹנֵי רָקִיעַ.

LANDES (HALAKHAH)

[1] *"Blessed ... creates everything"* The custom on Shabbat is for the prayer leader not to say this first line of the blessing aloud (*Tur*, by Jacob ben Asher, 1270–1340, Toledo, Spain, the major post-Maimonidean halakhic code; and commentary thereto, *P'rishah* by Joshua Hakohen Falk, 1555–1614, Poland, 281), lest the congregation say *amen* after it, for the entire prayer is considered a *b'rakhah arikhta* (pronounced b'rah-KHAH ah-REEKH-tah), "a long blessing" *(p. 77)*

unlocks the gates to the east every day, and opens the windows of the sky, who brings the sun out from its place, and the moon from where it abides, illumining the entire world and its inhabitants whom He created in mercy, [4] illumining the earth and those who dwell there in mercy, in his goodness forever renewing daily the work of creation. [5] The exalted ruler ever since, lauded, glorified, and extolled for days immemorial, [6] God immemorial, in your great mercy have mercy on us: lord, acting as our strength; rock, acting as our protector; defender, acting as our salvation; protector, acting on our behalf. [7] None is so valuable as You, and there is none other than You. There is nothing without You. Who is like You! [8] None is so valuable as You, Adonai our God, in this world, and there is none other than You, our king, in the life of the world-to-come. [9] There is nothing without You, our redeemer, in the days of the messiah, and none is like You, our savior, when the dead will be revived.

מוֹצִיא חַמָּה מִמְּקוֹמָה, וּלְבָנָה מִמְּכוֹן שִׁבְתָּה, וּמֵאִיר לָעוֹלָם כֻּלּוֹ וּלְיוֹשְׁבָיו שֶׁבָּרָא בְּמִדַּת רַחֲמִים. [4] הַמֵּאִיר לָאָרֶץ וְלַדָּרִים עָלֶיהָ בְּרַחֲמִים, וּבְטוּבוֹ מְחַדֵּשׁ בְּכָל יוֹם תָּמִיד מַעֲשֵׂה בְרֵאשִׁית. [5] הַמֶּלֶךְ הַמְרוֹמָם לְבַדּוֹ מֵאָז, הַמְשֻׁבָּח וְהַמְפֹאָר וְהַמִּתְנַשֵּׂא מִימוֹת עוֹלָם. [6] אֱלֹהֵי עוֹלָם, בְּרַחֲמֶיךָ הָרַבִּים רַחֵם עָלֵינוּ, אֲדוֹן עֻזֵּנוּ, צוּר מִשְׂגַּבֵּנוּ, מָגֵן יִשְׁעֵנוּ, מִשְׂגָּב בַּעֲדֵנוּ. [7] אֵין כְּעֶרְכְּךָ וְאֵין זוּלָתֶךָ; אֶפֶס בִּלְתֶּךָ, וּמִי דּוֹמֶה לָּךְ. [8] אֵין כְּעֶרְכְּךָ, יְיָ אֱלֹהֵינוּ, בָּעוֹלָם הַזֶּה; וְאֵין זוּלָתְךָ, מַלְכֵּנוּ, לְחַיֵּי הָעוֹלָם הַבָּא. [9] אֶפֶס בִּלְתְּךָ, גּוֹאֲלֵנוּ, לִימוֹת הַמָּשִׁיחַ; וְאֵין דּוֹמֶה לְךָ, מוֹשִׁיעֵנוּ, לִתְחִיַּת הַמֵּתִים.

BRETTLER (BIBLE)

emphasizing Judaism's monotheistic faith, according to which a single deity must be responsible for the opposites of light and darkness, peace and trouble. This polemic served little function in later periods, where, if anything, it was problematic since it explicitly attributes the creation of trouble to God, and for this reason was revised in the liturgy. Though deeply indebted to biblical precedents, the liturgy is not enslaved to the Bible, which it regularly revises to fit the changed needs of worshipers.

[2] *"All will gratefully acknowledge You"* The notion of "all" *(hakol)* praising God expands upon "every creature" *(kol hay'tsurim)*, above (see v. 17, "Every creature," p. 51), and is the theme of Psalm 148 (e.g., vv. 7–12, "Praise Adonai, O you who are on earth, all sea monsters and ocean depths, fire and hail, snow and smoke, storm wind … mountains and hills, all fruit trees and cedars, all wild and tamed beasts, creeping things and winged birds, all kings and peoples of the earth, all princes of the earth and its judges, youths and maidens alike, old and young together").

[2] *"Adonai is the most holy"* From Hannah's prayer, 1 Samuel 2:2.

[3] *"Unlocks the gates"* The astronomical vision here is typical of the ancient near east: a stable earth, with the sun and moon leaving their gates to move to their proper places. Such gates are not explicit in the Bible but are attested in the Dead Sea Scrolls and rabbinic literature. The general image depicted here is also found in Psalm 19:7, "His rising-place is at one end of heaven, and his circuit reaches the other." The concluding words, "in mercy" *(b'midat rachamim)*, as well as the following verse, emphasize that the universe does not function automatically, but only through God's beneficence and care for all of creation. Creation is thus not a one-time occurrence, but is continually perpetuated—God regularly distinguishes day from night.

[5] *"Ever since … for days immemorial"* As earthly kings build cities, God constructs the universe. The image of God as king is presupposed by the creation story, with which the Torah opens: like a contractor assembling a building crew, God tells his royal council, "Let *us* make humanity in our image" (Gen. 1:26). Through creation, God becomes king "ever since" and "for days immemorial." "Ever since" reflects Psalm 93:2, which explicitly announces, "Your throne stands firm ever since; from eternity You have existed."

[6] *"Your great mercy"* Our experience frequently is that the more powerful people become, the less compassion they have. Our prayer invokes a powerful but also compassionate deity.

[7] *"None is so valuable as You"* Again (see v. 11, "Who can compare to You," p. 50), we see God's incomparability. But this text goes farther, in that (unlike the Bible) it reflects the rabbinic claim that God's incomparability extends to "the world-to-come" *(olam haba*—a post-biblical idea); and to "the resurrection of the dead" *(t'chiyat hametim)*, a biblical idea that appears there only late and only rarely, as (most clearly)

in Daniel 12:2, "Many of those that sleep in the dust of the earth will awake, some to eternal life, others to reproaches, to everlasting abhorrence." The Rabbis inherit this late biblical notion and make it central to their theology.

———◆———

DORFF (THEOLOGY)

[3] *"Its inhabitants whom He created in mercy"* God's mercy is evident in creating human beings in the first place. As the Rabbis maintain:

> Rabbi Simon said: When the Holy Blessed One wished to create the first person, ... Benevolence advised his creation on the grounds that he would practice charity. Truth, however, said that he should not be created, for he is full of lies. Justice favored humanity's creation, saying that he would do many acts of justice. Peace objected to man's creation because he would be full of conflict. What did God do? He took hold of Truth, cast it to the ground [and created Adam]. (Gen. Rab. 8:5)

[8-9] *"The world-to-come ... in the days of the messiah ... when the dead will be revived"* In rabbinic theology, the "world-to-come" signified both messianic times (for all the world) and life after death (for each individual). The former denotes the end of human history when living conditions will be ideal, even though people will still be born, live, and die, and will still subscribe to membership in a nation. Life after death, however, promises resurrection someday in conditions very different from our own.

The Jewish hope for messianic times goes back at least as far as Isaiah (late eighth century B.C.E.), who foretells a time of universal peace for humans and for animals ("The wolf shall dwell with the lamb" [Isa. 11:6]). In addition:

> In the days to come ... the many peoples shall go and say: "Come, let us go up to the Mount of Adonai, to the House of the God of Jacob, that He may instruct us in his ways, and that we may walk in his paths." For instruction shall come forth from Zion, the word of Adonai from Jerusalem. Then He will judge among the nations and arbitrate for the many peoples, and they shall beat their swords into plowshares and their spears into pruning hooks. Nation shall not take up sword against nation; they shall never again know war." (Isa. 2:2–4)

Even at this relatively late date (late eighth century B.C.E.), the ambiguity between henotheism and monotheism (see "The God of gods," p. 30) recurs. Isaiah predicts a monotheistic world in which all nations worship Israel's God. His younger contemporary, Micah, however (Mic. 4:1–5), quotes Isaiah 2 verbatim but adds two verses that imply nations will worship their own gods while we Jews worship ours: "Though all the peoples walk each in the names of its gods, we will walk in the name of Adonai our God forever and ever."

They agree that God will ultimately rule from Jerusalem—a tenet that has become the core rationale for religious Zionism.

The messianic ideal that emerges from these and other prophetic passages—and then, from the Rabbis—includes the following elements:

1. Both (a) procedural and (b) substantive justice—that is, (a) justice in the court procedures by which people are tried, and (b) care for the poor, widowed, orphaned, and otherwise disadvantaged.
2. The triumph of Israel over her foes, and Israel's political independence.
3. The ingathering of Jewish exiles.
4. Universal knowledge of God's word.
5. Universal prosperity.
6. Healing of all disease.
7. Peace.

(For detail, see Elliot Dorff, *The Way Into Tikkun Olam [Repairing the World]* [Woodstock, VT: Jewish Lights, 2007], chap. 11.)

Unlike the messianic idea, which the Bible discusses again and again, life after death, the second idea discussed here, appears unambiguously only twice in the Bible: Isaiah 26:19 and Daniel 12:2. The Book of Isaiah actually has two parts, chapters 1–39 and 40–66. Part one was written by the Isaiah of the eighth century B.C.E.; part two comes from someone we call "Second Isaiah" who lived in Babylonia during the exile of the sixth century B.C.E. exile. Isaiah 26:19 is in the part that was composed by the original Isaiah, but because no other source affirms life after death from a period as early as that, scholars think the verse in question is a later addition, possibly as late as the second century B.C.E., when belief in life after death first appears, and when the Book of Daniel was written.

In the second and first century B.C.E., the Jewish polity was divided between Pharisees and Sadducees. Because of the sparse mention of the belief in life after death in the Bible, the Sadducees (who are associated with a literal reading of the Bible) denied it, asserting instead that after our deaths we live on only through our children and through the effects of what we did in life. The Pharisees, however (who are generally regarded as the earliest Rabbis), affirmed life after death. In a classic work of early American Jewish scholarship, Louis Finkelstein (*The Pharisees: The Sociological Background of Their Faith*, 2 vols. [Philadelphia: Jewish Publication Society, 1938, 1962]) plausibly suggested that the Pharisees' insistence on life after death derived from the fact that they represented the lower socioeconomic classes and were more keenly aware that in this life "the righteous suffer and the evil prosper [*tsadik v'ra lo, rasha v'tov lo*]" (Ber. 7a). By contrast, the upper-class Sadducees thought that their very prosperity was a sign of their righteousness and had no need to affirm a world other than this one.

For Jewish ideas about life after death, see Neil Gillman, *The Death of Death: Resurrection and Immortality in Jewish Thought* (Woodstock, VT: Jewish Lights, 2000); and Elie Kaplan Spitz, *Does the Soul Survive? A Jewish Journey to Belief in Afterlife, Past Lives and Living with Purpose* (Woodstock, VT: Jewish Lights, 2001).

◆

SHACHARIT ("MORNING SERVICE")

FRANKEL (A WOMAN'S VOICE)

and night? Not as the dance of the planetary spheres, a cosmic clock, or a grand celestial drama—but as a *domestic* scene: God "opens the gates to the east" and "opens the windows of the sky." Like an efficient *baleh busteh* ("homemaker"), God cracks open the windows to air out the house each day, letting in the fresh morning breeze and the warm sun; She changes the sheets, makes the beds, puts things to right. Each day She rolls up the blinds of night; each night, rolls them down again. How comfortable it is to inhabit a world that is so well-tended!

———◆———

GRAY (OUR TALMUDIC HERITAGE)

with both the attributes of justice and mercy, and may it endure!" Why then does the prayer refer to mercy alone? The answer lies in the text: the prayer does not read *midat harachamim* (literally, "*the* attribute of mercy"), but *midat rachamim* (literally, "attribute of mercy," without the definite article). The prayer is thus saying that God's decision to create, and thereby to initiate all existence, was undertaken out of God's generalized sense of love and compassion for the worlds that were being called into existence, not *the* "Attribute of Mercy" specifically. The general love applies to the cosmos; God's specific love is directed at the destiny of every individual human being.

———◆———

KUSHNER & POLEN (CHASIDISM)

to the first interpretation, when we realize that there is nothing devoid of God, we are awestruck by God's greatness. We whisper to ourselves, "Who am I to pray before One so great?" Indeed we enter a state of spiritual paralysis. In the words of Isaiah 53:3, "I am despised of humanity" *(chadal ishim)*. This is a raw, self-abasing, even debilitating kind of humility.

But then, if we continue to ponder the nature of God's greatness, we realize that we ourselves are part of this awesome divine organism. Thus the first phrase, "None is so valuable as You," results in awestruck silence, but with the second, "there is none other than You," comes the realization that there is nothing *but* God. Since we ourselves are part of God, our prayers merely return words of praise back into the divine being. We effectively become a dimension of the divine, speaking its own joy.

———◆———

LANDES (HALAKHAH)

that culminates only with the last line (v. 20, included in Volume 1, *The Sh'ma and Its Blessings*, p. 43), *Barukh atah … yotser ham'orot* ("Blessed are You, Adonai, creator of the lights"). Only then does one say *amen*, which is intended to apply to the entire prayer.

⁶*The* Amidah *("Standing" Prayer): Talking to God* Generally we are very careful to fulfill the requirement *lismokh g'ullah lit'fillah* (pronounced lis-MOKH g'-oo-LAH li-t'-fee-LAH)—"to connect [the blessing on redemption, the last of the Sh'ma's morning blessings] to the *T'fillah* [the *Amidah*, which follows]." This means to allow no interruption between the last line of this final blessing after the *Sh'ma* ("Blessed are You … who redeemed Israel") and the first blessing of the *Amidah*. Interestingly, some halakhic authorities are under the opinion that this does not apply to Shabbat. The explanation is implicit from the proximity of two psalm verses that form the basis for the practice in the first place: the last verse of Psalm 19, "May the words of my mouth and the prayer of my heart be acceptable to You, Adonai, my rock and my redeemer [*go'ali*]"; and the first verse of Psalm 20, "May Adonai answer you in the time of trouble." The two verses connect redemption to God's response "in time of trouble." Since, however, Shabbat is by definition *not* a time of trouble, and, indeed, on Shabbat we do not focus on "trouble," the rationale for this practice falls away. Not everyone agrees with this reasoning, but in cases of compelling liturgical need—adding responses to *Kaddish*, *Bar'khu*, and *K'dushah*—one may indeed, on Shabbat, interrupt (*R'ma* on O. Ch. 111:1, *Mishneh B'rurah*, subsection 8 and 9, as well as *Be'ur Hahalakhah* at that citation).

◆

L. HOFFMAN (HISTORY)

    all of creation praises God.

2. The second ("God, Master" [*El Adon*]) is a poem picturing the angels and the entire array of heaven praising God (see p. 79).

3. In the final section, "To God who rested from all work" (*La'el asher shavat*), we find a midrashic treatment of Psalm 92, "A song for the Sabbath Day," personifying Shabbat as an entity that itself praises God (see p. 87).

²*"All will gratefully acknowledge You* [hakol yodukha] …. *God, master* [El Adon] [*p. 79*]"* In virtually all manuscripts, these two liturgical staples for Shabbat morning occur together, as if two parts to a single composition. Clearly their style differs—*El Adon* is a poem; *Hakol yodukha* is not. But they both reflect *Merkavah* (literally, "chariot") mysticism, which used liturgy to transport the worshiper to the heavenly realm where angels surround God's chariot declaring, *Kadosh kadosh kadosh* ("holy, holy, holy"). (For detail, see Volume 1, *The Sh'ma and Its Blessings*, pp. 42–65.)

In context, then, the "All" of "All will gratefully acknowledge You" includes not just humans but angels too, as well as heavenly bodies like stars and planets, which were imagined as having a soul and being unfettered, like the angels, by earthly existence.

[2] *"All* [hakol] *will praise You"* The word *hakol* comes first, to match the ending word in the line before—a common poetic device in classical liturgical poetry.

———◆———

J. HOFFMAN (TRANSLATION)

one here, and one immediately below, to capture the structure of the Hebrew.

[3] *"Opens"* Birnbaum's "cleavest the windows" seems too literal to us. Ellen Frankel (see Frankel, p. 76) suggests "cracks open," on the analogy of opening the windows just a bit to air out a house in the morning.

[8] *"None is so valuable"* In verse 2 ("Adonai is the most holy") we rejected "none" for the Hebrew *ein*, but here we use it. It still fails to capture the breadth of the Hebrew, but we have no choice. We can hardly say (on the analogy of the above), "You are the most valuable...."

———◆◆◆———

B. *El Adon* (God, Master [of All Creation]")

¹ God, master of all creatures, blessed and praised by the mouth of all that breathes: his grandeur and greatness fill the world. Wisdom and knowledge surround Him.

² Exalted above the holy beings, and adorned in glory above chariots, with honor and integrity before his throne, love and mercy before his glory.

³ Great are the lights that our God created: He created them with wisdom and understanding and insight. He gave them might and power, to have dominion around the earth.

⁴ Full of brilliance they emanate radiance. Their brilliance is beautiful throughout the world, happy when they rise and joyful when they set, reverently doing their creator's will.

⁵ They render honor and glory to his name, celebration and joy to his reign. He called to the sun and it shone forth light, He saw and affixed the form of the moon.

⁶ The entire army on high gives Him praise; the serafim and the ofanim and holy beings, splendor and greatness—

¹ אֵל אָדוֹן עַל כָּל הַמַּעֲשִׂים בָּרוּךְ וּמְבֹרָךְ בְּפִי כָּל נְשָׁמָה; גָּדְלוֹ וְטוּבוֹ מָלֵא עוֹלָם דַּעַת וּתְבוּנָה סוֹבְבִים אוֹתוֹ.

² הַמִּתְגָּאֶה עַל חַיּוֹת הַקֹּדֶשׁ וְנֶהְדָּר בְּכָבוֹד עַל הַמֶּרְכָּבָה; זְכוּת וּמִישׁוֹר לִפְנֵי כִסְאוֹ חֶסֶד וְרַחֲמִים לִפְנֵי כְבוֹדוֹ.

³ טוֹבִים מְאוֹרוֹת שֶׁבָּרָא אֱלֹהֵינוּ יְצָרָם בְּדַעַת בְּבִינָה וּבְהַשְׂכֵּל; כֹּחַ וּגְבוּרָה נָתַן בָּהֶם לִהְיוֹת מוֹשְׁלִים בְּקֶרֶב תֵּבֵל.

⁴ מְלֵאִים זִיו וּמְפִיקִים נֹגַהּ נָאֶה זִיוָם בְּכָל הָעוֹלָם; שְׂמֵחִים בְּצֵאתָם וְשָׂשִׂים בְּבוֹאָם עוֹשִׂים בְּאֵימָה רְצוֹן קוֹנָם.

⁵ פְּאֵר וְכָבוֹד נוֹתְנִים לִשְׁמוֹ צָהֳלָה וְרִנָּה לְזֵכֶר מַלְכוּתוֹ; קָרָא לַשֶּׁמֶשׁ וַיִּזְרַח אוֹר רָאָה וְהִתְקִין צוּרַת הַלְּבָנָה.

⁶ שֶׁבַח נוֹתְנִים לוֹ כָּל צְבָא מָרוֹם, תִּפְאֶרֶת וּגְדֻלָּה, שְׂרָפִים וְאוֹפַנִּים וְחַיּוֹת הַקֹּדֶשׁ–

BRETTLER (BIBLE)

[1] *"God … blessed"* The notion that heavenly bodies offer praise to God is biblical, found clearly in Isaiah 6, where serafim, a type of angel, call back and forth, "Holy, holy, holy! *Adonai ts'va'ot! His presence fills all the earth!"* In the post-biblical period, this idea is extended. For example, the Dead Sea Scrolls contain a prayer called Words of the Luminaries, probably a non-sectarian prayer used widely by many groups, that just happened to be preserved at Qumran. Throughout the ancient near east, astral bodies were frequently identified also as deities, so their praise to God reflected obeisance to a greater power. *(p. 82)*

DORFF (THEOLOGY)

[6] *"The entire army on high gives Him praise* [shevach not'nim lo kol ts'va marom]; *the serafim and the ofanim and holy beings, splendor and greatness"* Philip Birnbaum points out that after mentioning explicitly the sun and the moon, the poet alludes to God's rule *(p. 83)*

ELLENSON (MODERN LITURGIES)

[1] *"God, master of all creatures"* Reform and Liberal prayer books have shown a great deal of ambivalence toward this prayer. On the one hand, many Reform and Liberal authors are comfortable with the manifest content that celebrates God as the creator *(p. 83)*

FRANKEL (A WOMAN'S VOICE)

[4] *"Radiance* [nogah]*"* Composed by early mystics, this prayer *(El Adon)* alludes to the sun, the moon, and the five major planets known in the ancient world: Saturn, Venus, Mercury, Jupiter, and Mars. Like the peoples surrounding them, the Jews "read" the heavens to divine the future. But to rationalize any conflict between astrology and monotheism, they reasoned that the sun, moon, planets, and stars were to be regarded as divine agents, expressing God's will as it played out in human lives. *(p. 84)*

B. *El Adon* (God, Master [of All Creation]")

[1] God, master of all creatures, blessed and praised by the mouth of all that breathes: his grandeur and greatness fill the world. Wisdom and knowledge surround Him.

[2] Exalted above the holy beings, and adorned in glory above chariots, with honor and integrity before his throne, love and mercy before his glory.

GRAY (OUR TALMUDIC HERITAGE)

[1] *"God, master"* David Abudarham (fourteenth-century Spain) locates some interesting numbers in this poem. The first line of verse 1 contains 10 words. The second line of verse 1 through the end of verse 5 (9 lines total) contains 8 words per line, for a total of 72 words. Finally, verse 6 consists of 12 words. Abudarham interprets this to mean that by means of the most ineffable name of *72* letters, God gave the Torah (consisting of the *10* Commandments), to the *12* tribes of Israel.

[5] *"He called to the sun and it shone forth light, He saw and affixed the form of the moon"* Rabbi Shimon ben Pazi pondered the ill fit between two parts of Genesis 1:16, which begins, "And God made the two great lights" (referring to the sun and moon), but then continues, "the great light [the sun] to rule the day, and the small light [the moon] to rule the night." Why are both sun and moon referred to initially as "great lights" if the moon is immediately demoted to the status of "small light"? The answer is given in an

אֵל אָדוֹן עַל כָּל הַמַּעֲשִׂים בָּרוּךְ וּמְבֹרָךְ בְּפִי כָל נְשָׁמָה; גָּדְלוֹ וְטוּבוֹ מָלֵא עוֹלָם דַּעַת וּתְבוּנָה סוֹבְבִים אוֹתוֹ. [1]

הַמִּתְגָּאֶה עַל חַיּוֹת הַקֹּדֶשׁ וְנֶהְדָּר בְּכָבוֹד עַל הַמֶּרְכָּבָה; זְכוּת וּמִישׁוֹר לִפְנֵי כִסְאוֹ חֶסֶד וְרַחֲמִים לִפְנֵי כְבוֹדוֹ. [2]

etiological story. The moon—initially large—was said to have asked God how it is possible for two kings to use one crown. Sensing the moon was wondering about the equality in size of the sun and itself, God told the moon to become smaller. The moon was outraged; just because it raised an appropriate issue about size, should it be the one to have to diminish itself? To this, God responded that—unlike the sun—the moon would rule both day and night (in that the moon can be seen by both day and night, *(p. 85)*

L. HOFFMAN (HISTORY)

THE SECOND ADDITION TO THE SHABBAT YOTSER: A POEM PICTURING THE ANGELS AND ENTIRE ARRAY OF HEAVEN PRAISING GOD. FOR THE OTHER TWO ADDITIONS, SEE PP. 69, 87.

[1] *"God, master* [El Adon]*"* The daily service here contains an alphabetic acrostic (*E*[*alef*]*l b*[*et*]*arukh g*[*imel*]*'dol d*[*alet*]*e'ah ...*) that assigns a single word to each letter of the alphabet (see Volume 1, *The Sh'ma and Its Blessings*, pp. 55). On Shabbat *El Adon* takes its place, providing each letter with an entire line.

The lines are crafted so that the first has 10 words; the last has 12; and in between, there are 9 lines with 8 words each, for a total of 72 (8 x 9). The author was an advocate of a school of thought called *Merkavah* mysticism (from as early as second to third [?] centuries C.E. *(p. 85)*

J. HOFFMAN (TRANSLATION)

[1] *"God, master"* This is an expanded version of the weekday acrostic metrical poem that we translated, "Almighty Blessed Great Diviner" (see Volume 1, *The Sh'ma and Its Blessings*, p. 41.) In this more complex poem, where the acrostic is assigned by entire lines, we abandon the attempt to provide a parallel acrostic in English, and translate more literally.

[1] *"Master"* Birnbaum's "Lord," with a capital "L," reflects the similarity between the Hebrew word *(p. 86)*

3 Great are the lights that our God created: He created them with wisdom and understanding and insight. He gave them might and power, to have dominion around the earth.

4 Full of brilliance they emanate radiance. Their brilliance is beautiful throughout the world, happy when they rise and joyful when they set, reverently doing their creator's will.

5 They render honor and glory to his name, celebration and joy to his reign. He called to the sun and it shone forth light, He saw and affixed the form of the moon.

6 The entire army on high gives Him praise; the serafim and the ofanim and holy beings, splendor and greatness—

3 טוֹבִים מְאוֹרוֹת שֶׁבָּרָא אֱלֹהֵינוּ יְצָרָם בְּדַעַת בְּבִינָה וּבְהַשְׂכֵּל; כֹּחַ וּגְבוּרָה נָתַן בָּהֶם לִהְיוֹת מוֹשְׁלִים בְּקֶרֶב תֵּבֵל.

4 מְלֵאִים זִיו וּמְפִיקִים נֹגַהּ נָאֶה זִיוָם בְּכָל הָעוֹלָם; שְׂמֵחִים בְּצֵאתָם וְשָׂשִׂים בְּבוֹאָם עוֹשִׂים בְּאֵימָה רְצוֹן קוֹנָם.

5 פְּאֵר וְכָבוֹד נוֹתְנִים לִשְׁמוֹ צָהֳלָה וְרִנָּה לְזֵכֶר מַלְכוּתוֹ; קָרָא לַשֶּׁמֶשׁ וַיִּזְרַח אוֹר רָאָה וְהִתְקִין צוּרַת הַלְּבָנָה.

6 שֶׁבַח נוֹתְנִים לוֹ כָּל צְבָא מָרוֹם, תִּפְאֶרֶת וּגְדֻלָּה, שְׂרָפִים וְאוֹפַנִּים וְחַיּוֹת הַקֹּדֶשׁ-

---

BRETTLER (BIBLE)

[1] *"God, master"* Alluding to the vision of the divine chariot *(merkavah)* in Ezekiel 1. Though the word "chariot" never appears there, that is clearly what is intended. We find ministering angels *(chayot)* and even a throne (1:5, 1:26). This apparently bizarre vision, difficult to fathom, played a major role in early Jewish rabbinic mysticism.

[1] *"Wisdom and knowledge [da'at ut'vunah]"* From Proverbs 3:19, "Adonai founded the earth by wisdom; He established the heavens by understanding," but in the Bible, wisdom and understanding may be personified entities, even deities.

[2] *"Love and mercy"* Possibly based on Psalm 89:15, "Righteousness and justice are the base of your throne; steadfast love and faithfulness stand before You," which may imply that the words "righteousness," "justice," "love," and "faithfulness" were physically inscribed on God's divine throne, much like an Egyptian cartouche (inscriptions bearing the names of Egyptian kings).

³*"Great … with wisdom"* [*Ed. Note:* The Hebrew for "great" here is *tovim*, normally translated as "good." Hence, comment by Brettler; for our translation "great," see J. Hoffman, "Great *(tovim)* are the lights."] A joint allusion to the first creation story in Genesis 1, where everything created is good, and Proverbs 3:19–20, where the world was created with wisdom. Post-biblical works regularly conflate biblical accounts.

³*"To have dominion"* Based on Genesis 1:16–18, "God made the two great lights, the greater light to dominate the day and the lesser light to dominate the night, and the stars … to dominate the day and the night…."

⁴*"Brilliance* [ziv]" A word found several times in the Aramaic sections of the Book of Daniel, and borrowed from Aramaic into Hebrew.

⁴*"Happy when they rise"* From Psalm 19:6, where the sun is compared to a bridegroom.

⁴*"Reverently doing their creator's will"* Based on Psalm 103:21, "Bless Adonai, all his hosts, his servants who do his will." The point is that these bodies, though powerful and perhaps even in some sense divine, cannot act autonomously, and thus do not threaten a monotheistic world-view.

⁵*"They* [*the lights*] *render honor"* See Psalm 148:2–3, "Praise Him, all his angels, praise Him, all his hosts. Praise Him, sun and moon, praise Him, all bright stars."

— ◆ —

DORFF (THEOLOGY)

over the planets through the initial letters of the words in v. 6: *SH*[*evach*] for *SHabtai* (Saturn); *N*[*ot'nim*] for *Nogah* (Venus); *K*[*ol*] for *Kokhav* (Mercury); *TS*['*va*] for *TSedek* (Jupiter); and *M*[*arom*] for *Ma'adim* (the red one, Mars).

— ◆ —

ELLENSON (MODERN LITURGIES)

of an orderly universe. On the other, it was composed by Jewish mystics known as *Yordei Merkavah*—dated variously, anywhere from the third to the eighth century—whose nonrational approach to Judaism was anathema to many modern prayerbook editors, and virtually every line of the prayer contains mystical allusions for those familiar with their doctrines. Consequently, both the 1819 and 1845 liturgies of the Hamburg Temple omitted this prayer, as did the *Olath Tamid* (1858) of David Einhorn, here in America. In contrast, the more liturgically conservative Abraham Geiger (Germany, 1854 and 1870) and Isaac Mayer Wise (United States, 1857) retained it, even though they surely did not subscribe to any of the mystical allusions it contained.

Fortunately, it can be read successfully without acknowledging its deeper mystical ideas. They included it as simply a nice poem.

Later on (1895/6), the North American Reform *Union Prayer Book* purged this prayer, as did the otherwise conservative 1997 British Liberal *Forms of Prayer for Jewish Worship*, the 1996 British Reform *Lev Chadash*, and the 2001 German *Das Juedische Gebetbuch*. However, the turn toward tradition in modern liberal Judaism as well as the fascination that many modern Jews have with mysticism have prompted recent American and Israeli Reform prayer books to add the prayer back in. The prayer books doing so include the 1975 North American Reform *Gates of Prayer*, the (1982) Israeli Reform *Ha'avodah Shebalev*, and the most recent manifestation of contemporary American Reform liturgy, *Mishkan T'filah* (2006). In Europe, too, we see the tendency toward inclusion in newly composed Reform liturgies—for example, the 1996 Dutch *Tov L'hodot* and the 1997 French *Siddour Taher Libeinu*.

———◆———

FRANKEL (A WOMAN'S VOICE)

Nogah—from the root *n.g.h*, meaning "to shine brightly"—is the Hebrew name for Venus. Throughout the classical and ancient near eastern world, Venus was worshiped as the goddess of love, and often of war as well. To the Babylonians she was known as Ishtar; to the Canaanites, Anat; to the Sumerians, Inanna. She was a complicated mythic figure, characterized by contradiction and paradox—depicted as both virginal and promiscuous, matronly and bloodthirsty. A similar ambivalence characterized ancient patriarchal attitudes toward women in general, for Jews too, not just pagans.

In the Talmud and then in the folklore of medieval Europe, Venus came to be associated astrologically with the qualities of grace, beauty, and passion, and was believed to play a critical role in conception and fertility. These elements were of particular importance in women's lives. Thus Friday was a favorite wedding day in eastern Europe because it was Venus's day, and it was hoped that she would bless the new union with many children.

But Venus was not always benign. In fact, in central Europe (and in some parts of Poland), Jews observed a ceremony called *Hollekreisch*, during which a name was bestowed on a newborn. It is likely that *Hollekreisch* derives from Holle, a Teutonic demon-witch who preyed on babies in the night. This figure is similar to Lilith, a figure from Jewish legend who also threatened the lives of newborns. Because of this resemblance, Holle became central to a Jewish ceremony in which Jews shouted out her name and tossed the baby in the air three times—to scare the witch off.

However, like her ancient near eastern counterparts, the demonic Holle also appears in German folklore as the goddess of love. And as such, she also found a positive place in Jewish folklore, particularly in the lives of women. A fifteenth-century Hebrew-Yiddish love recipe instructs:

Obtain an egg on a Thursday, laid by a jet-black hen which has never before laid an egg, and bury it after sunset that day at a crossroads. Leave it there for three days, dig it up after sunset, sell it and buy a mirror with the money. Bury the mirror in the same place that evening in the name of Venus. Sleep on that spot for three nights, then dig up the mirror. He who gazes in it will love you! (From Joshua Trachtenberg, *Jewish Magic and Superstition* [Philadelphia: Jewish Publication Society, 1939, 2004], p. 43)

◆————————

GRAY (OUR TALMUDIC HERITAGE)

whereas the sun can only be seen in the day). Hardly mollified, the moon pointed out that its light during the day is as insignificant as the light of a candle in the afternoon. After further argument, God implicitly admitted having wronged the moon; to atone for the error, a sacrifice was demanded of Israel on Rosh Chodesh—on God's (!) behalf (Num. 28:15). The sacrifice consists of a young male goat, said in the verse to be offered literally "for sin for God" *(l'chatat l'Adonai)*. Midrashically, the Rabbis read the phrase as implying "for God's sin," that sin being the diminution of the moon's size.

◆————————

L. HOFFMAN (HISTORY)

See "All will praise You [*hakol yodukha*].... God, master [*El Adon*]," p. 69). We do not know if he saw symbolic significance to these numbers, but members of a twelfth- to thirteenth-century mystical school *(Chasidei Ashkenaz)* did. Ten is for the 10 Commandments; 12 is for the twelve tribes of Israel, and 72 corresponds to the number of letters in one of God's several ineffable names.

2–6 "The holy beings [chayot hakodesh] ... *chariots* [merkavah] ... *before his glory* [lifnei k'vodo].... *gives Him praise* [shevach notnim lo]" These (and other terms) immediately identify the poem as emanating from the *Yordei Merkavah*, sometimes called "chariot" mystics *(merkavah* means "chariot"), a school of thought that may have begun as early as the second or third century in Eretz Yisrael. Its doctrine emphasized the affective impact of prayer and its ability to induce a trancelike state that would transport worshipers to the outermost heavens. There they would join the angels around God's throne of glory (pictured as a chariot), proclaiming, "Holy holy holy." (For detail, see Volume 1, *The Sh'ma and Its Blessings*, pp. 42–65.) The "holy beings" *(chayot hakodesh)* are the angels; "chariot" *(merkavah)* is the chariot or throne. "Glory" *(k'vodo)* is an error—most manuscripts have *kisei k'vodo*, God's "*throne of* glory," before which the angels offer praise. Hence, the last line: *shevach notnim lo*, "gives him [God] praise."

◆————————

J. HOFFMAN (TRANSLATION)

for "lord" *(adon)* and "[the] Lord" *(Adonai)*. But although the poet ultimately has in mind Adonai, he means here to identify Adonai with the concept of lord, as in "lord of the manor," the manor here being the universe. The Hebrew here must mean "lord" in the sense of "master."

[1] *"Blessed* [barukh] *and praised* [m'vorakh]" Both Hebrew words here come from the same root. If we had a convenient way to write it in English, we would prefer "bless'd" and "blessed" (one syllable and two, respectively).

[1] *"Grandeur* [godlo] *and greatness* [tuvo]" "Grandeur" is a stretch. Birnbaum's "greatness and goodness" more closely approximates the meaning of each word individually, but the downward transition from "great" to "good" in English destroys the poetry of the Hebrew, which consciously moves from the lesser characteristic to the more important one.

[3] *"Great* [tovim] *are the lights"* From the same root as "greatness," above (see "Grandeur and greatness"). In Hebrew, the word *tov* was chosen here because it starts with the relatively rare letter *tet*, and a *tet*-word was needed for the acrostic.

[3] *"Insight"* Following Birnbaum.

[3] *"To have dominion around the earth"* The less awkward "to rule the world" sounds too much like a comic book story.

[4] *"Rise"* Literally, "leave." Ancient imagery has the celestial bodies leaving their homes when they are first seen and returning home when they cease to be visible.

[6] *"Serafim and the ofanim"* Two kinds of angels. Serafim reappear in the *K'dushat Hashem*, v. 3, p. 93.

◆ ◆ ◆

c. *La'el Asher Shavat* ("To God Who Rested")

¹To God who rested from all work on the seventh day. He ascended to sit upon his throne of glory, ²wrapping the day of rest in splendor, calling the Sabbath day a delight. ³This is how the seventh day is praised, for on it God rested from all his work. ⁴And the seventh day offers praise with these words: "A musical psalm for the Sabbath day. It is good to praise Adonai." ⁵Therefore let all of his creatures extol and praise God, let them ascribe praise and honor and greatness to God, the king, creator of all, who in his holiness bestows rest on his People Israel on the holy Sabbath day. ⁶May your name, Adonai our God, be sanctified, as You are magnified in heaven above and on earth below. ⁷Be blessed, our deliverer, for the excellent work of your hands, and for the glowing lights that You created; they will glorify You.

לְאֵל אֲשֶׁר שָׁבַת מִכָּל הַמַּעֲשִׂים ¹ בַּיּוֹם הַשְּׁבִיעִי; הִתְעַלָּה וְיָשַׁב עַל כִּסֵּא כְבוֹדוֹ; ²תִּפְאֶרֶת עָטָה לְיוֹם הַמְּנוּחָה, עֹנֶג קָרָא לְיוֹם הַשַּׁבָּת. ³זֶה שֶׁבַח שֶׁל יוֹם הַשְּׁבִיעִי, שֶׁבּוֹ שָׁבַת אֵל מִכָּל מְלַאכְתּוֹ. ⁴וְיוֹם הַשְּׁבִיעִי מְשַׁבֵּחַ וְאוֹמֵר: מִזְמוֹר שִׁיר לְיוֹם הַשַּׁבָּת טוֹב לְהוֹדוֹת לַיָי. ⁵לְפִיכָךְ יְפָאֲרוּ וִיבָרְכוּ לָאֵל כָּל יְצוּרָיו; שֶׁבַח, יְקָר וּגְדֻלָּה יִתְּנוּ לָאֵל מֶלֶךְ, יוֹצֵר כֹּל, הַמַּנְחִיל מְנוּחָה לְעַמּוֹ יִשְׂרָאֵל בִּקְדֻשָּׁתוֹ בְּיוֹם שַׁבַּת קֹדֶשׁ. ⁶שִׁמְךָ יְיָ אֱלֹהֵינוּ יִתְקַדַּשׁ, וְזִכְרְךָ מַלְכֵּנוּ יִתְפָּאַר, בַּשָּׁמַיִם מִמַּעַל וְעַל הָאָרֶץ מִתָּחַת. ⁷תִּתְבָּרַךְ, מוֹשִׁיעֵנוּ, עַל שֶׁבַח מַעֲשֵׂה יָדֶיךָ, וְעַל מְאוֹרֵי אוֹר שֶׁעָשִׂיתָ; יְפָאֲרוּךָ סֶּלָה.

BRETTLER (BIBLE)

[1] *"To God who rested ... He ascended"* In the first creation story (Gen. 1:1–2:4a), God creates the world in six days and rests on the seventh. But the prayer adds the notion that God was too busy to sit down while creating, and so was enthroned only after that primeval Shabbat. Psalm 93:2 depicts a different image—God enthroned forever ("your throne stands firm from of old").

[2] *"Splendor* [tiferet] *... delight* [oneg]*"* No biblical text calls Shabbat *tiferet*. *Oneg* occurs only once, in Isaiah 58:13, a relatively late (post-exilic) composition that emphasizes the positive *(p. 90)*

DORFF (THEOLOGY)

[5] *"Creator of all ... bestows rest on his People Israel"* Note again the juxtaposition of the universal with the particular (see *"The breath of every living being ... our king,"* p. 44). God is "the creator of all," but gives Israel Shabbat. That is also the import of Exodus 31:16–17, used (1) before the Friday evening *(p. 91)*

ELLENSON (MODERN LITURGIES)

[1] *"To God who rested from all work"* The first Reform prayer book *(Gebetbuch)* of the Hamburg Temple (1819) already had made the decision to retain only the last lines of this prayer, beginning with the words, "May your name, Adonai our God, be sanctified" *(p. 91)*

FRANKEL (A WOMAN'S VOICE)

[1] *"To God who rested"* This prayer praises God for the gift of Shabbat, our weekly day of rest modeled on the seventh day of creation, when God rested from the labors of creation. Here is one more example of *imitatio dei*, the human privilege of being created in the divine image and the responsibility that such an exalted state entails. Just as God calls the Sabbath "a delight," so, too, the Jewish People enjoy this day freed from toil.

But for many Jewish women, *(p. 91)*

c. La'el Asher Shavat ("To God Who Rested")

[1] To God who rested from all work on the seventh day. He ascended to sit upon his throne of glory, [2] wrapping the day of rest in splendor, calling the Sabbath day a delight. [3] This is how the seventh day is praised, for on it God rested from all his work. [4] And the seventh day offers praise with these words: "A musical psalm for the Sabbath day. It is good to praise Adonai." [5] Therefore let all of his creatures

GRAY (OUR TALMUDIC HERITAGE)

[2] *"Wrapping the day of rest in splendor"* Abudarham (fourteenth-century Spain) sees this as an allusion to the *mitzvah* of dressing better on Shabbat than on the weekday. His interpretation goes back to the Yerushalmi, where Rabbi Simlai lectured in public about the need for specially festive Shabbat attire. His lecture affronted poorer scholars who could not afford to purchase special Shabbat wear. Rabbi Simlai advised that if they could not change all their clothes for Shabbat, they should at least change

something about the way they wore their usual clothes (PT Peah 8:8, 21b).

[2] *"Calling the Sabbath day a delight"* Abudarham sees this as an allusion to the requirement that Shabbat be honored with food and drink. (See Volume 7, *Shabbat at Home*, pp. 118, 123 [Gray, "Food and meals"].)

◆

L. HOFFMAN (HISTORY)

THE FINAL SHABBAT ADDITION TO THE YOTSER, A MIDRASHIC TREATMENT OF PSALM 92, "A SONG FOR THE SABBATH DAY," PERSONIFYING SHABBAT AS AN ENTITY THAT ITSELF PRAISES GOD. FOR THE OTHER TWO ADDITIONS, SEE PP. 69, 79.

[4] *"'A musical psalm for the Sabbath day. It is good to praise Adonai'"* Rabbinic prayer can sometimes be seen as a branch of midrash. Like midrash, prayer also began orally. Prayers were spoken aloud by a prayer leader, and midrash was used as sermons. Like the *(p. 92)*

[1]לָאֵל אֲשֶׁר שָׁבַת מִכָּל הַמַּעֲשִׂים בַּיּוֹם הַשְּׁבִיעִי; הִתְעַלָּה וְיָשַׁב עַל כִּסֵּא כְבוֹדוֹ; [2]תִּפְאֶרֶת עָטָה לְיוֹם הַמְּנוּחָה, עֹנֶג קָרָא לְיוֹם הַשַּׁבָּת. [3]זֶה שֶׁבַח שֶׁל יוֹם הַשְּׁבִיעִי, שֶׁבּוֹ שָׁבַת אֵל מִכָּל מְלַאכְתּוֹ. [4]וְיוֹם הַשְּׁבִיעִי מְשַׁבֵּחַ וְאוֹמֵר: מִזְמוֹר שִׁיר לְיוֹם הַשַּׁבָּת טוֹב לְהוֹדוֹת לַיָי. [5]לְפִיכָךְ יְפָאֲרוּ וִיבָרְכוּ לָאֵל כָּל יְצוּרָיו; שֶׁבַח,

J. HOFFMAN (TRANSLATION)

[1] *"Rested"* The verb "rested" *(shavat)* comes from the same root that gives us "Shabbat," the day of rest.

[2] *"Delight* [oneg]" Or, perhaps: Calling the Sabbath day "Delight." *Oneg* is used in many congregations to name the snack served after services on Friday night: *oneg* or (more fully) *oneg Shabbat*.

[3] *"How the seventh day is praised"* Birnbaum's "distinction of the seventh day" is nicely poetic, but immediately after (*m'shabe'ach*—see "Offers praise") we need "praise" to match the noun *(shevach)* here. The whole point is the play on words, which we need to reproduce in our English (see L. Hoffman, p. 92). *(p. 92)*

extol and praise God, let them ascribe praise and honor and greatness to God, the king, creator of all, who in his holiness bestows rest on his People Israel on the holy Sabbath day. [6] May your name, Adonai our God, be sanctified, as You are magnified in heaven above and on earth below. [7] Be blessed, our deliverer, for the excellent work of your hands, and for the glowing lights that You created; they will glorify You.

יְקָר וּגְדֻלָּה יִתְּנוּ לְאֵל מֶלֶךְ, יוֹצֵר כֹּל, הַמַּנְחִיל מְנוּחָה לְעַמּוֹ יִשְׂרָאֵל בִּקְדֻשָּׁתוֹ בְּיוֹם שַׁבַּת קֹדֶשׁ. [6]שִׁמְךָ יְיָ אֱלֹהֵינוּ יִתְקַדַּשׁ, וְזִכְרְךָ מַלְכֵּנוּ יִתְפָּאַר, בַּשָּׁמַיִם מִמַּעַל וְעַל הָאָרֶץ מִתָּחַת. [7]תִּתְבָּרַךְ, מוֹשִׁיעֵנוּ, עַל שֶׁבַח מַעֲשֵׂה יָדֶיךָ, וְעַל מְאוֹרֵי אוֹר שֶׁעָשִׂיתָ; יְפָאֲרוּךָ סֶּלָה.

BRETTLER (BIBLE)

rather than the negative aspects of Shabbat.

[4] *"A musical psalm for the Sabbath day"* Quoting the introduction to Psalm 92. That psalm does not suggest that the Sabbath day itself is reciting it, though some verses early in the psalm—like "You have gladdened me by your deeds, Adonai; I shout for joy at your handiwork" (v. 5)—allow for that reading.

[5] *"Honor [y'kar] and greatness [g'dulah] to God, the king"* In Esther 1:4, *y'kar ug'dulah* are attributed to the earthly king.

[5] *"Holy Sabbath"* See Exodus 31:14, "You must keep my Sabbath for this is a sign between me and you ... that you may know that I, Adonai, have consecrated you. You shall keep the Sabbath, for it is holy for you."

[6] *"May your name [shimkha, from shem, 'name'] ... be sanctified, as You [zikhr'kha, from zekher, meaning, literally, 'name'] are magnified"* Parallelism based on Exodus 3:15, where God reveals his special name to Moses: "This shall be my *shem* forever, this my *zekher* for all eternity." The exact nuance of *zekher* there continues to be debated; it is unclear if it means the same as "name."

[7] *"Be blessed ... they will glorify You"* The use of the post-biblical word pair from the roots *b.r.kh* and *p.'.r* recalls similar uses earlier in this composition, helping to tie it all together.

[7] *"Work of your hands, and ... glowing lights"* From Psalm 19:2, "The heavens declare

the glory of God, the sky proclaims his handiwork." But the poet here expands on praise given specifically by the luminaries.

———◆———

DORFF (THEOLOGY)

Amidah, (2) as part of the Sabbath morning *Amidah*, and (3) as part of *Kiddush* for Sabbath lunch: the Sabbath is specifically "between Me and the children of Israel." (See Volume 9, *Welcoming the Night: Minchah and Ma'ariv [Afternoon and Evening Prayer]*, pp. 107 and 109.)

———◆———

ELLENSON (MODERN LITURGIES)

to the end, "and for the glowing lights that You created; they will glorify You." Isaac Mayer Wise followed exactly the precedent of Hamburg in his *Minhag America* (1857). The desire to create an abbreviated service probably prompted this move and led virtually all other Reform Siddurim—with the exception of both the 1854 and 1870 editions of Abraham Geiger's *D'var Yom B'yomo* (Germany), the contemporary Israeli *Ha'avodah Shebalev* (1982), and the 1997 French *Siddour Taher Libeinu*—to omit this prayer altogether. Conservative and Reconstructionist prayer books have retained it in its entirety, in part, possibly, because of the familiar tune to which it is sung.

———◆———

FRANKEL (A WOMAN'S VOICE)

especially mothers, the Sabbath is not a day of pure "delight." The hours leading up to Shabbat bring stress and burden: shopping, cleaning, cooking, washing dishes, setting a festive table, washing and dressing the children in their Shabbat best—then during the Sabbath day itself, preparing and serving elaborate meals (often to guests as well as family), and caring for exhausted children until they settle into bed.

Are these acts, too, *imitatio dei*? Although this prayer tells us that on the first Shabbat so long ago, God "ascended to sit upon his throne of glory," we can't be sure that this was always the case. Perhaps for God, too, Shabbat only eventually evolved into a day of rest.

The prayer concludes by blessing God for "the excellent work of your hands." How well Jewish women understand those words! So, yes, women's labors for the sake of and on Shabbat are a form of *imitatio dei*, a reflection of the holy. As a Yiddish proverb aptly puts it: "God couldn't be everywhere, so He made mothers."

———◆———

L. HOFFMAN (HISTORY)

sermons, then, ancient prayers sometimes use midrashic style to make their point.

Here is a prime example. The Bible introduces Psalm 92 as "the song for the seventh day," meaning the psalm intended for Temple recitation on Shabbat. Our prayer pictures *everything* God created—not just angels and humans—praising God. Since God created time, each day of the week must join the chorus of praise. The author of our prayer, therefore, creatively misreads "song *for* the seventh day" as "song *of* [belonging to] the seventh day." The seventh day, personified, says, "It is good to praise Adonai."

———◆———

J. HOFFMAN (TRANSLATION)

[3] *"Offers praise* [m'shabe'ach]" See preceding comment, "How the seventh day is praised."

[4] *"Praise* [l'hodot]" Or "gratefully acknowledge." This is not the word for "praise" that we just saw *(shevach, m'shabe'ach)*, but here is a biblical citation, so we translate it the same way we did for Psalm 95. See J. Hoffman, "Praise," v. 2, in Volume 8, *Kabbalat Shabbat (Welcoming Shabbat in the Synagogue)*, p. 63.

[6] *"You"* Birnbaum's "your fame" is another way of approaching the dilemma presented by the Hebrew *zekher*, literally "memory," which really just serves to poetically modify "You." Once again, we opt for idiomatic English at the expense of literal translation of one of the Hebrew words. See above, "You".

[7] *"Deliverer"* Or "savior."

[7] *"Excellent"* We translate in accordance with Volume 1, *The Sh'ma and Its Blessings*, p. 42. Another option in this context would be "glorious."

———◆ ◆ ◆———

C. THE *AMIDAH* ("STANDING" PRAYER): TALKING TO GOD

I. *K'DUSHAT HASHEM* ("SANCTIFICATION OF [GOD'S] NAME"): DECLARING GOD'S HOLINESS

¹ Let us sanctify your name on earth as it is sanctified in the heavens on high, as written by your prophet: "They called out one to another:

² 'Holy, holy, holy is the Lord of hosts. The whole earth is full of his glory.'"

³ Then in a mighty and powerful great loud voice they make their voice heard. Rising toward the serafim, from across the way they offer blessing:

⁴ "The glory of Adonai is blessed from his place."

⁵ Our king, appear to us from your place and reign over us, for we await You! ⁶ When will You reign over Zion? Soon, in our day, You will dwell there forever. ⁷ You will be magnified and sanctified in Jerusalem your city in all generations and for all eternity. ⁸ And our eyes will behold your kingdom, as is written in your songs of glory by David, your servant of righteousness:

⁹ "Adonai will reign forever, your God, Zion, for all generations. Halleluyah."

¹⁰ For all generations we will tell of your greatness and for all of eternity proclaim your holiness. ¹¹ Your praise, our God, will never depart our mouths, for You are a sovereign God, great and holy. ¹²*Blessed are You, Adonai, the holy God.

[**From Rosh Hashanah to Yom Kippur, substitute the following:*]

¹³ Blessed are You, Adonai, the holy king.

נְ¹קַדֵּשׁ אֶת שִׁמְךָ בָּעוֹלָם כְּשֵׁם שֶׁמַּקְדִּישִׁים אוֹתוֹ בִּשְׁמֵי מָרוֹם, כַּכָּתוּב עַל יַד נְבִיאֶךָ: וְקָרָא זֶה אֶל זֶה וְאָמַר:

²קָדוֹשׁ, קָדוֹשׁ, קָדוֹשׁ יְיָ צְבָאוֹת; מְלֹא כָל הָאָרֶץ כְּבוֹדוֹ.

³אָז בְּקוֹל רַעַשׁ גָּדוֹל, אַדִּיר וְחָזָק, מַשְׁמִיעִים קוֹל, מִתְנַשְּׂאִים לְעֻמַּת שְׂרָפִים, לְעֻמָּתָם בָּרוּךְ יֹאמֵרוּ:

⁴בָּרוּךְ כְּבוֹד יְיָ מִמְּקוֹמוֹ.

⁵מִמְּקוֹמְךָ מַלְכֵּנוּ תוֹפִיעַ וְתִמְלֹךְ עָלֵינוּ, כִּי מְחַכִּים אֲנַחְנוּ לָךְ. ⁶מָתַי תִּמְלֹךְ בְּצִיּוֹן, בְּקָרוֹב בְּיָמֵינוּ לְעוֹלָם וָעֶד תִּשְׁכּוֹן. ⁷תִּתְגַּדַּל וְתִתְקַדַּשׁ בְּתוֹךְ יְרוּשָׁלַיִם עִירְךָ לְדוֹר וָדוֹר וּלְנֵצַח נְצָחִים. ⁸וְעֵינֵינוּ תִרְאֶינָה מַלְכוּתֶךָ, כַּדָּבָר הָאָמוּר בְּשִׁירֵי עֻזֶּךָ, עַל יְדֵי דָוִד מְשִׁיחַ צִדְקֶךָ:

⁹יִמְלֹךְ יְיָ לְעוֹלָם, אֱלֹהַיִךְ צִיּוֹן לְדֹר וָדֹר; הַלְלוּיָהּ.

¹⁰לְדוֹר וָדוֹר נַגִּיד גָּדְלֶךָ, וּלְנֵצַח נְצָחִים קְדֻשָּׁתְךָ נַקְדִּישׁ, ¹¹וְשִׁבְחֲךָ אֱלֹהֵינוּ מִפִּינוּ לֹא יָמוּשׁ לְעוֹלָם וָעֶד, כִּי אֵל מֶלֶךְ גָּדוֹל וְקָדוֹשׁ אָתָּה. ¹²בָּרוּךְ אַתָּה, יְיָ, הָאֵל הַקָּדוֹשׁ.

[**From Rosh Hashanah to Yom Kippur, substitute the following:*]

¹³בָּרוּךְ אַתָּה, יְיָ, הַמֶּלֶךְ הַקָּדוֹשׁ.

BRETTLER (BIBLE)

[1] *"Let us sanctify"* The community's recitation of "Let us sanctify" reflects the human desire to parallel the divine retinue's act of sanctifying God. Although the Bible knows nothing of the idea of *sanctifying* God on earth to match what is done in heaven, Psalm 148:1–12 calls upon God *to be praised* from the heavens and earth, equally (cf. Ps. 103:20–22). A Dead Sea Scroll hymn likewise suggests that people praise God alongside the angels (F. G. Martinez, *The Dead Sea Scrolls Translated*, p. 332; 1QH XI21–22).

(p. 97)

DORFF (THEOLOGY)

[2, 4] *"Holy, holy, holy is the Lord of hosts. The whole earth is full of his glory.... The glory of Adonai is blessed from his place"* These biblical verses (Isaiah 6:3 and Ezekiel 3:12) speak of the total otherness of God—God's holiness, or separateness, from every human quality. Two theological points arise. First, if God is really totally other, how can we know Him? Torah depicts God in human terms when it speaks, for (p. 98)

ELLENSON (MODERN LITURGIES)

Shacharit K'dushat Hashem American Reform Judaism did away with the *Musaf* service, so all North American Reform Siddurim—*Union Prayer Book* (1895/6), *Gates of Prayer* (1975), and *Mishkan T'filah* (2006)—compose a *Shacharit K'dushat Hashem* (p. 99)

FRANKEL (A WOMAN'S VOICE)

[1] *"Let us sanctify your name"* Beyle Hurvits wrote the following *t'khine* (Yiddish prayer for women) to be recited here (before the *K'dushah*), from the beginning of the month of Elul until Yom Kippur. She promises her readers that these penitential prayers, combined with hearing the blowing of the shofar during this forty-day period, will reward them with "instant merit."

> Near you, God, there is no night,
> And candles are not needed beside You,
> (p. 100)

I. K'DUSHAT HASHEM ("SANCTIFICATION OF [GOD'S] NAME"): DECLARING GOD'S HOLINESS

[1] Let us sanctify your name on earth as it is sanctified in the heavens on high, as written by your prophet: "They called out one to another:

[2] 'Holy, holy, holy is the Lord of hosts. The whole earth is full of his glory.'"

[3] Then in a mighty and powerful great loud voice they

GRAY (OUR TALMUDIC HERITAGE)

[2] *"Holy, holy, holy"* David Kimchi (Provence, c. 1160–1235) interprets each occurrence of "holy" as a different aspect of existence: the first refers to the transcendent world of the divine; the second to galaxies, stars, and planets; and the third to the world in which we live. Just as the divine and heavenly worlds praise God, so do human beings here on earth. Although occupying the most "lowly world" *(olam hashafel)*, we are nevertheless the equivalents of those who offer praise in the two more

exalted realms of existence.

[4] *"The glory of Adonai is blessed from his place"* See Volume 6, *Tachanun and Concluding Prayers*, p. 119 (Gray "Blessed be the glory").

[9] *"Adonai will reign forever"* Midrash T'hillim (Midrash on Psalms) 146:9 interprets this verse (Psalm 146:10) to mean that it is the righteous here on earth who crown God king. This interpretation is explicable in light of the psalm as a whole, which praises those who pursue justice on behalf of

נְקַדֵּשׁ אֶת שִׁמְךָ בָּעוֹלָם כְּשֵׁם שֶׁמַּקְדִּישִׁים אוֹתוֹ [1] בִּשְׁמֵי מָרוֹם, כַּכָּתוּב עַל יַד נְבִיאֶךָ: וְקָרָא זֶה אֶל זֶה וְאָמַר:

קָדוֹשׁ, קָדוֹשׁ, קָדוֹשׁ יְיָ צְבָאוֹת; מְלֹא כָל הָאָרֶץ [2] כְּבוֹדוֹ.

others and who feeds the hungry (v. 7). God is similarly described as loving the righteous (v. 8), and doing acts of justice (vv. 7–9). No wonder the "coronation" of God is proclaimed by the righteous.

[12–13] *"Blessed are You, Adonai, the holy God / Blessed are You, Adonai, the holy king"* A talmudic discussion (Ber. 12b) cites Rav (third century) as advising us to change "holy God," the usual wording here, to "holy king" during the Ten Days of Repentance (between Rosh Hashanah and *(p. 101)*

L. HOFFMAN (HISTORY)

WITH THE SH'MA AND ITS BLESSINGS BEHIND US, WE MOVE ON TO THE SECOND OF THE THREE MAJOR SERVICE RUBRICS, THE AMIDAH. WE WILL SAY THE AMIDAH TWICE ON SHABBAT MORNING, HERE IN SHACHARIT (THE MORNING SERVICE), AND AGAIN IN MUSAF (THE ADDITIONAL SERVICE). IN BOTH CASES THE READER'S REPETITION OF THE THIRD BENEDICTION, THE K'DUSHAT HASHEM ("SANCTIFICATION OF [GOD'S] NAME") STANDS OUT. FOR THE PARALLEL MUSAF BLESSING, SEE PP. 119–120.

[1] *"Let us sanctify your name"* This third blessing of the *Amidah* proclaims God's holiness, but following biblical precedent *(p. 101)*

J. HOFFMAN (TRANSLATION)

[1] *"Let us sanctify your name"* In Hebrew, the entire line is redolent with the poetic repetition of the sounds *sh'm*—the assonance is missing from our English translation. (For detail, see Volume 2, *The Amidah*, p. 93.)

[6] *"Dwell there"* Literally, just "dwell."

[6] *"Forever"* So reads the Hebrew. The point is that soon God will begin the eternal process of dwelling.

[7] *"You will be"* Or, "may you be." This is a persistent problem in translating Hebrew into English, because Hebrew is almost always ambiguous in this regard. *(p. 103)*

make their voice heard. Rising toward the serafim, from across the way they offer blessing:

4 "The glory of Adonai is blessed from his place."

5 Our king, appear to us from your place and reign over us, for we await You! 6 When will You reign over Zion? Soon, in our day, You will dwell there forever. 7 You will be magnified and sanctified in Jerusalem your city in all generations and for all eternity. 8 And our eyes will behold your kingdom, as is written in your songs of glory by David, your servant of righteousness:

9 "Adonai will reign forever, your God, Zion, for all generations. Halleluyah."

10 For all generations we will tell of your greatness and for all of eternity proclaim your holiness. 11 Your praise, our God, will never depart our mouths, for You are a sovereign God, great and holy. 12 *Blessed are You, Adonai, the holy God.

[*From Rosh Hashanah to Yom Kippur, substitute the following:]

13 Blessed are You, Adonai, the holy king.

³אָז בְּקוֹל רַעַשׁ גָּדוֹל, אַדִּיר וְחָזָק, מַשְׁמִיעִים קוֹל, מִתְנַשְּׂאִים לְעֻמַּת שְׂרָפִים, לְעֻמָּתָם בָּרוּךְ יֹאמֵרוּ:

⁴בָּרוּךְ כְּבוֹד יְיָ מִמְּקוֹמוֹ.

⁵מִמְּקוֹמְךָ מַלְכֵּנוּ תוֹפִיעַ וְתִמְלֹךְ עָלֵינוּ, כִּי מְחַכִּים אֲנַחְנוּ לָךְ. ⁶מָתַי תִּמְלֹךְ בְּצִיּוֹן, בְּקָרוֹב בְּיָמֵינוּ לְעוֹלָם וָעֶד תִּשְׁכּוֹן. ⁷תִּתְגַּדַּל וְתִתְקַדַּשׁ בְּתוֹךְ יְרוּשָׁלַיִם עִירְךָ לְדוֹר וָדוֹר וּלְנֵצַח נְצָחִים. ⁸וְעֵינֵינוּ תִרְאֶינָה מַלְכוּתֶךָ, כַּדָּבָר הָאָמוּר בְּשִׁירֵי עֻזֶּךָ, עַל יְדֵי דָוִד מְשִׁיחַ צִדְקֶךָ:

⁹יִמְלֹךְ יְיָ לְעֹלָם, אֱלֹהַיִךְ צִיּוֹן לְדֹר וָדֹר; הַלְלוּיָהּ.

¹⁰לְדוֹר וָדוֹר נַגִּיד גָּדְלֶךָ, וּלְנֵצַח נְצָחִים קְדֻשָּׁתְךָ נַקְדִּישׁ, ¹¹וְשִׁבְחֲךָ אֱלֹהֵינוּ מִפִּינוּ לֹא יָמוּשׁ לְעוֹלָם וָעֶד, כִּי אֵל מֶלֶךְ גָּדוֹל וְקָדוֹשׁ אָתָּה. ¹²בָּרוּךְ אַתָּה, יְיָ, הָאֵל הַקָּדוֹשׁ.

[*From Rosh Hashanah to Yom Kippur, substitute the following:]

¹³בָּרוּךְ אַתָּה, יְיָ, הַמֶּלֶךְ הַקָּדוֹשׁ.

BRETTLER (BIBLE)

¹ *"On earth* [ba'olam]*"* See "Adonai will reign forever [*l'olam*]," below.

¹ *"Heavens* [sh'mei] *on high* [marom]*"* Literally "heavens of heavens." This is typical biblical style: two words that are largely synonymous (*shamayim* = "heavens" and *marom* = "on high" or "heavens") are juxtaposed to express a superlative.

¹ *"As written by your prophet"* From Isaiah 6:3. (See comments on "Be blessed our rock" in Volume 1, *The Sh'ma and Its Blessings*, p. 56.)

³ *"Mighty and powerful great loud voice ... serafim"* From the heavenly vision of Ezekiel 3:12–13, "Then a spirit carried me away, and behind me I heard a great roaring sound...." The serafim (an angelic type) are absent from Ezekiel's vision but are present in Isaiah's (chap. 6). Our prayer conflates the two. In fact, the idea that the phrase "blessed from his place" (v. 4), from Ezekiel, is said "from across the way" (v. 3, *l'umatam*) is based on the idea that, in Isaiah 6:3, the serafim call "one to another."

³ *"From across the way"* Suggesting, perhaps, an antiphonal response between the earth-bound sanctification of God and the angelic praise in heaven.

⁵ *"Appear ... and reign"* The *K'dushah* emphasizes the kingship of God, a common biblical motif, but from the perspective of the person praying, that kingship is not evident. Verses 5–8 appeal to God to demonstrate divine sovereignty in Jerusalem. They borrow from Ezekiel's vision of the war of Gog and Magog (38:23): "Thus will I manifest my greatness and my holiness, and make Myself known in the sight of many nations. And they shall know that I am Adonai."

⁹ *"Adonai will reign forever* [l'olam]*, your God, Zion, for all generations. Halleluyah."* Alternatively, "May Adonai reign forever ...," meant to express a wish or desire that God will be forever sovereign. The previous two verses (from Isaiah 6 and Ezekiel 3) were chosen because they were understood to be part of the libretto of the heavenly praise of God. This verse, taken from the conclusion to Psalm 146, suggests praise also because it pictures God as a reigning monarch and, by implication, receiving praise from his angelic servants. Additionally, *l'olam* ("forever") nicely mirrors the word *ba'o-lam* ("on earth") in the opening sentence of the blessing.

¹⁰ *"For all generations we will tell of your greatness"* Although a conclusion specifically of the *K'dushah*, this paragraph functions also as a summary for all three of the first blessings, as it refers to God's greatness, the theme of the first and second blessings, and his holiness ("your greatness ... your holiness"; "great and holy"). Traditionally, the first three blessings are seen as a unit. They follow biblical style in that they offer God praise before the petitions that will follow.

———◆———

DORFF (THEOLOGY)

example, of God's "mighty hand and outstretched arm" (e.g., Exod. 13:9, 32:11; Deut. 4:34) or God's "face" (e.g., Exod. 33:14–15, 33:20; Deut. 34:10), but how can it do that if God is truly unlike human beings?

This question did not bother the authors of the Bible, which is replete with anthropomorphisms. So too is rabbinic literature, though the Rabbis must have had some inkling of the problem because they go out of their way to claim (thirty-two times [!] in the Talmud—e.g., Ber. 31a; Yev. 71a) that "the Torah is written in the language of human beings." Human beings have no choice but to relate to God in terms of human characteristics.

This issue did disturb some medieval philosophers, however, especially Maimonides, who thought depictions of God in human terms would diminish God. He therefore resoundingly denied the corporeality of God—that is, that God has a body. Sometimes he interpreted biblical references to God's form (e.g., hand, foot) figuratively—as a means of communicating a more lofty divine attribute (e.g., God's power). Usually he took such descriptions "negatively"—to say that God has "a mighty hand and an outstretched arm" is to say that God is not weak; to say that God has a face is to say that God is not faceless to us, as if unconcerned with our lives (Maimonides, *Guide for the Perplexed*, part I, esp. chaps. 21, 26, 28, 36–37, 46–47, 52, 55, 58–61 [on negative attributes]).

One problem with this approach is that the Bible and the Rabbis did not flinch from using positive attributes for God. Transforming them all into negative attributes seems to distort their original intent. Also, it is not clear that Maimonides has gained much in this transformation. If God is *not* weak, for example, does that not at least imply that God is strong, thus amounting to the same thing?

A more popular philosophical way to understand human-like depictions of God is through the logic of similes and metaphors. When, for example, Homer speaks of "the fingers of dawn," nobody assumes that the sun has fingers. That is obvious to us because we have direct experience of the dawn and know that it does not have fingers. With God, however, we do not have direct experience. This makes it much harder to identify those images that fit God well and those that do not, and it also makes it harder to avoid identifying God with our picture of Him rather than understanding that the images we use do not describe divine reality. Especially when they have used a very human or humbling image of God, the Rabbis stipulate *kiv'yakhol*, "as it were," as if saying "God, as it were, [is this or that]" (e.g., Meg. 21a; Gen. Rab. 12:1). Indeed, that phrase is used 375 times in the Midrash Aggadah. But short of that kind of explicit reminder, how can we use images without straining the bounds of appropriateness and meaning?

This problem persists in fundamentalist versions of religion, often with disastrous consequences, as, for example, in asserting that we should go to war because God is "a man of war" (Exod. 15:3) and God's own name is "Adonai of armies [hosts]" e.g., Isa. 47:4, 48:2; Jer. 10:16, 31:35; Amos 4:13).

Consequently, it remains crucial even for us to distinguish metaphors from literal reality. Coming, as they must, from our limited human perspective, our claims about God are only *metaphorically* true. We should be careful not to make idols of our limited divine imagery. For more on this issue, see Elliot N. Dorff, *Knowing God: Jewish Journeys to the Unknowable* (Northvale, NJ: Jason Aronson, 1996), chapter seven.

A second theological issue is our understanding of what "the glory of God" means. Abraham Joshua Heschel (*God in Search of Man*, [New York: Farrar, Straus and Giroux, 1955], p. 82) identifies it with God's goodness, based on Exodus 33:18–19, "He [Moses] said, 'Oh, let me behold your presence [*kavod*, "glory"]!' And He [God] answered, 'I will make all my goodness pass before you....'" This would mean that Isaiah and Ezekiel were impressed with the beneficence, or moral quality, of God. The Hebrew word for "glory" *(kavod)*, however, comes from the same root that gives us *kaved*, "heavy." *Kavod*, then, implies God's heaviness, weightiness, or importance—the very existence, power, and ubiquitous presence of God in human life.

But even so, it is not God's might alone that we proclaim, for power is morally neutral and can be used for downright brutal ends; it is, rather, the moral character of God's power that we acknowledge. Thus the two meanings of God's *kavod* are complementary; what we proclaim is God's power *and* goodness.

◆

ELLENSON (MODERN LITURGIES)

that is a composite of passages taken from the traditional *Shacharit* and *Musaf* versions. In addition, *Union Prayer Book* and *Gates of Prayer* add Psalm 8:10 from the Festival parallel: *Adir adireinu ...*, "God our Strength, God our Lord, how excellent is Thy Name in all the earth."

5–6 *"Reign over us ... over Zion"* The antipathy of classical Reform Judaism toward Zion and any mention of Jewish national restoration in the Land of Israel caused nineteenth-century Reform prayerbook authors to regard the phrases, "When will You reign over Zion?" (v. 6) and "You will be magnified and sanctified in Jerusalem your city" (v. 7) as ideologically problematic. The issue was addressed in different ways.

The Hamburg Temple *Gebetbuecher* ("prayerbooks") of 1819 and 1845 resolved the "problem" by deleting the entire traditional content of the Sabbath morning *K'dushah* altogether and substituted in its stead the *K'dushah* for *Musaf*. Isaac Mayer Wise (*Minhag America*, 1857) went further. He virtually removed the traditional *K'dushat Hashem* altogether, retaining only the lines, "Thou art holy, and holy is Thy Name. The saints glorify Thee every day. Selah. Praised art Thou, O God, most holy Lord." In contrast, David Einhorn's *Olath Tamid* (1858) kept most of it intact but omitted the paragraph beginning, "Our king, appear to us from your place and reign over us" (v. 5). These nineteenth-century liturgists served as influential precedents for later Reform liturgies. Thus many contemporary liberal Siddurim—the British Liberal *Forms of Prayer for Jewish Worship* (1997), the Dutch *Tov L'hodot* (1996), and the

SHACHARIT ("MORNING SERVICE")

German *Das Juedische Gebetbuch* (2001)—that have no ideological difficulty whatsoever with affirming the importance and centrality of the State of Israel in modern Jewish life have nevertheless all adopted the Hamburg model and have included the *Shabbat Musaf K'dushah* in their *Shacharit* services in lieu of the traditional *Shacharit* one. Others—the North American *Union Prayer Book* (1895/6), *Gates of Prayer* (1975), and *Mishkan T'filah* (2006)—retain much of the *Shacharit* wording but omit the paragraph beginning, "Our king, appear to us from your place" (v. 5), despite the obvious pro-Zionist stances of these prayer books, with which they agree. The British *Lev Chadash* (1996), while including the first lines of this prayer ("Our king, appear to us from your place"), simply ends with, "Because we are waiting for You."

Nineteenth-century Abraham Geiger retained the remainder of the prayer while removing the "offensive" references to Zion and Jerusalem. Marcus Jastrow, often cited as an early forerunner of American Conservative Judaism (in his *Avodath Yisrael*, 1885) substituted "When will You reign over all the world in your glory?" for "When will You reign over Zion?" He then continued in this universalistic vein, further denationalizing the prayer by omitting "in Jerusalem your city" and writing instead, "on all who sanctify your name."

[8] *"David, your servant of righteousness"* As a messianic theme attached to the Davidic dynasty, this has proved troubling to a number of liberal liturgists. Even the relatively conservative Marcus Jastrow omitted it from his *Avodath Yisrael*, as did the Reconstructionists in their 1965 Siddur and in their later *Kol Haneshamah* (1996).

---◆---

FRANKEL (A WOMAN'S VOICE)

For You light up the whole world with Your light.
And the morning speaks of Your mercy,
And the night speaks of Your truth,
And all creatures acknowledge Your wonder.
God, You help us every day.

Who can speak of the great wonder
That You might impart to the pious men on their day,
In the place where all the people of creation will sit
For Your one day is a thousand years
And Your day is longer than the whole of the world's existence.
And You are forever in eternity,
You outlive all Your creation,
And You remain eternal,
And as You live eternally,
So, too, do Your servants
Live in eternal life.

And how holy You are.
Everyone sanctifies You

In heaven three times a day
And on earth.
And not only do the angels say
"Holy, holy, holy"
But so do Your holy people, Israel
Sanctify Your name by saying
"Holy, holy, holy."
You are sanctified, Lord.
Amen.

(From Devra Kay, *Seyder Tkhines: The Forgotten Book of Common Prayer for Jewish Women* [Philadelphia: Jewish Publication Society, 2004], pp. 224–225)

— ◆ —

GRAY (OUR TALMUDIC HERITAGE)

Yom Kippur). Others disagree. The dispute continued at least into the early fourth century, where Rav's view is championed by Rabbah. Eventually the Talmud settles the dispute by peremptorily proclaiming, "The law follows Rabbah." This anonymous determining note—like others of its kind in the Babylonian Talmud—could be as late as the post-talmudic geonic period (c. eighth to eleventh centuries). In any event, it settles our practice, as codified by *Rambam* (*T'fillah* 10:13) and the *Shulchan Arukh* (O. Ch. 582).

— ◆ —

L. HOFFMAN (HISTORY)

where God's name is equivalent to God's very being, the blessing is known as *K'dushat Hashem*, "Sanctification of the Name," and the version we have here begins, "Let us sanctify your *name*."

This is just one of many versions that prayer leaders once pioneered. In an age before the widespread use of writing and, therefore, with no written prayer text to consult, they made up new compositions, sometimes week after week, using common prayer idioms and textual precedents they had memorized from the Bible. Without prayer books, worshipers mostly listened and answered *amen*.

Most of these improvised prayers died out. What we still have are the "lucky" ones that eventually got written down and saved. Later still, when prayer books arose, the surviving alternatives were apportioned among various prayers—in this case, among different *Amidah*s as "reader's repetitions." That is why the reader's repetition of *K'dushat Hashem* varies so widely, not only from service to service (Shabbat differs from weekdays, for instance, and *Musaf* from *Shacharit*), but also from rite to rite (Sefardim, for example, as opposed to Ashkenazim).

Testimony to its standing as the most important of all the *Amidah*'s blessings, the *K'dushat Hashem* (colloquially, just *K'dushah*—pronounced k'-doo-SHAH, but popularly, k'-DOO-shah) features a reader's repetition that is a separate composition from what the congregation has just said silently. Early rabbinic prayer sought to emulate the angels who were believed to circle God's throne of glory, praising God as "holy, holy, holy." Since that is the theme of the *K'dushah*, early prayer leaders put more energy into it than into any other prayer. That is also why we have not just one but three instances of a *K'dushah* in the liturgy: not just (1) here in the *Amidah*, but also (2) in the *Yotser* (in the first blessing before the *Sh'ma*—see Volume 1, *The Sh'ma and Its Blessings*, pp. 42–43) and (3) the *K'dushah D'sidra*, a *K'dushah* that followed the Torah reading and still occurs near the end of the *Shacharit* service, whether the Torah is read that day or not (see Volume 6, *Tachanun and Concluding Prayers*, p. 110).

Classical poets of fifth- to sixth-century Eretz Yisrael emphasized the *K'dushat Hashem* in their compositions. They wrote many kinds of liturgical poetry, but the most famous was called a *k'dushta* (popularly pronounced k'-DOOSH-tah). It had nine parts spread out as insertions throughout the first three blessings of the *Amidah*; the last seven of them were placed within the *K'dushah*, allowing the poem to reach its climax there. Palestinian poets who founded the *k'dushta* wrote hundreds of them, with verbal complexity that makes it hard even today to understand their content, and with internal references to the Torah and *Haftarah* readings for every holiday and Shabbat—in a "triennial cycle," moreover, which demanded new poems every Shabbat not just for one year but for (roughly) three! We now limit this poetry (called *piyyut*; pl., *piyyutim*—pronounced pee-YOOT, pee-yoo-TEEM) to holy days (that is why holy day liturgy is longer than what we are used to for Shabbat—it has so many *piyyutim* in it). An example is the familiar *Un'taneh Tokef* (pronounced oo-n'-TAH-neh TOH-kehf), now a stand-alone poem for Rosh Hashanah and Yom Kippur, but originally the climactic conclusion (known as a *siluk*, pronounced see-LOOK) of a nine-poem *k'dushta*. Given all this attention to the *K'dushat Hashem*, it is no wonder that many successful versions of the reader's repetition managed to survive the centuries and find their way into different services and rites.

We reproduce here the standard Ashkenazi version, in which reference to the angels in Isaiah 6:3 (vv. 1–2) is prefaced by, "Let us sanctify your name on earth as it is sanctified in the heavens on high." The Sefardi parallel reads: *Nakdishakh v'na'aritsakh k'no'am si'ach sod sarfei kodesh, ham'shal'shim l'kha k'dushah*, "Let us declare your awe and holiness as in the council of holy serafim who offer a three-fold *k'dushah* [holy, holy, holy] to You." With a few small changes, that version appears in the Ashkenazi *Musaf* service (see p. 123).

² *"Holy, holy, holy* [Kadosh kadosh kadosh]" The threefold repetition of "holy" attracted Jewish-Christian polemic. Christians claimed it demonstrated the reality of the trinity: "holy [is the Father]; holy [is the son]; holy [is the holy spirit]." Jews therefore felt obliged to explain the triple usage differently. One early (and lasting) interpretation can be found in the *K'dushah D'sidra* (see Volume 6, *Tachanun and*

Concluding Prayers, pp. 110–127): "Holy in the heavens on high, his divine abode, holy upon the earth, his mighty work, and holy to the ends of eternity is Adonai of hosts." The first two instances of "holy" denote space—the heavenly world above and our earthly world below; the third refers to time.

A later, medieval interpretation replaced the temporal reference with a third spatial one. *R'dak* (David Kimchi, Provence, 1160–1235) says:

> They [the angels] recite "holy" three times, referring to three worlds. The upper world, the intermediate world, and the lower world, that being this world where the most exalted creature is humankind, the point being that his [God's] holiness is beyond all three worlds. In two worlds, the angels declare God's holiness and exalt Him with praise. Human beings do likewise in the lower world.

The notion of an area of space entrusted specifically to human beings has theological significance. The classical understanding of the *K'dushah* assumed the need for human beings to ascend to the angels if they were to recite God's holiness. For *R'dak*, however, our human praise remains earthbound but has value precisely because the angels cannot praise God from here. Only we can. Rather than aspire to be angelic, we represent an important species in our own right, a unique and altogether necessary part of God's divine plan.

◆

J. HOFFMAN (TRANSLATION)

[8] *"Songs of glory"* That is, the psalms. But because the Hebrew alludes to them obliquely, so does our English. Also, the Hebrew word *oz* may be "glory" or "victory." It is not any of the words we translated above as "glory."

[8] *"Servant of righteousness"* Or "righteous servant," but we want to maintain the parallel structure between "songs of glory" and "servant of righteousness."

◆ ◆ ◆

II. *K'DUSHAT HAYOM* ("SANCTIFICATION OF THE DAY"): DECLARING SABBATH HOLINESS

[1] Moses will be pleased with what he received as his portion, when You called him a faithful servant, [2] crowning him completely as he stood before You on Mount Sinai. [3] He brought down two tablets of stone in his hand and on them was written to keep Shabbat. It is also written in your Torah:

[4] The children of Israel shall keep Shabbat, observing Shabbat throughout their generations as an eternal covenant. [5] It is an eternal sign between Me and the children of Israel, for in six days Adonai made heaven and earth, and on the seventh day He rested.

[6] Adonai our God, You did not give it to the nations of other lands, and, our king, You did not bequeath it to idol worshipers. And gentiles will not dwell in its rest. You gave it to Israel your people in love, to the descendants of Jacob whom You chose. [7] A people who sanctifies the seventh day, they will all be satisfied and delight in your goodness. [8] You loved the seventh day and sanctified it, calling it the favorite of days, in memory of acts of creation.

[9] Our God and our ancestors' God, accept our rest, sanctify us through your commandments, and grant us a share in your Torah. [10] Satisfy us with your goodness, and gladden us with your salvation. And purify our heart to serve You in truth. [11] And, Adonai our God, lovingly and adoringly grant us as our inheritance your holy Shabbat, that all of Israel, who sanctify your name, might rest on it. [12] Blessed are You, Adonai, who sanctifies Shabbat.

[1] יִשְׂמַח מֹשֶׁה בְּמַתְּנַת חֶלְקוֹ, כִּי עֶבֶד נֶאֱמָן קָרָאתָ לּוֹ; [2] כְּלִיל תִּפְאֶרֶת בְּרֹאשׁוֹ נָתַתָּ, בְּעָמְדוֹ לְפָנֶיךָ, עַל הַר סִינָי. [3] וּשְׁנֵי לוּחוֹת אֲבָנִים הוֹרִיד בְּיָדוֹ, וְכָתוּב בָּהֶם שְׁמִירַת שַׁבָּת, וְכֵן כָּתוּב בְּתוֹרָתֶךָ:

[4] וְשָׁמְרוּ בְנֵי יִשְׂרָאֵל אֶת הַשַּׁבָּת, לַעֲשׂוֹת אֶת הַשַּׁבָּת לְדֹרֹתָם בְּרִית עוֹלָם. [5] בֵּינִי וּבֵין בְּנֵי יִשְׂרָאֵל אוֹת הִיא לְעוֹלָם, כִּי שֵׁשֶׁת יָמִים עָשָׂה יְיָ אֶת הַשָּׁמַיִם וְאֶת הָאָרֶץ, וּבַיּוֹם הַשְּׁבִיעִי שָׁבַת וַיִּנָּפַשׁ.

[6] וְלֹא נְתָתוֹ, יְיָ אֱלֹהֵינוּ, לְגוֹיֵי הָאֲרָצוֹת; וְלֹא הִנְחַלְתּוֹ, מַלְכֵּנוּ, לְעוֹבְדֵי פְסִילִים; וְגַם בִּמְנוּחָתוֹ לֹא יִשְׁכְּנוּ עֲרֵלִים; כִּי לְיִשְׂרָאֵל עַמְּךָ נְתַתּוֹ בְּאַהֲבָה, לְזֶרַע יַעֲקֹב אֲשֶׁר בָּם בָּחָרְתָּ. [7] עַם מְקַדְּשֵׁי שְׁבִיעִי, כֻּלָּם יִשְׂבְּעוּ וְיִתְעַנְּגוּ מִטּוּבֶךָ. [8] וְהַשְּׁבִיעִי רָצִיתָ בּוֹ וְקִדַּשְׁתּוֹ, חֶמְדַּת יָמִים אוֹתוֹ קָרָאתָ, זֵכֶר לְמַעֲשֵׂה בְרֵאשִׁית.

[9] אֱלֹהֵינוּ וֵאלֹהֵי אֲבוֹתֵינוּ, רְצֵה בִמְנוּחָתֵנוּ; קַדְּשֵׁנוּ בְּמִצְוֹתֶיךָ, וְתֵן חֶלְקֵנוּ בְּתוֹרָתֶךָ; [10] שַׂבְּעֵנוּ מִטּוּבֶךָ, וְשַׂמְּחֵנוּ בִּישׁוּעָתֶךָ; וְטַהֵר לִבֵּנוּ לְעָבְדְּךָ בֶּאֱמֶת; [11] וְהַנְחִילֵנוּ, יְיָ אֱלֹהֵינוּ, בְּאַהֲבָה וּבְרָצוֹן שַׁבַּת קָדְשֶׁךָ, וְיָנוּחוּ בָהּ יִשְׂרָאֵל מְקַדְּשֵׁי שְׁמֶךָ. [12] בָּרוּךְ אַתָּה, יְיָ, מְקַדֵּשׁ הַשַּׁבָּת.

BRETTLER (BIBLE)

[1] *"His portion* [matnat chelko], *when You called him a faithful servant"* In the Bible, "his portion" refers to Moses's status as God's "servant" *(eved)*. Elsewhere it means Shabbat itself, which is viewed as a gift *(matanah)*, in part because of Exodus 16:29, "Adonai has given [*natan*] you Shabbat."

[1] *"Faithful servant"* Based on Numbers 12:7, "My *servant* Moses ... is *faithful.*"

[2] *"Crowning him ... on Mount Sinai"* This image of Moses as king on Mount Sinai is not biblical, even though a variety of texts give Moses a royal role in general. Deuteronomy 33:5 may explicitly call Moses, *(p. 109)*

DORFF (THEOLOGY)

[1] *"Moses will be pleased"* That is, pleased with the gift of Torah. Elsewhere, the Rabbis discuss the "yoke of the commandments" *(ol hamitzvot)*, thus acknowledging the burdens that Torah imposes, but not here and, in fact, not in most of Jewish liturgy, which prefers the *(p. 110)*

ELLENSON (MODERN LITURGIES)

[1] *"Moses will be pleased"* In keeping with the naturalistic theological positions of its founders, the Reconstructionist Movement (*Kol Haneshamah*, 1996) omits this paragraph, taking issue with "crowning him completely" because of its reference to Moses appearing *(p. 111)*

FRANKEL (A WOMAN'S VOICE)

[12] *"Who sanctifies Shabbat"* One of the principal differences between the Shabbat *Amidah* and the weekday version is that the former contains only a single blessing in its center as opposed to the thirteen contained in the weekday prayer. That single *b'rakhah*—blessing God for sanctifying Shabbat—expresses our hope that we truly enjoy rest on this day. The four paragraphs leading up to the final *chatimah* celebrate Shabbat as a divine gift to the Jewish people and call upon *(p. 112)*

II. K'DUSHAT HAYOM ("SANCTIFICATION OF THE DAY"): DECLARING SABBATH HOLINESS

[1] Moses will be pleased with what he received as his portion, when You called him a faithful servant, [2] crowning him completely as he stood before You on Mount Sinai. [3] He brought down two tablets of stone in his hand and on them was written to keep Shabbat. It is also written in your Torah:

[4] The children of Israel shall keep Shabbat, observing

GRAY (OUR TALMUDIC HERITAGE)

Shacharit K'dushat Hayom The Shabbat *Amidah* consists of the normal three introductory and concluding blessings, but only one intermediary blessing instead of the usual thirteen for weekdays. This Shabbat blessing, "Sanctification of the Day" (*K'dushat Hayom*), ends, "Blessed are You, Adonai, who sanctifies Shabbat" (*Barukh atah Adonai m'kadesh hashabbat*). The Talmud asks for scriptural proof to support our notion that the Shabbat *Amidah* *(p. 112)*

KUSHNER & POLEN (CHASIDISM)

[1] "*Moses will be pleased with what he received as his portion* [Yismach moshe b'matnat chelko]" The Jerusalem kabbalist Chayim Yosef David Azulai (d. 1806) is known as the CHIDA—an acronym from the first letters of his name (the "Y" of Yosef is rendered as an "I" in English transcription). In the Siddur where some of his teachings are expounded (*Siddur Chida*), we are told that when Moses received the Torah on Sinai, he merited 1,000 lights. Citing an old midrashic tradition,   *(p. 114)*

L. HOFFMAN (HISTORY)

WE SAY THE AMIDAH TWICE ON SHABBAT MORNING, HERE IN SHACHARIT (THE MORNING SERVICE), AND AGAIN IN MUSAF (THE ADDITIONAL SERVICE). IN BOTH CASES, THE THIRTEEN MIDDLE BLESSINGS OF THE WEEKDAY AMIDAH ARE REPLACED BY A K'DUSHAT HAYOM ("SANCTIFICATION OF THE DAY"), A SINGLE BLESSING DECLARING THE DAY'S HOLINESS. FOR THE PARALLEL MUSAF BLESSING(S), SEE PP. 132–133, 146–147.

[1-3] "*Moses will be pleased* [yismach moshe] ... *two tablets* [Torah]" This version of the *K'dushat Hayom* ("Sanctification of the Day," the middle blessing of the   *(p. 117)*

¹יִשְׂמַח מֹשֶׁה בְּמַתְּנַת חֶלְקוֹ, כִּי עֶבֶד נֶאֱמָן קָרֵאתָ לּוֹ; ²כְּלִיל תִּפְאֶרֶת בְּרֹאשׁוֹ נָתַתָּ, בְּעָמְדוֹ לְפָנֶיךָ, עַל הַר סִינָי. ³וּשְׁנֵי לוּחוֹת אֲבָנִים הוֹרִיד בְּיָדוֹ, וְכָתוּב בָּהֶם שְׁמִירַת שַׁבָּת, וְכֵן כָּתוּב בְּתוֹרָתֶךָ: ⁴וְשָׁמְרוּ בְנֵי יִשְׂרָאֵל אֶת הַשַּׁבָּת, לַעֲשׂוֹת אֶת הַשַּׁבָּת לְדֹרֹתָם בְּרִית עוֹלָם. ⁵בֵּינִי וּבֵין בְּנֵי יִשְׂרָאֵל אוֹת הִיא

LANDES (HALAKHAH)

[1] "*Moses will be pleased* [yismach moshe]" Halakhic authorities connect the three *Amidot* of Shabbat—Friday night's *Ma'ariv*, Shabbat morning's *Shacharit*, and Shabbat afternoon's *Minchah*. (*Musaf*, for reasons to be explained later [see "There we will offer," v. 5, p. 132], is in a different category). Each of the three has the same basic seven-blessing structure, featuring a middle blessing that concludes, *Barukh atah Adonai m'kadesh hashabbat*, "Blessed   *(p. 115)*

J. HOFFMAN (TRANSLATION)

[1] "*When*" Commonly, "because." Although that is one option, the logic seems reversed. Moses "will be pleased with what he received," but not *because* he was called a faithful servant.

[3] "*Hand*" Presumably, in his hands. Interestingly, in a similar context (Exod. 32:19), the printed text (the *k'tiv*) of the Torah refers to Moses's "hand," while a Masoretic note corrects the Hebrew to read (the *k'ri*) "hands."

[4] "*Children of Israel*" We translate this literally. Another possibility would be the more colloquial "Israelites."

[4] "*Observing*" Literally, "doing." The Hebrew verb from the root `[ayin].s.h, literally to "do" or "make,"   *(p. 118)*

Shabbat throughout their generations as an eternal covenant. [5] It is an eternal sign between Me and the children of Israel, for in six days Adonai made heaven and earth, and on the seventh day He rested.

[6] Adonai our God, You did not give it to the nations of other lands, and, our king, You did not bequeath it to idol worshipers. And gentiles will not dwell in its rest. You gave it to Israel your people in love, to the descendants of Jacob whom You chose. [7] A people who sanctifies the seventh day, they will all be satisfied and delight in your goodness. [8] You loved the seventh day and sanctified it, calling it the favorite of days, in memory of acts of creation.

[9] Our God and our ancestors' God, accept our rest, sanctify us through your commandments, and grant us a share in your Torah. [10] Satisfy us with your goodness, and gladden us with your salvation. And purify our heart to serve You in truth. [11] And, Adonai our God, lovingly and adoringly grant us as our inheritance your holy Shabbat, that all of Israel, who sanctify your name, might rest on it. [12] Blessed are You, Adonai, who sanctifies Shabbat.

לְעוֹלָם, כִּי שֵׁשֶׁת יָמִים עָשָׂה יְיָ אֶת הַשָּׁמַיִם וְאֶת הָאָרֶץ, וּבַיּוֹם הַשְּׁבִיעִי שָׁבַת וַיִּנָּפַשׁ.

[6] וְלֹא נְתַתּוֹ, יְיָ אֱלֹהֵינוּ, לְגוֹיֵי הָאֲרָצוֹת; וְלֹא הִנְחַלְתּוֹ, מַלְכֵּנוּ, לְעוֹבְדֵי פְסִילִים; וְגַם בִּמְנוּחָתוֹ לֹא יִשְׁכְּנוּ עֲרֵלִים; כִּי לְיִשְׂרָאֵל עַמְּךָ נְתַתּוֹ בְּאַהֲבָה, לְזֶרַע יַעֲקֹב אֲשֶׁר בָּם בָּחָרְתָּ. [7] עַם מְקַדְּשֵׁי שְׁבִיעִי, כֻּלָּם יִשְׂבְּעוּ וְיִתְעַנְּגוּ מִטּוּבֶךָ. [8] וְהַשְּׁבִיעִי רָצִיתָ בּוֹ וְקִדַּשְׁתּוֹ, חֶמְדַּת יָמִים אוֹתוֹ קָרָאתָ, זֵכֶר לְמַעֲשֵׂה בְרֵאשִׁית.

[9] אֱלֹהֵינוּ וֵאלֹהֵי אֲבוֹתֵינוּ, רְצֵה בִמְנוּחָתֵנוּ; קַדְּשֵׁנוּ בְּמִצְוֹתֶיךָ, וְתֵן חֶלְקֵנוּ בְּתוֹרָתֶךָ; [10] שַׂבְּעֵנוּ מִטּוּבֶךָ, וְשַׂמְּחֵנוּ בִּישׁוּעָתֶךָ; וְטַהֵר לִבֵּנוּ לְעָבְדְּךָ בֶּאֱמֶת; [11] וְהַנְחִילֵנוּ, יְיָ אֱלֹהֵינוּ, בְּאַהֲבָה וּבְרָצוֹן שַׁבַּת קָדְשֶׁךָ, וְיָנוּחוּ בָהּ יִשְׂרָאֵל מְקַדְּשֵׁי שְׁמֶךָ. [12] בָּרוּךְ אַתָּה, יְיָ, מְקַדֵּשׁ הַשַּׁבָּת.

BRETTLER (BIBLE)

at the end of this life, "king," but the verse is ambiguous.

⁴ *"The children of Israel shall keep Shabbat"* From Exodus 31:16–17, an excerpt from a larger section legislating Shabbat observance. These two verses are chosen because they emphasize the role of Shabbat as a "sign" *(ot)* and "covenant" *(b'rit)*. The surrounding verses, which highlight capital punishment for Shabbat violation, are omitted from our prayer.

⁴ *"Keep Shabbat"* Shabbat is not a burden; it was given to chosen Israel in love, and all other nations, identified here as idolaters, enjoy no benefit from it. By contrast, Isaiah 56:6–7 envisions non-Israelites observing Shabbat.

⁷ *"Will all be satisfied and delight"* Based on Isaiah 58:14, in reference to Shabbat: "Then you can delight [*titanag*] in Adonai." Isaiah 58:13–14 are structured in a measure-for-measure fashion: "If you call Shabbat a 'delight'" then "you will delight in Adonai."

⁸ *"Sanctified it"* The notion of Shabbat being the only sanctified day is explicit in the first creation story (Gen. 2:3), suggesting that it is God's favorite day, even though this idea of favoritism is never explicit in the Bible.

⁹ *"Accept our rest"* The Hebrew, *r'tseh vim'nuchateinu*, "accept our rest," is a play on *r'tseh v'minchateinu*, "accept our offerings." Shabbat replaces the defunct sacrificial system.

⁹ *"Sanctify us through your commandments"* "Your commandments" likely refers specifically to the Shabbat commandment(s), which are connected to God's sanctification of Israel, announced in Exodus 31:13: "Speak to the Israelite people and say: … "Keep my Sabbaths … that you may know that I Adonai have sanctified you." (Elsewhere, however, Israel is told to sanctify itself, rather than have God sanctify it.)

¹⁰ *"Satisfy us with your goodness [tovekha, also understood as 'bounty'])"* A request for eschatological redemption, paraphrasing the description of the ideal future in Jeremiah 31:14, "And my people shall enjoy my full bounty"(*tuvi*, a form of the word *tuvekha*).

¹⁰ *"Purify our heart"* God must purify the heart of a sinner—as in Psalm 51:4, "Purify me of my sin." In some biblical texts God is expected to do so only in the future ideal time, and for the whole people Israel, not individuals—as in Jeremiah 33:8, "And I will purge them of all the sins which they committed against Me"; or Ezekiel 36:25, "I will sprinkle clean water upon you, and you shall be clean."

¹¹ *"Grant us our inheritance … who sanctify your name"* The paragraph concludes by returning to themes and phrases found in its opening lines (vv. 6–7)—"inheritance" and "sanctify"—but with a twist: here, Israel sanctifies God, while earlier (v. 7), they sanctified "the seventh day." Sanctification of Shabbat is a recognition of God as creator;

however, so is a sanctification of God, secondarily.

[12] *"Who sanctifies Shabbat"* Here, as in Genesis 2:3 ("God blessed the seventh day and declared it holy"), it is God who sanctifies Shabbat, while above (v. 7), following other biblical texts, Israel does so. We find the latter also in Jeremiah 17:27, "Obey my command to hallow the Sabbath day." Our prayer combines both biblical notions, but by ending as it does, it gives priority to the idea that Shabbat is intrinsically holy, sanctified by God, not just by us.

◆

Dorff (Theology)

tone of gratitude for Torah—the gift of a loving God who (like a parent) wishes to guide our lives. (See Volume 1, *The Sh'ma and Its Blessings*, pp. 69–71; and Volume 9, *Welcoming the Night: Minchah and Ma'ariv [Afternoon and Evening Prayer]*, pp. 58–61.)

[4] *"The children of Israel shall keep Shabbat"* Shabbat is a sign *(ot)* of the covenant between God and Israel. This is the reason that *t'fillin* are not worn on Shabbat: *t'fillin* too are such a sign *(ot)* (Exod. 13:9, 13:16; Deut. 6:8, 11:18), so would be redundant then (and, by extension, on the other biblical holy days as well [Eruv. 96a; *Shulchan Arukh*, O. Ch. 31:1]). On weekdays, when we get caught up in our work, we need concrete symbols like the *tallit, t'fillin,* and *m'zuzah.* The third paragraph of the *Sh'ma* (Num. 15:37–41) twice specifies this psychological process: we attach a tassel to our garments so as to "look at it and recall all the commandments of Adonai and observe them" (Num. 15:39), and in case we did not get the point the first time, the next verse (15:40) repeats the purpose of the tassel—"so that you will be reminded to observe all My commandments and to be holy to your God."

Shabbat observance is identified here as *imitatio dei* ("imitating God"): we rest as God did on the seventh day of creation (the reason provided in the Decalogue, as given in Exod. 20:8–11). The second version of the Decalogue (Deut. 5:12–15), however, links Shabbat to the Exodus from Egypt. (See my comments in Volume 7, *Shabbat at Home,* pp. 92, 96–98, 160.)

[6] *"Adonai our God, You did not give it [Shabbat] to the nations of other lands"* Sometimes a donor presents a gift to multiple recipients. When given to just one party, however, it marks a special relationship between donor and recipient. By providing Israel alone with Shabbat, God distinguished Israel as a people with whom God has an especially loving relationship.

According to the Rabbis, God also made a "Noahide" covenant with all humanity—named after Noah, the Bible's "everyman," who preceded Abraham and Sarah, the first Jews. It consists of just seven commandments (Tosefta A.Z. 8:4; San. 56b), while the Jewish covenant has 613 (e.g., *Makkot* 23b; Gen. Rab. 24:5; Exod. Rab. 32:1, 33:7; Num. Rab. 13:15–16, 14:9, 18:21). The deeper a relationship is, the more duties it imposes. (Compare your responsibility to a stranger in the street who asks you for directions, to acquaintances, then colleagues, and finally, immediate family.) We Jews are therefore especially grateful for the gift of Shabbat, which allows us to celebrate our relationship with God, like a weekly honeymoon with our divine spouse. (See Volume 7, *Shabbat at Home*, pp. 156, 159–160; and Volume 9, *Welcoming the Night: Minchah and Ma'ariv [Afternoon and Evening Prayer]*, pp. 106, 109.)

Whoever wrote this prayer knew that Christians observe a day of rest. Depending on the prayer's dating, the author may have known the Muslim day of rest as well. Those Sabbaths do not undermine the Jewish claim of uniqueness, however, for each of those religions celebrates its own uniqueness in its explanation of its Sabbath. For Christians, Sunday is the Lord's Day, when Jesus was resurrected. For Muslims, Friday is Jummah, the Day of Gathering (*Koran*, Sura 62), set on Friday because that was the day that the first human was created.

[9] *"Our God and our ancestors' God, accept our rest"* Shabbat is not just for relaxation, nor even just for reconnection with God and our Jewish community. It is ultimately a day set aside (1) in obedience to God's commandment; (2) in thanksgiving for creation; and (3) in recognition of God's ownership of the world and, therefore, his right to determine when and how we may use it. Thus the end of the blessing ("Blessed are you, Adonai, who sanctifies Shabbat") speaks of *God* hallowing the day. Whether we observe Shabbat or not, God has made that day holy.

This is counterintuitive to modern consciousness, which measures all things—Shabbat included—in terms of human fulfillment. But the liturgy portrays Shabbat not as a panacea for human well-being, but as a commandment of God, who has hallowed it to remind us of our indebtedness to Him for all of creation.

———◆———

ELLENSON (MODERN LITURGIES)

with head aglow bringing the Ten Commandments down from Mount Sinai. The editor explains, "The sharpness of the imagery suggests a literal belief in Sinai rather than an affirmation of its mythic truth." Instead, basing itself on a prayer from the *Birkhat Hashachar* (see Volume 5, *Birkhat Hashachar [Morning Blessings]*, p. 158), it substitutes, "Happy are we, how fortunate our lot, how pleasing is our destiny, how lovely our inheritance! Happy are we to be at rest upon the seventh day," as an affirmation of the joy inherent in Jewish religious tradition.

[6] *"You did not bequeath it to idol worshipers"* The two Hamburg Temple prayer books, the two Siddurim of Abraham Geiger, and Isaac Mayer Wise's *Minhag America*—all from the nineteenth century, and all relatively traditional—retained the rest of this prayer but omitted these particular lines. Their authors felt that this passage contained "invidious" and "deprecatory" references to gentiles that were inappropriate for the modern setting.

⁶ *"Gentiles"* Literally, "the uncircumcised." Isak Noa Mannheimer (1793–1865), rabbi of the *Stadttempel* in Vienna, in his 1843 *Tefillot Yisrael—Gebete der Israeliten*, spoke for many when he denounced this word as especially offensive to his moral tastes. He substituted *r'sha'im* ("evildoers") in Hebrew and *Suender* ("sinners") in German. In so doing, he set a precedent for later Conservative liturgy in the United States, as the 1946 American Conservative *Sabbath and Festival Prayerbook* made the same change. The current American Conservative prayer book, *Siddur Sim Shalom* (1985), restored the original Hebrew *arelim*, but without literal translation in the English. In so doing, *Sim Shalom* displayed a Conservative tendency to retain the Hebrew text of the received Ashkenazi rite while employing creative translation (or non-translation in this instance) to address issues deemed theologically or ideologically troublesome.

———◆———

FRANKEL (A WOMAN'S VOICE)

us to be satisfied with this reward. Shabbat is variously described as "a gift" *(matanah)*, "an everlasting covenant" *(b'rit olam)*, "a heritage" *(nachalah)*, and "a remembrance of creation" *(zikaron l'ma'aseh v'reshit)*.

As Jewish women continue to add to an already overfull dance card—as carpool drivers, synagogue volunteers, leaders and shleppers in women's organizations, working professionals, sandwich-generation caretakers, major-domos of the household, bodies beautiful, and culture vultures—we would do well to accept this weekly gift. It's a regular chance to reboot ourselves and bring more sanity into our lives.

———◆———

GRAY (OUR TALMUDIC HERITAGE)

should consist only of seven blessings, especially the unique central one. Rabbi Chalafta ben Shaul answers that they correspond to the seven times that the word *kol* ("voice") appears in Psalm 29. True, Psalm 29 has no direct connection to Shabbat, but it ends with the verse, "Adonai will give strength to God's [lit., his] people; Adonai will bless God's [lit., his] people with peace." This blessing of strength and peace is taken to be the equivalent of God's sanctifying Shabbat. Shabbat is therefore a time of rejuvenation, leading to our renewed peace and strength.

¹ *"Moses will be pleased with what he received* [b'matnat] *as his portion"* Why is Moses said to be pleased in "the gift of" *(b'vmatnat)* his portion? Why not just say he was pleased with "his portion"? Moreover, why mention at all that Moses "was pleased"? What else would we expect? The Talmud (Shab. 10b) interprets Exodus 31:13 ("in order that you may know that I am Adonai who sanctifies you") as part of an imagined charge from God to Moses. God tells Moses to inform Israel of a wonderful gift

(*matanah*) called "Shabbat." Abudarham (fourteenth-century Spain) says that "Moses will be pleased" recollects the fact that Shabbat is a "gift" that God gave via Moses to the Jewish People.

The Midrash (Exod. Rab. 1:32) suggests another interpretation. When Moses grew up, he went out "to his brothers" and "saw their burdens" (Exod. 2:11). The midrash interprets "their burdens" as the ceaseless toil by the Israelite slaves, without a day of rest. Upon noticing this, Moses approached Pharaoh, pointing out that generally speaking, a slave who does not rest one day per week will die. By not allowing Israel to rest, Pharaoh was killing them! When Pharaoh acceded to Moses's request, Moses had it scheduled for the very day that became Shabbat.

In his *Etz Yosef* commentary on the midrash, Chanokh Zundel (d. 1867) adds that when God later selected as Shabbat the very day that Moses had selected, "Moses was pleased."

³ *"And on them was written to keep Shabbat* [v'khatuv bahem sh'mirat Shabbat]" "Keeping Shabbat" alludes to Deuteronomy 5:12 ("Keep [*sh'mor*] the Sabbath day to keep it holy"), rather than Exodus 20:8, "Remember [*z'khor*] the Sabbath day to keep it holy." Abudarham explains why the Deuteronomy version says "keep" rather than "remember." Imagine Person A giving a present to Person B, who promptly loses it and asks A to replace it. As A does so, A would likely say, "Be especially careful with it this time!" The same applies to Shabbat. God initially commanded, "Remember [the Sabbath day]," but shortly after, the Torah recounts its public desecration by the man who gathered wood then (Num. 15:32–36). Now *sh'mor* ("keep," sometimes translated as "observe") can also mean "watch over" or "be careful with." So when God reiterated the Shabbat law in Deuteronomy, God added the caution, "Be careful with Shabbat!"

⁵ *"Between Me and the children of Israel"* Rabbi Yochanan in the name of Rabbi Shimon bar Yochai used this phrase ("Between Me and the children of Israel") to indicate the special status of Shabbat among all the other *mitzvot*. God gave all the other *mitzvot* to Israel publicly, but Shabbat was given privately—"between Me [privately] and the children of Israel" (Beitsah 16a).

⁵ *"And on the seventh day He rested* [shavat vayinafash]" Rabbi Shimon ben Lakish taught that God gives each Jew an extra soul on *Erev Shabbat* and takes it back on Saturday night. The removal of the extra soul is alluded to by the phrase *shavat VaYiNaFaSH*, which is read midrashically as *shavat VoY-NeFeSH*. Voy ("woe") to the soul *(nefesh)*, which will have to depart (Beitsah 16a).

⁷ *"They will all be satisfied and delight in your goodness* [kulam yisb'u v'yitangu mituvekha]" Rabbi Barukh Halevi Epstein points out that this phrase is backwards: Shouldn't the Jewish people be said to "delight" (*v'yitangu* [from the root for *oneg*, '[ayin].n.g, "joy," as in *oneg Shabbat*, "the joy of Shabbat"]) prior to being "satisfied" (*yisb'u*)? If we are already sated with joy *(oneg)*, how can we be expected to rejoice any more? His answer is that the Sabbath joy referred to here is not the physical pleasures

of eating and drinking—as to which we could legitimately say that the liturgical phrase is backwards—but the spiritual pleasures such as Torah study. When it comes to spiritual matters, no matter how sated we are, we can always—through further study—rejoice even more. Epstein ingeniously relates this interpretation to the teaching of Rabbi Yochanan in the name of Rabbi Yose that whoever "brings about Sabbath joy" (*m'aneg*, from the same root as *oneg*) is given (from God) an "inheritance without constraints," meaning boundless reward. Rabbi Yochanan proves this point through a close reading of Isaiah 58:14, "Then you will be joyful [*titanag*, like *oneg*] in Adonai, and He will cause you to ride on the heights of the earth, and He will feed you the inheritance of your father Jacob." The verse singles out the inheritance of Jacob, not of Abraham or Isaac, for their inheritances were geographically limited to the boundaries of the Land of Israel. God will feed the people specifically the inheritance of Jacob, of whom it is said (Gen. 28:14) that he will spread out (without bounds!) to the west, east, north, and south (Shab. 118a–b). The Sabbath joy for which the boundless divine reward will be received is spiritual and, therefore, boundless, just as God promised Jacob.

———◆———

KUSHNER & POLEN (CHASIDISM)

Azulai reminds us that Adam was originally a big *alef*. In Hebrew, the letter *alef* has the numerical value of 1. If, however, it has a *merkha*, an apostrophe-like trope, after it, then the *alef* represents 1,000. So both Adam and Moses originally had 1,000 lights each. They were both big *alef*s.

Alas, with the worship of the golden calf, Moses and all Israel were diminished. Of Moses's original crown of 1,000 lights, 999 were taken away, leaving him with only 1 (represented by a single small *alef*). Indeed, the last letter of the first word of *Vayikra* (Leviticus) in every Torah scroll is written smaller (*alef z'ira*) than all the other letters. And this tiny *alef* hints at Moses's only remaining single light after the "fall" of his people.

On the Sabbath, however, the other 999 lights are returned to Moses, and this is the reason, explains Azulai, that Moses is so "pleased with his portion." And, because Moses was an *eved ne'eman*, a faithful servant and leader of Israel, he naturally asks, "How can I keep all these Sabbath lights for myself? I must find a way to share them with my people." Indeed, on the Sabbath we celebrate Moses's magnanimity: Moses took great pleasure not simply in a missing light being returned to him but also in the possibility of further bestowing it upon his people Israel, providing a *k'lil tiferet*, "crowning" Israel (not himself) "completely" with recovered lights.

[6] *"You did not give it [Shabbat] to the nations of other lands, and … You did not bequeath it to idol worshipers"* Israel ben Shabbetai, the Maggid of Kozienice (d. 1814), in his *Avodat Yisro'el* (Jerusalem, 1999, *Likkutim*, 267), noted these two parallel phrases, which seem so obviously redundant. Surely "the nations of other lands" includes "idol worshipers." He then answers his own question. Those who worship idols are not

necessarily confined to the "nations of other lands." Some of them are even among the people of Israel! Indeed, there are many Jews who acknowledge God's sovereignty but do so in order to secure for themselves a place in the world-to-come or to attain a higher level of prophetic insight or other such laudable spiritual gifts. But, alas, such acknowledgment arises from an ulterior motive. God is the *Ein Sof* (literally, "no end"), the "One who cannot be bounded in any way." But even service to God, if offered with an ulterior motive, effectively superimposes upon God some concrete and bounded form. And thus, even though the goal of such service be spiritual, by seeking a concrete end, such service transforms the holy One, as it were, into an idol! Because the service has an end, a goal, it deprives God of God's endlessness (if you will, God's *Ein Sof*-ness). Indeed, the only fitting goal of serving God is to take pleasure in God's pleasure—in the words of the Chasidic maxim, let your service be to bring pleasure to the *Shekhinah*.

Similarly, Moshe Idel (*Hasidism: Between Ecstasy and Magic* [Albany: State University of New York Press, 1995], p. 214) cites Asher Zevi of Ostraha, who teaches, "He who directs all his deeds in order to create delight in his Creator, he draws down the *aleph*, the symbol of the Ruler of the World, in all his deeds. But if he takes the delight for himself (alone), not in order to create a delight in his Creator, he is separating the *aleph*, the Ruler of the world."

[10] *"And purify our heart to serve You in truth* [v'taher libenu l'ovd'kha b'emet]*"* Rabbi Zev Wolf of Zhitomir (in his *Or Ham'ir*) recounts a surprising teaching he once heard from the Baal Shem Tov about the performance of religious acts (*Siddur Baal Shem Tov*, pp. 396–97, *Parashat Sh'mot*). There are many *chasidim* who devote themselves to elaborate regimens of religious practice: fasting, immersion in the *mikvah*, and devoting many hours to study Torah and to pray. And their primary goal in performing these and similar actions is to attain the *ru'ach hakodesh*, the "holy spirit," or a *giluy eliyahu*, a "revelation of Elijah." But, cautions the Besht, the angels only laugh at such a person! For what good could it do a person to chase after such spiritual states when his heart is still missing *d'vekut* ("cleaving" to God). For, indeed, if you cleave to God in truth and simplicity, and thereby certainly attain high spiritual states, those states will no longer be of any importance to you.

---◆---

LANDES (Halakhah)

are you, Adonai, who sanctifies Shabbat." But each service has its own distinctive version of the paragraph that introduces this blessing. The *Tur* (Jacob ben Asher, 1270–1340, Spain; see O. Ch. 292) sees their common theme as the nature of Shabbat in cosmic history:

1. Friday night (which begins *Atah kidashta*, "You sanctified") depicts *Shabbat Bereshit* as "the Sabbath of Creation ... the end of creation of heaven and earth."
2. Shabbat morning (which begins *Yismach moshe*, "Moses will be pleased") depicts

Shabbat shel matan torah, "the Sabbath of the giving of Torah," as it states, "crowning him completely as he stood before You on Mount Sinai" (v. 2).

3. Shabbat *Minchah* (which begins *Atah echad*, "You are One") depicts *Shabbat shel atid lavo*, "the Sabbath of the world-to-come," as it states a description of unity and *m'nuchah*, "serenity," that can only be fully realized at the end of time.

Abudarham (fourteenth-century Spain) envisions a progression of the bride and groom, symbolic of Shabbat and the People Israel:

1. *Atah kidashta* ("You sanctified") on Friday night is *Kiddushin* (pronounced kee-doo-SHEEN), the first part of the marriage service, where bride and groom become uniquely sanctified to each other.
2. *Yismach moshe* ("Moses will be pleased") of Saturday morning is the utter *simchah*, the pure "joy," that the married couple shares. Abudarham includes *Musaf* too; it means "addition" (as in "additional service") and hints at the *tosefet k'tubah*, the "additional" clauses traditionally added to the standard *k'tubah* (the "wedding document").
3. *Atah echad* ("You are One") of *Minchah* refers to *yichud* (pronounced yee-KHOOD), the seclusion and (throughout antiquity and the Middle Ages) the actual physical union of the couple at the end of the wedding service.

The Shabbat *Amidah* is noteworthy also by what it lacks: the middle blessings of petition (see Volume 2, *The Amidah*, "Prayer as Petition: The Philosophic Basis for Halakhic Prayer," pp. 1–8). Halakhah, however, follows Rabbah bar Abbuha's ruling in the Talmud (Ber. 21a), to the effect that someone who mistakenly begins one of the petitions must complete it (*Shulchan Arukh*, O. Ch. 268:2). The reason given in the Talmud is that petitions were put aside on Shabbat "so that that we should not trouble a worshiper, because of the honor due to Shabbat" (*d'lah atrachuhu mishum k'vod shabbat*). The idea is that reciting so many benedictions is a *tircha*, a "bother" or "trouble," so we reduce the middle twelve (actually thirteen) benedictions to one, thereby honoring the rest due Shabbat. In short, the Shabbat *Amidah* is an abridged service! Therefore, if one returns to the more extended service, unintentionally, one needs to finish the particular blessing that one has begun.

Abudarham explains the omission of petitions as our not wanting to remind people of what they lack and thereby providing psychic pain on Shabbat. This attractive explanation, however, does not explain the halakhah of finishing a petition once one has started it.

All this refers to private prayer. The repetition by the prayer leader (the *sh'liach tsibbur*)—known as *chazarat hashats*—is different. Regarding that prayer, one immediately stops upon being reminded that a mistake has been made, and one returns to the Shabbat prayer. The difference is that the *sh'liach tsibbur* is literally the "agent of the community" who has been "contracted" to say the Shabbat, not the weekday prayer (*Siddur Y'sodei Y'shurun*, Shabbat, p. 386, of R. Gedalia Felder, chief authority of the Centrist Orthodox Rabbinate in North America; Toronto, 1921–1991).

[1] *"When You called him* [Moses] *a faithful servant* [eved ne'eman]*"* Only at the very end of the Torah, the end of Moses's life (Deut. 34:5), is Moses called "servant of God." God does call him earlier (Num. 12:7) "my servant Moses," but only here does Torah add "of God." This, say the Rabbis (Shav. 47b), is the highest level of all: "A servant of the King is a king" *(eved melekh melekh).* (See the *G'ra*, [the Vilna Gaon, Lithuania, 1720–1797], *Aderet Eliyahu*, Deuteronomy *Ofan* 2.)

[3-4]*"It is also written* [v'khen katuv] *... The children of Israel shall keep Shabbat"* Why is the prooftext from Exodus 31 here instead of the Decalogue? Rabbi Chayim of Brisk agrees that the covenantal nature of Shabbat is derived from the Decalogue, but Exodus 31 is an extra verse that drums the lesson home. *V'khen katuv* should be understood as, "and *furthermore* it is written" (the stenciled notes of the commentary of the *Griz*, the Gaon Rabbi Isaac Z'ev [Soloveitchik] on the Torah, #138, late nineteenth and early to mid-twentieth century, Lithuania, Israel, quoting his father Rabbi Chayim).

> They fixed just the first verse of *Sh'ma* [to be recited] for it is the essence of [declaring] the unity of the Kingdom of Heaven.... The *K'dushah* of *Musaf* is therefore called *K'dushah Rabbah* [pronounced k'-doo-SHAH rah-BAH, but, commonly k'-DOO-shah RAH-bah, meaning "the Great *K'dushah*"], referring to the recitation of the *Sh'ma*, because it is the essence of the [acceptance of the] Kingdom of Heaven and also because we mention within it the *G'ulah* [final redemption], "He shall redeem us in mercy," for by the merit of the Sabbath we shall be redeemed.

◆

L. HOFFMAN (HISTORY)

Amidah, proclaiming the uniqueness of Shabbat holiness) entered the liturgy relatively late. Even in the tenth century, though widespread, it was by no means universal. Writing a century later, *Rashi* himself (our preeminent founder of Franco-German Jewish culture, d. 1105) challenged it as having no apparent connection to Shabbat morning. Nowhere does the Bible portray Moses being especially "pleased" then.

Several medieval rabbis leapt to the defense of *Yismach Moshe. Rashi's* illustrious grandson, Rabbeinu Tam (c. 1100–1171), supposed Moses received pleasure Saturday morning because that was when he received the Torah.

A particularly creative approach depicted negotiations between Moses and Pharaoh. Having witnessed the Israelites' suffering, Moses urged Pharaoh to give the Israelites a day of rest. All other nations have such a day, he argued, so Israel is entitled to one as well; besides, the Israelite slaves would become more productive the six other days of the week. Another version has Moses link Saturday etymologically to Saturn, the planet said to preside over times when work is not productive. In any event, when invited to choose a day, Moses named Shabbat. Freeing the Israelites for a day of rest, and having it coincide with Shabbat, gave Moses special pleasure every Shabbat morning. *Yismach Moshe* therefore belongs in the Shabbat morning *Amidah*.

◆

J. HOFFMAN (TRANSLATION)

seems out of context here. Usually one "keeps" Shabbat; one does not "do" it (Deut. 5:15 is the only other biblical exhortation to "do Shabbat"). Perhaps the verb "to do" is chosen here to emphasize the parallel nature of the covenant. God "did" (see below, "Made") six days of work and we "do" Shabbat.

⁵ *"For in six days"* Others, "that...." The preposition we use matters. "A sign ... that [in six days Adonai made heaven and earth]" implies that we keep Shabbat to *demonstrate* God's creation of heaven and earth. "A sign ... for [in six days, etc.]" implies that the *reason* we keep Shabbat is that God created. In the first case, Shabbat is a sign of God's activity. In the second, though it is still a sign (since the Bible says it is), the purpose of the sign remains unstated.

⁵ *"Made"* This is the same verb in Hebrew from the root `[ayin].s.h that we translated above as "observing" and that means, more generally, "to do."

⁵ *"Rested"* The Hebrew contains two verbs for "to rest" here. The first is from the root for "Shabbat." The second, probably reflecting nuances we have not fully appreciated, comes from the root *n.f.sh*, commonly translated as "soul," but more accurately understood as referring to the physical aspect of human life (see Volume 1, *The Sh'ma and Its Blessings*, pp. 100–102).

⁶ *"Other lands"* Literally, "the lands."

⁶ *"Dwell in its rest"* Birnbaum's "enjoy" expresses the same point. But the Hebrew offers the more poetic "dwell," and we translate accordingly.

⁷ *"Seventh day"* Literally, "the seventh," (here and in verse 8) a construction possible in Hebrew but not English. "The seventh" in Hebrew can also mean "the seventh one" or "the seventh thing that we are talking about."

⁸ *"In memory"* Hebrew, *zekher*, related to the word *zikaron*. Both words come from the root *z.kh.r*, which means not only "to remember," but also "to point out," "highlight," "mention," or "call to mind." The related Arabic root, *z.k.r*, retains these additional meanings.

◆ ◆ ◆

2 Musaf ("Additional Service")

A. THE *AMIDAH* ("STANDING" PRAYER): TALKING TO GOD

I. *K'DUSHAT HASHEM* ("SANCTIFICATION OF [GOD'S] NAME"): DECLARING GOD'S HOLINESS

¹Let us declare your awe and holiness as in the conversations of the inner council of holy serafim who declare your name holy with "holy," as written by your prophet: "They called out one to another:

²'Holy, holy, holy is the Lord of hosts. The whole earth is full of his glory.'"

³His glory fills the earth. His servants ask one another, "Where is the place with his glory?" From across the way they offer blessing:

⁴"The glory of Adonai is blessed from his place."

⁵From his place may He turn in mercy and be gracious to the people that proclaim his name one, evening and morning, every day, forever, twice in love reciting the *Sh'ma*:

⁶"Hear, O Israel, Adonai is our God; Adonai is One."

⁷He is our God. He is our father. He is our king. He is our deliverer. And He will again proclaim to us in mercy before the eyes of

נַעֲרִיצְךָ וְנַקְדִּישְׁךָ כְּסוֹד שִׂיחַ שַׂרְפֵי ¹ קֹדֶשׁ הַמַּקְדִּישִׁים שִׁמְךָ בַּקֹּדֶשׁ, כַּכָּתוּב עַל יַד נְבִיאֶךָ וְקָרָא זֶה אֶל זֶה וְאָמַר:

²קָדוֹשׁ, קָדוֹשׁ, קָדוֹשׁ יְיָ צְבָאוֹת; מְלֹא כָל הָאָרֶץ כְּבוֹדוֹ.

³כְּבוֹדוֹ מָלֵא עוֹלָם; מְשָׁרְתָיו שׁוֹאֲלִים זֶה לָזֶה אַיֵּה מְקוֹם כְּבוֹדוֹ; לְעֻמָּתָם בָּרוּךְ יֹאמֵרוּ—

⁴בָּרוּךְ כְּבוֹד יְיָ מִמְּקוֹמוֹ.

⁵מִמְּקוֹמוֹ הוּא יִפֶן בְּרַחֲמִים, וְיָחֹן עַם הַמְיַחֲדִים שְׁמוֹ; עֶרֶב וָבֹקֶר, בְּכָל יוֹם תָּמִיד, פַּעֲמַיִם בְּאַהֲבָה שְׁמַע אוֹמְרִים—

⁶שְׁמַע יִשְׂרָאֵל, יְיָ אֱלֹהֵינוּ, יְיָ אֶחָד.

⁷הוּא אֱלֹהֵינוּ, הוּא אָבִינוּ, הוּא מַלְכֵּנוּ, הוּא מוֹשִׁיעֵנוּ, וְהוּא יַשְׁמִיעֵנוּ בְּרַחֲמָיו

all the living: "... to be your God."

[8] "I am Adonai your God."

[9] In your holy scriptures it is written:

[10] "Adonai will reign forever, your God, Zion, for all generations. Halleluyah."

[11] For all generations we will tell of your greatness, and for all of eternity proclaim your holiness.

[12] Your praise, our God, will never depart our mouths for You are a sovereign God, great and holy. [13] *Blessed are You, Adonai, the holy God.

*[*From Rosh Hashanah to Yom Kippur, substitute the following:]*

[14] Blessed are You, Adonai, the holy king.

שֵׁנִית לְעֵינֵי כָּל חָי: לִהְיוֹת לָכֶם לֵאלֹהִים–

[8]אֲנִי יְיָ אֱלֹהֵיכֶם.

[9]וּבְדִבְרֵי קָדְשְׁךָ כָּתוּב לֵאמֹר:

[10]יִמְלֹךְ יְיָ לְעֹלָם, אֱלֹהַיִךְ צִיּוֹן לְדֹר וָדֹר; הַלְלוּיָהּ.

[11]לְדוֹר וָדוֹר נַגִּיד גָּדְלֶךָ, וּלְנֵצַח נְצָחִים קְדֻשָּׁתְךָ נַקְדִּישׁ.

[12]וְשִׁבְחֲךָ אֱלֹהֵינוּ מִפִּינוּ לֹא יָמוּשׁ לְעוֹלָם וָעֶד, כִּי אֵל מֶלֶךְ גָּדוֹל וְקָדוֹשׁ אָתָּה. [13]בָּרוּךְ אַתָּה, יְיָ, הָאֵל הַקָּדוֹשׁ.

*[*From Rosh Hashanah to Yom Kippur, substitute the following:]*

[14]בָּרוּךְ אַתָּה, יְיָ, הַמֶּלֶךְ הַקָּדוֹשׁ.

BRETTLER (BIBLE)

[1] *"Let us declare your awe and holiness"* Following Isaiah 29:23b, "Men will declare the holy One of Jacob holy and stand in awe of the God of Israel."

[1] *"Inner [sod]"* In the Bible, *sod* usually refers to the divine council with whom God consults on occasion. Prophets are sometimes imagined as being part of this *sod*. Secondarily, it means the decisions of this council and thus develops a secondary meaning of "secret" or "inner." In context here, the image of a divine king and His "cabinet" of advisors, we render it an "inner" (not "secret") council.   *(p. 125)*

DORFF (THEOLOGY)

[2] *"Holy, holy, holy"* See "Holy, holy, holy …," p. 94; and in Volume 2, *The Amidah*, pp. 84–93.

[5] *"That proclaim his name one, evening and morning"* We request blessing because we recite the *Sh'ma* twice daily. But why does that merit God's favor? One possibility is theological: by proclaiming God "One," we acknowledge God's reality. Even we human beings like it when others know who we really are. Another possibility is moral: because God is One, there can be only one standard of right and wrong. The unity of God thus creates morality. Our actions are not just pragmatically motivated to please some pagan god and avoid the wrath of another; they aim at realizing the

singular standard of behavior that the One true God establishes.

[11] *"For all generations we will tell of your greatness"* Our acknowledgment of God's uniqueness and sovereignty repeats a claim made by generations of Jews before us. This historicity strengthens our claim, for we are not relying on our own insights and experience alone, but on those of our ancestors as well. Further, we announce our intention to bequeath this world-view to generations yet to come.

———◆———

I. K'DUSHAT HASHEM ("SANCTIFICATION OF [GOD'S] NAME"): DECLARING GOD'S HOLINESS

[1] Let us declare your awe and holiness as in the conversations of the inner council of holy serafim who declare your name holy with "holy," as written by your prophet: "They called out one to another:

[2] 'Holy, holy, holy is the Lord of hosts. The whole earth is full of his glory.'"

[3] His glory fills the earth. His servants ask one

GRAY (OUR TALMUDIC HERITAGE)

[6] *"Hear, O Israel, Adonai is our God; Adonai is One [shema yisrael Adonai Elohenu Adonai echad]"* An eighth-century scholar named Pirkoi ben Baboi, who was a student of a student of the great Yehudai Gaon (Gaon of Baghdad, c. 750), reports a tradition that the Byzantine Christian empire that had ruled the Land of Israel once forbade Jews from reciting the *Sh'ma* (presumably because they saw its declaration of monotheism as an affront to the Christian   *(p. 126)*

KUSHNER & POLEN (CHASIDISM)

[1] *"Let us declare your awe"* In the Sefardi rite used by Chasidim, the *Musaf K'dushah* begins differently: "A crown [*keter*] they shall give You—the angels above, together with your people Israel assembled here below." (For full text, see L. Hoffman, v. 1, p. 129.) Because it starts with the word *keter* ("crown"), it is referred to as the *K'dushat Keter*, the Coronation Sanctus (or "sanctification"). And while not found in the standard Ashkenazi prayer book, this hallmark of Chasidic *(p. 126)*

L. HOFFMAN (HISTORY)

ON SHABBAT (AND HOLIDAYS), AN ADDITIONAL SERVICE (MUSAF) IS INSERTED BEFORE THE CONCLUDING PRAYERS. IT CONSISTS PRIMARILY OF AN AMIDAH. AS WITH THE MORNING AMIDAH, THE THIRD BLESSING, THE K'DUSHAT HASHEM ("SANCTIFICATION OF GOD'S NAME"), RECEIVES SPECIAL ATTENTION. FOR THE PARALLEL SHACHARIT BLESSING, SEE P. 93.

Musaf The Shabbat *Musaf* service is largely just an extra *Amidah*. In keeping with the rabbinic notion that, in general, the *Amidah* was ordained to replace defunct Temple sacrifices, *(p. 128)*

[1] נַעֲרִיצְךָ וְנַקְדִּישְׁךָ כְּסוֹד שִׂיחַ שַׂרְפֵי קֹדֶשׁ הַמַּקְדִּישִׁים שִׁמְךָ בַּקֹּדֶשׁ, כַּכָּתוּב עַל יַד נְבִיאֶךָ וְקָרָא זֶה אֶל זֶה וְאָמַר:

[2] קָדוֹשׁ, קָדוֹשׁ, קָדוֹשׁ יְיָ צְבָאוֹת; מְלֹא כָל הָאָרֶץ כְּבוֹדוֹ.

[3] כְּבוֹדוֹ מָלֵא עוֹלָם; מְשָׁרְתָיו שׁוֹאֲלִים זֶה לָזֶה אַיֵּה

J. HOFFMAN (TRANSLATION)

[1] *"Let us declare your awe and holiness"* This introductory line is a variation on that in *K'dushat HaShem* for Shabbat morning (see p. 93). Here we have a new word, "awe," and a variation on the previous one ("holiness" instead of "sanctify"). In Hebrew the two words are more closely related.

[1] *"As in"* More literally, just "as."

[1] *"Conversations"* Or "words," as in Birnbaum. But the Hebrew *si'ach* is more specific than simply "words," and we need something compatible with *sod*, an "inner council." "Deliberations" might also work.

[1] *"With 'holy'"* Implying that "holy" is what they say when they *(p. 131)*

LANDES (HALAKHAH)

[1] *"Let us declare your awe and holiness"* The beginning of the third blessing (*K'dushat Hashem*) recited by the prayer leader (*sh'liach tsibbur*) in the repetition of the *Musaf Amidah* (this repetition is known as *chazarat hashats* [pronounced khah-zah-raht hah-SHaTS—SHaTS is an acronym for *SH'liach Tsibbur*]). Volume 2, *The Amidah* (pp. 5–8), discusses the independent value of both private and communal prayer, as expressed in the repetition by the prayer leader, who literally represents *(p. 127)*

another, "Where is the place with his glory?" From across the way they offer blessing:

4 "The glory of Adonai is blessed from his place."

5 From his place may He turn in mercy and be gracious to the people that proclaim his name one, evening and morning, every day, forever, twice in love reciting the *Sh'ma*:

6 "Hear, O Israel, Adonai is our God; Adonai is One."

7 He is our God. He is our father. He is our king. He is our deliverer. And He will again proclaim to us in mercy before the eyes of all the living: "… to be your God."

8 "I am Adonai your God."

9 In your holy scriptures it is written:

10 "Adonai will reign forever, your God, Zion, for all generations. Halleluyah."

11 For all generations we will tell of your greatness, and for all of eternity proclaim your holiness.

12 Your praise, our God, will never depart our mouths for You are a sovereign God, great and holy.
13 *Blessed are You, Adonai, the holy God.

*[*From Rosh Hashanah to Yom Kippur, substitute the following:]*

14 Blessed are You, Adonai, the holy king.

מָקוֹם כְּבוֹדוֹ; לְעֻמָּתָם בָּרוּךְ יֹאמֵרוּ—

⁴בָּרוּךְ כְּבוֹד יְיָ מִמְּקוֹמוֹ.

⁵מִמְּקוֹמוֹ הוּא יִפֶן בְּרַחֲמִים, וְיָחֹן עַם הַמְיַחֲדִים שְׁמוֹ; עֶרֶב וָבֹקֶר, בְּכָל יוֹם תָּמִיד, פַּעֲמַיִם בְּאַהֲבָה שְׁמַע אוֹמְרִים—

⁶שְׁמַע יִשְׂרָאֵל, יְיָ אֱלֹהֵינוּ, יְיָ אֶחָד.

⁷הוּא אֱלֹהֵינוּ, הוּא אָבִינוּ, הוּא מַלְכֵּנוּ, הוּא מוֹשִׁיעֵנוּ, וְהוּא יַשְׁמִיעֵנוּ בְּרַחֲמָיו שֵׁנִית לְעֵינֵי כָּל חָי: לִהְיוֹת לָכֶם לֵאלֹהִים—

⁸אֲנִי יְיָ אֱלֹהֵיכֶם.

⁹וּבְדִבְרֵי קָדְשְׁךָ כָּתוּב לֵאמֹר:

¹⁰יִמְלֹךְ יְיָ לְעוֹלָם, אֱלֹהַיִךְ צִיּוֹן לְדֹר וָדֹר; הַלְלוּיָהּ.

¹¹לְדוֹר וָדוֹר נַגִּיד גָּדְלֶךָ, וּלְנֵצַח נְצָחִים קְדֻשָּׁתְךָ נַקְדִּישׁ.

¹²וְשִׁבְחֲךָ אֱלֹהֵינוּ מִפִּינוּ לֹא יָמוּשׁ לְעוֹלָם וָעֶד, כִּי אֵל מֶלֶךְ גָּדוֹל וְקָדוֹשׁ אָתָּה. ¹³בָּרוּךְ אַתָּה, יְיָ, הָאֵל הַקָּדוֹשׁ.

*[*From Rosh Hashanah to Yom Kippur, substitute the following:]*

¹⁴בָּרוּךְ אַתָּה, יְיָ, הַמֶּלֶךְ הַקָּדוֹשׁ.

BRETTLER (BIBLE)

[1] *"Holy serafim* [sarfei; *sing.,* seraf]*"* A kind of divine being or angel, described only in Isaiah 6, which is quoted here. Elsewhere, a *seraf* is a type of snake; how these two meanings relate is uncertain.

[3] *"His glory fills the earth* [olam].... *Where is the place with his glory?"* In biblical Hebrew, *olam* refers only to space ("the world"), but in rabbinic Hebrew, it may denote time as well ("forever"). Here it clearly means space, possibly paraphrasing Psalm 72:19, where *olam* as time is paralleled to *eretz* meaning space: "Blessed is his glorious name forever [*l'olam*]; his glory fills the whole world [*eretz*]." The more common biblical idea, however, is that God's glory is especially localized at the Temple, and at its predecessor, the Tabernacle. For example, after the latter is completed, "the Presence of Adonai filled the Tabernacle" (Exod. 40:35), and in reference to the Solomonic Temple, "the Presence of Adonai filled the House of Adonai" (1 Kings 8:11). There is thus some confusion in the Bible about whether God's glory is universal or localized. This explains why God's ministering servants *(m'shartim)* can ask, "Where is the place with his glory?"

[4] *"From his place"* See above, v. 3, "His glory fills the earth." God's "glory" is primarily in his (heavenly) Temple, but can spread out from there, especially if Israel acts properly, by accepting and declaring true monotheism.

[5] *"Proclaim his name one* [m'yachadim sh'mo]*"* A late biblical idea, although no actual phrase related to *m'yachadim sh'mo* appears in the Bible. This is because what became the central *Sh'ma* declaration (Deut. 6:4) in rabbinic times played no special role in the biblical period.

[7] *"He is our God ... our deliverer"* The beginning of this verse, "our God" *(eloheinu)* deliberately picks up the previous line's "Adonai is our God." It then continues with three divine epithets, where, in Hebrew, each is longer than the previous one—a pattern called "the law of increasing members."

[7] *"Proclaim to us in mercy"* The English cannot capture the word play between *moshi'enu* ("our deliverer") and *yashmi'enu* ("proclaim to us"). The latter implies that God will again cause his voice to be heard, just as at Sinai (see Deut. 4:36, "From the heavens He let you hear his voice"). But this time the revelation will be more universal in nature. The universal idea occurs in eschatological prophecies like Isaiah 30:30, "Adonai will make his majestic voice heard." Our prayer is a request for the coming of the ideal future age.

[8] *"I am Adonai your God"* This phrase appears almost fifty times in the Bible, especially in what is called the Holiness Code, Leviticus 17–26, a post-exilic document composed by the priestly class. Found also in eschatological passages (e.g., Ezek. 34:30, 39:22, 39:28), it fits the content of the last few lines—Adonai as God, king, and savior of Israel will be unmistakably prominent in the eschatological age.

[9] *"Your holy scriptures"* A reference to the Bible. As such, it does not occur in the

Bible itself, although Psalm 105:42, "Mindful of his holy word [*d'var kodsho*] to his servant Abraham," may be a biblical prototype.

[10] *"Adonai will reign"* From Psalm 146:10. In the original context, the verb is ambiguous, implying either *"may* Adonai reign" or "Adonai *will* reign." Our prayer uses it as a proof text, which has to mean, "Adonai *will* reign."

———◆———

GRAY (OUR TALMUDIC HERITAGE)

trinity). He reports (with disapproval) that the Jews there sneaked it into *Musaf*, where it would not be noticed by governmental spies. Twelfth-century Ashkenazi sources from the school of *Rashi (Machzor Vitry, Siddur Rashi*, and *Sefer Hapardes)* report in the name of other Geonim (Sar Shalom or Moshe) that this new *Sh'ma* eventually entered the *K'dushah* of every *Shacharit Amidah*, both Shabbat and weekdays. This Palestinian innovation did not penetrate Babylonian liturgy, which adopted just the more limited practice of adding the *Sh'ma* in *Musaf* of Shabbat and *N'illah* of Yom Kippur. Sar Shalom is said to have reported that when the ban on the *Sh'ma* was nullified, so that it could be said again in its proper place, the innovation of saying it in *Musaf* was retained in order to publicize the miracle of the decree's nullification for future generations.

———◆———

KUSHNER & POLEN (CHASIDISM)

liturgy reveals an important dimension of Jewish spirituality. Like the Ashkenazi rite, it too invites the entire congregation to join with the angelic chorus above in sanctifying God; but it goes even further by permitting the worshiper to literally give God a crown. Ordinary Jews are thereby empowered to exert a direct impact on the godhead itself.

This image of crowning God goes all the way back to the beginnings of Jewish mysticism. We find evidence of it in the Qumran scrolls and *Heikhalot* ("heavenly palaces") literature, where the worshiper participates in "an act of daily coronation of God" (Arthur Green, *Keter: The Crown of God in Early Jewish Mysticism* [Princeton, NJ: Princeton University Press], p. 12). In the *s'firot* system of the Iberian kabbalists, *Keter*, "Crown," becomes the highest of the ten *s'firot*. Indeed, in some systems, *Keter* is identical with the *Ein Sof* (the "One Without End" or the "One of Nothingness" itself) and is said to contain the deepest secret of the divine mystery.

Yerachmiel Yisro'el Yitzhak Danziger (d. 1910) of Alexander (near Lodz, Poland), in his *Yismach Yisro'el* (93–94), relates a story he once heard that every day before prayer, the Holy Yehudi of Przysucha would bid farewell to those he loved. For such was the intensity of his encounter with God that he assumed he might actually die. Some say he ascended all the way to *Keter* itself!

Indeed, the way to channel blessing is to attain the top three highest *s'firot*: *Binah* ("intuition"), *Chokhmah* ("insight"), and *Keter* ("crown") or (the parallel term) *Ein Sof* (the "One Without End" itself). Once there, the worshiper becomes a clear and open channel for blessing. But first he or she must attain a state of *bitul hayesh* (literally, "annihilating what is"), emptying oneself of all selfhood. This is surely a form of egodeath and seems to be why the Holy Yehudi assumed he might die in prayer. For in this way the worshiper attains *Ayin* ("nothingness") and thereby becomes only a channel for the divine flow of blessing.

And why does the liturgy (Sefardi) say, "Your people, Israel, assembled here below"? Because each one of us feels humbled in the presence of the other. We contemplate the uniqueness of each one of the other worshipers. We are astonished and humbled to realize that every member of the congregation has a precious gift to offer—a gift utterly beyond our own capacities. In their presence, we feel as nothing before everyone else. And this loss of selfhood is precisely what crowns God. And that's why we begin the *K'dushah* with *keter*, the "crown."

◆

LANDES (HALAKHAH)

the community as its agent. In this regard, *Musaf* seems to have had its own destiny. The *Bet Yosef* (Joseph Caro, author of *Shulchan Arukh*, 1488–1575, Turkey, Greece, Safed, on the *Tur*, O. Ch. 491) quotes the Ribash (Isaac ben Sheshet Perfet, 1326–1408, Barcelona) as saying that in Aragon, Spain, the prayer leader recited the *Amidah* along with the community—in effect, one shared recitation that obliterated the distinction between private and communal. This was done because most of the worshipers were illiterate and could not easily pray from a prayer book, especially the complicated weekly *Musaf* payer. Rabbi Gedalia Felder (1921–1991, leading centrist Traditional Halakhic Decider and chief legal authority of the Centrist Orthodox Rabbinate in North America; Toronto, *Y'sodei Y'shurun*, Shabbat, p. 481) cites Maimonides as ordaining this practice in Egypt for the same reason and emphasizing his own concern regarding neglect of this prayer. Evidently this practice was observed only for that locale and for that period of time. Subsequently, Egypt reverted to the practice of reciting two *Amidah*'s (private and communal) for *Musaf* as well.

[6] *"Hear, O Israel"* In his *Sefer Hamanhig*, Abraham ben Nathan Hayarchi of Lunel (1155–1215) discusses the importance of the *Sh'ma* here. He traces its presence to an ancient decree by the Sassanian king Yezdegard of Babylonia, who forbade it from being said in its usual places: *Shacharit* and *Ma'ariv*, the morning and evening liturgy. The Jews were forced to postpone it until after royal informers left the synagogue. Since *Musaf* could be said at any point during the day, it was inserted in the *Musaf K'dushah*. "And even though the decree was annulled, the repairing ordinance [to say *Sh'ma* in the *K'dushah* of *Musaf*] was retained" (*Sefer Hamanhig*, Laws of Sabbath 43). (See extensive notes by Yitzchak Rafael in Mosad Harav Kook edition, p. 171, which traces this explanation to the Geonic period.)

Additionally, he notes a new name for this *K'dushah*:

They fixed just the first verse of *Sh'ma* [to be recited] for it is the essence of [declaring] the unity of the Kingdom of Heaven.... The *K'dushah* of *Musaf* is therefore called *K'dushah Rabbah* [pronounced k'-doo-SHAH rah-BAH, but, commonly k'-DOO-shah RAH-bah, meaning "the Great *K'dushah*"], referring to the recitation of the *Sh'ma*, because it is the essence of the [acceptance of the] Kingdom of Heaven and also because we mention within it the *G'ulah* [final redemption], "He shall redeem us in mercy," for by the merit of the Sabbath we shall be redeemed.

———◆———

L. HOFFMAN (HISTORY)

Musaf is generally explained as a substitute for the additional Shabbat and holiday sacrifices specifically. But this explanation is suspect.

The idea that the *Amidah* arose to replace sacrifice is an *ex post facto* interpretation, intended to assuage the feeling of loss caused by the destruction of the Temple. Were we to require an *Amidah* only in place of sacrifices, we would have no evening *(Ma'ariv)* *Amidah*, since there was no evening sacrifice—a fact fully recognized by third-century Rabbis, who had inherited an evening *Amidah* and then, afterward, when it was said to replace sacrifices, had to question its necessity. The "extra" evening *Amidah* remained but was theoretically labeled "optional" *(r'shut)* because it had no corresponding sacrifice. (See Volume 9, *Welcoming the Night: Minchah and Ma'ariv*, pp. 27–29.)

Musaf is first mentioned in connection with the *ma'amad*, an institution associated with, but separate from, the Temple cult. Supervision of the daily communal sacrifice is said to have been assigned according to geography. When a given area's turn arrived, it would dispatch to Jerusalem a delegation of officiating priests (called a *mishmar*, pronounced mish-MAHR) along with some laypeople (called a *ma'amad*, pronounced mah-ah-MAHD) to observe the proceedings. Other laypeople (also called a *ma'amad*) remained home and met for an *Amidah* at the times that the sacrifices were being offered. Their prayers included a *Musaf*. *Musaf* therefore was linked to the additional offering, in that it occurred parallel to it but was not originally a stand-in for it.

The *Amidah* seems to have two origins. Insofar as it was part of the *ma'amad* ritual, it was connected to the sacrifices. But the *Ma'ariv Amidah* must have arisen independently.

How can we harmonize these two diverse origins?

The earliest rabbinic liturgy had three mandatory units: the *Sh'ma* and Its Blessings, the *Amidah*, and the reading of Torah. The *Sh'ma* is a creed-like statement *about* God; the Torah reading (which had no accompanying prayers yet) was a confrontation *with* God through God's word; so the *Amidah* alone consisted of prayers *to* God. The desire to speak directly *to* God is what led to an *Amidah*, even though it waited until the late first century for its final topics to be codified, and even later for its wording to be standardized. (For detail, see "How the *Amidah* Began: A Jewish Detective Story," Volume 2, *The Amidah*, pp. 17–36.)

The *timing* of public prayer arose in two ways: first, through the demand to say the *Sh'ma* "when you lie down and when you rise up," that is, *Shacharit* and *Ma'ariv*; and, second, to parallel the sacrifices going on in Jerusalem—*Shacharit*, *Minchah*, and (on fast days) when the Temple gates finally closed *(N'illah)*. Since people were reciting an evening *Sh'ma* anyway, they added an *Amidah* to be able to speak to God as they did at other services.

When the Rabbis looked back on their liturgy after the Temple's demise, the *Amidah* became falsely associated with *replacing* the cult, rather than just *accompanying* it. The *Ma'ariv Amidah* proved problematic but was retained, because it was already present, and then declared optional in theory.

Musaf, then, began as a parallel to the sacrificial system; it was later explained as a replacement for it.

In practice, today, by the time *Musaf* begins, people are usually anxious to go home for lunch. In some synagogues, therefore, people daven their way through *Musaf* as rapidly as possible—the whole thing takes only fifteen to twenty minutes. Reconstructionist synagogues replace the lengthy *Amidah* with a short "recollection of" *(zekher l')* *Musaf*. Many Conservative congregations shorten it by adopting what is called the *Hoeche K'dushah* (pronounced HAY-kh' k'-DOO-shah), a means of avoiding a full repetition of the *Amidah*. Reform Jews omit *Musaf* altogether—a decision influenced also by the explicit connection to sacrifices in the *Musaf K'dushat Hayom* (the fourth benediction—see "The hand turned against your Temple [*hayad shenishtalchah b'mikdashekha*]," p. 149).

But American practice has worked to lengthen *Musaf* rather than shorten it. In large synagogues that celebrate a bar/bat mitzvah every Shabbat morning, the bulk of the congregation does not arrive until the Torah reading, where the bar/bat mitzvah is featured. With few people present before that, prayer leaders hurry through *Shacharit* to reach the Torah reading as quickly as possible. Cantors may not even bother to lead the service until *Musaf* (when a large congregation is finally present), and then draw *Musaf* out at some length. *Musaf* is thereby converted into the most important part of the morning ritual, even though it was intended to be just what its name implies: the *additional* offering of prayer, not the primary service of Shabbat morning.

[1] *"Let us declare your awe and holiness"* Sefardi liturgy supplies this for the morning service (see "Let us sanctify your name," p. 93). The parallel Sefardi version for *Musaf* reads: *Keter yitnu l'kha, Adonai Eloheinu, malakhim hamonei malah, im am'kha yisra'el k'vutsei matah, yachad kulam k'dushah l'khah y'shaleishu, kadavar ha'amur al yad n'viekha, v'kara zeh el zeh v'amar kadosh, kadosh, kadosh.* "Adonai our God, the angels (massed above) along with your people Israel (banded together below) will give You a crown. All of them, together, will recite 'holiness' *(k'dushah)* three times, following the model of which your prophet speaks, 'They called out one to the other: Holy, Holy, Holy....'"

[5–6] *"Twice ... Hear, O Israel [Pa'amayim ... Sh'ma Yisra'el]"* The "official" place for the *Sh'ma* in the synagogue service is after the Call to Prayer for the morning and evening services *(Shacharit* and *Ma'ariv)*, where it appears in full—not just this single biblical line (Deut. 6:4) but as part of three longer biblical citations, and with accompanying blessings that define the classical Jewish belief in God (see Volume 1, *The Sh'ma and Its Blessings*). But on three other occasions in the liturgy, the opening line (from Deut. 6:4—what we have here) is found alone: (1) in the early morning service (see Volume 5, *Birkhot Hashachar [Morning Blessings]*, p. 158); (2) as the Torah is removed from the ark (see Volume 4, *Seder K'riat Hatorah [The Torah Service]*, p. 79); and 3) here, in the *K'dushat Hayom* of *Musaf*.

In 1925 scholar Jacob Mann argued that these extra appearances of the *Sh'ma* entered the service because of "religious persecution." He got the idea from medieval sources that cited occasions when Christian or Zoroastrian rulers (in the Land of Israel under Byzantine rulership and in Babylonia under Sasanians, respectively) banned the *Sh'ma*. Its thoroughgoing monotheism was said to imply a critique of the trinity (for Christians) and dualism (for Zoroastrians). Unable to say the *Sh'ma* officially, say our sources, Jews "sneaked" it in surreptitiously where government spies who attended services would not have noticed it.

Mann's theory is still widely reported as true, partly because of the medieval sources that back it up, but also because the theory has appealed to authors who have experienced anti-Semitism firsthand. But Mann's claim is almost certainly false. He made the mistake of trusting his sources, as if medieval authorities would have known what happened in late antiquity. In fact, we know more about classical Jewish history than they did. Their appeal to "persecution" as a justification for these "extra" recitations of the *Sh'ma* is probably a convenient fiction.

They faced a halakhic problem: On the one hand, the *Sh'ma* is biblically mandated "when you lie down and when you rise up"—hence its official appearance in the evening and morning services. On the other hand, the *Sh'ma* was already being said elsewhere—despite the rule against prayer redundancy. Authorities had, therefore, to explain away the custom to say the *Sh'ma* three "extra" times.

Precedent for a somewhat similar liturgical change could be found in the Talmud, which explains the extra day of festivals (in the diaspora) by the circumstances that governed calendrical calculations. Jewish months are lunar, averaging 29½ days in length (the time it takes for the moon to circle the earth). In practice, they must be either 29 or 30 days long, and whichever it is determines the setting of that month's festivals. The Mishnah recalls a time when witnesses would appear in the Jerusalem court to testify that they saw the new moon the night before—either on the evening of the 30th (in which case the prior month would be declared 29 days long) or the next night (so that the prior month would have had 30 days in all). The sighting was relayed throughout the Jewish world by runners. Most Jewish festivals appear on the full moon, two weeks after the sighting, by which time, presumably, the runners would successfully have reached the outskirts of the Land of Israel. Jews in Babylonia, however, would have no way of knowing whether the new month had been declared on the 30th or the 31st. That is why festivals in the diaspora have an extra day: communities there keep two days, one in case the new month had begun after 29 days of the old one, and another in case it had fallen the day after.

This discussion is carried in the Talmud of Babylonia, where the extra day was still being kept. But by that time the calendar was calculated mathematically, so that Jews were setting the New Moon without dependence on runners. Logically, there was no longer any need for an extra festival day in the diaspora, but the Talmud ruled that it should be retained anyway, if only out of respect for custom.

Medieval Jews applied that ruling to the "extra" recitations of *Sh'ma*. The persecutions that had occasioned them had ceased, but custom dictated retaining them anyway.

We are not sure, therefore, how the *Sh'ma* was added three "extra" times. But at least here, and in the Morning Blessings *(Birkhot Hashachar)*, it is likely that we have no extra recitation at all. It is a *statement* that we make, testifying to the fact that we do, in fact, say the *Sh'ma* twice daily *(pa'amayim)* as commanded. In the course of making that statement, the first line of the *Sh'ma* gets cited. (For detail, see Volume 10, *Birkhot Hashachar [Morning Blessings]*, pp. 10–16.)

───◆───

J. HOFFMAN (TRANSLATION)

declare God holy. Another option is "with holiness," but in context it is not clear what that would mean. Another likely possibility is "who declare your name holy in the Holy [part of the divine place]."

[3] *"Earth"* Or "world" or "universe," but we need "earth" to preserve the connection between this verse and the last (v. 2), which says, "The whole earth is full of his glory." Still, the prayer highlights the connection between earth and heaven, so the translation "earth," implying the earth alone, is not without problems.

[3] *"Where is the place with"* Translated literally. We do not shorten the translation to just "where is" because we want to preserve the connection between this line and the next (v. 4, "… from his place").

[7] *"Deliverer … proclaim"* The Hebrew word for "proclaim," *yashmi'a*, sounds like the Hebrew for "deliverer," *moshi'ah*. (As is frequently the case, the similarity is more immediately evident to those who know Hebrew and who therefore naturally focus on the consonants.) A vaguely similar English example would be: "He reviles his enemies as he lets us relive our victories."

[9] *"In your holy scriptures"* Or "your holy words."

[11] *"For all generations"* Better, "in each and every generation" or "from generation to generation," but here and immediately below we repeatedly have idioms representing eternity, each beginning with the Hebrew *l'*, which we render with the English "for."

─────◆ ◆ ◆─────

II. *K'DUSHAT HAYOM* ("SANCTIFICATION OF THE DAY"): DECLARING SABBATH HOLINESS

[1] You instituted Shabbat, loved its offerings, commanded us regarding its ceremonies and the order of its libations. [2] Those who delight in it will always possess glory, those who taste it earn life, and those who love its words choose greatness. [3] Then from Sinai they were commanded about it. Adonai our God, You commanded us to offer an additional offering on it, as is appropriate. [4] Adonai our God and our ancestors' God, may You find it favorable to bring us back up to our land in joy, and plant us within our borders. [5] There we will offer before You the offerings that are our obligation, the *tamid* offerings in the right order and the *musaf* offerings in the right way. [6] And we will perform and offer this Shabbat *musaf* before You in love, in accordance with your will and your commandment, as You wrote about us in your Torah, transcribed by Moses your servant and dictated by your very self:

[7] On the day of Shabbat, two perfect year-old lambs, two-tenths of a measure of choice flour, a meal-offering mixed with oil, and its libation. [8] The Shabbat *olah* every Shabbat, and its libation on top of the *olah*.

[9] Those who keep Shabbat and who call it a delight will rejoice in your kingdom. A people who sanctifies the seventh day, they will all be satisfied and delight in your goodness. You loved the seventh day and sanctified it, calling it the favorite of days, in memory of acts of creation.

[10] Our God and our ancestors' God, accept our rest, sanctify us through your commandments, and grant us a share in your

[1] תִּ כַּנְתָּ שַׁבָּת, רָצִיתָ קָרְבְּנוֹתֶיהָ, צִוִּיתָ פֵּרוּשֶׁיהָ עִם סִדּוּרֵי נְסָכֶיהָ. [2] מְעַנְּגֶיהָ לְעוֹלָם כָּבוֹד יִנְחָלוּ; טוֹעֲמֶיהָ חַיִּים זָכוּ; וְגַם הָאוֹהֲבִים דְּבָרֶיהָ גְּדֻלָּה בָּחָרוּ. [3] אָז מִסִּינַי נִצְטַוּוּ עָלֶיהָ. וַתְּצַוֵּנוּ, יְיָ אֱלֹהֵינוּ, לְהַקְרִיב בָּהּ קָרְבַּן מוּסַף שַׁבָּת כָּרָאוּי. [4] יְהִי רָצוֹן מִלְּפָנֶיךָ, יְיָ אֱלֹהֵינוּ וֵאלֹהֵי אֲבוֹתֵינוּ, שֶׁתַּעֲלֵנוּ בְשִׂמְחָה לְאַרְצֵנוּ, וְתִטָּעֵנוּ בִּגְבוּלֵנוּ; [5] וְשָׁם נַעֲשֶׂה לְפָנֶיךָ, אֶת קָרְבְּנוֹת חוֹבוֹתֵינוּ, תְּמִידִים כְּסִדְרָם וּמוּסָפִים כְּהִלְכָתָם. [6] וְאֶת מוּסַף יוֹם הַשַּׁבָּת הַזֶּה נַעֲשֶׂה וְנַקְרִיב לְפָנֶיךָ, בְּאַהֲבָה, כְּמִצְוַת רְצוֹנֶךָ, כְּמוֹ שֶׁכָּתַבְתָּ עָלֵינוּ בְּתוֹרָתֶךָ, עַל יְדֵי מֹשֶׁה עַבְדֶּךָ, מִפִּי כְבוֹדֶךָ, כָּאָמוּר:

[7] וּבְיוֹם הַשַּׁבָּת, שְׁנֵי כְבָשִׂים בְּנֵי שָׁנָה תְּמִימִם; וּשְׁנֵי עֶשְׂרֹנִים סֹלֶת, מִנְחָה בְּלוּלָה בַשֶּׁמֶן, וְנִסְכּוֹ. [8] עֹלַת שַׁבָּת בְּשַׁבַּתּוֹ, עַל עֹלַת הַתָּמִיד וְנִסְכָּהּ.

[9] יִשְׂמְחוּ בְמַלְכוּתְךָ שׁוֹמְרֵי שַׁבָּת וְקוֹרְאֵי עֹנֶג, עַם מְקַדְּשֵׁי שְׁבִיעִי, כֻּלָּם יִשְׂבְּעוּ וְיִתְעַנְּגוּ מִטּוּבֶךָ; וּבַשְּׁבִיעִי רָצִיתָ בּוֹ וְקִדַּשְׁתּוֹ, חֶמְדַּת יָמִים אוֹתוֹ קָרָאתָ, זֵכֶר לְמַעֲשֵׂה בְרֵאשִׁית.

Torah. [11] Satisfy us with your goodness, and gladden us with your salvation. And purify our heart to serve You in truth. [12] And, Adonai our God, lovingly and adoringly grant us as our inheritance your holy Shabbat, that all of Israel, who sanctify your name, might rest on it. [13] Blessed are You, Adonai, who sanctifies Shabbat.

[10]אֱלֹהֵֽינוּ וֵאלֹהֵי אֲבוֹתֵֽינוּ, רְצֵה בִמְנוּחָתֵֽנוּ; קַדְּשֵֽׁנוּ בְּמִצְוֹתֶֽיךָ, וְתֵן חֶלְקֵֽנוּ בְּתוֹרָתֶֽךָ; [11]שַׂבְּעֵֽנוּ מִטּוּבֶֽךָ, וְשַׂמְּחֵֽנוּ בִּישׁוּעָתֶֽךָ; וְטַהֵר לִבֵּֽנוּ לְעָבְדְּךָ בֶּאֱמֶת: [12]וְהַנְחִילֵֽנוּ, יְיָ אֱלֹהֵֽינוּ, בְּאַהֲבָה וּבְרָצוֹן שַׁבַּת קָדְשֶֽׁךָ, וְיָנֽוּחוּ בָהּ יִשְׂרָאֵל מְקַדְּשֵׁי שְׁמֶֽךָ. [13]בָּרוּךְ אַתָּה, יְיָ, מְקַדֵּשׁ הַשַּׁבָּת.

BRETTLER (BIBLE)

[1] *"You instituted Shabbat"* The additional *(musaf)* offerings for Shabbat are enumerated in Numbers 28:9–10 (quoted at the end of this prayer). Its beginning is a reverse acrostic; though the Bible contains many acrostics, none of them go backwards.

[2] *"Those who delight in it ... who taste it ... who love its words"* A rabbinic adaptation of biblical parallelism, though it is in three parts rather than the typical two, and the sections are of different sizes. It begins with a paraphrase of Isaiah 58:13, "If you call Shabbat 'delight' [*oneg*, from the same root as *m'angeha*], Adonai's holy day 'honored.'" *(p. 137)*

DORFF (THEOLOGY)

[4] *"May You find it favorable"* The traditional liturgy requests the restoration of our homeland and Temple so that we can again fulfill the Torah's command to offer the *musaf* sacrifice. The Talmud, however, is ambivalent about the idea of restoring sacrifices. "Prayer," says Rabbi *(p. 138)*

ELLENSON (MODERN LITURGIES)

Musaf K'dushat Hayom Authors of all non-Orthodox prayer books in the modern era have regarded the manifest content of the *Musaf K'dushat Hayom*, with its prayers for the restoration of the Temple and its sacrificial offerings, as extremely problematic. *(p. 139)*

FRANKEL (A WOMAN'S VOICE)

[5] *"We will offer before You the offerings that are our obligation"* The principal characteristic of the *K'dushat Hayom* in the *Musaf Amidah* is its focus on sacrifices *(korbanot)*. In fact, this additional service derives its name from the additional sacrifice (the *musaf*) required on Shabbat and holidays. Jewish tradition adds this second *Amidah* as a symbolic substitution for the extra sacrifice that was offered as long as the Temple stood. Orthodox prayer books call for the *(p. 141)*

I. *K'DUSHAT HAYOM* ("SANCTIFICATION OF THE DAY"): DECLARING SABBATH HOLINESS

[1] You instituted Shabbat, loved its offerings, commanded us regarding its ceremonies and the order of its libations. [2] Those who delight in it will always possess glory, those who taste it earn life, and those who love its words choose greatness. [3] Then from Sinai they were commanded about it. Adonai our God, You commanded us to offer an

GRAY (OUR TALMUDIC HERITAGE)

[1–3] *"You instituted Shabbat.... Then from Sinai they were commanded about it* [tikanta Shabbat ... az misinai nitstavu aleha]" A reverse alphabetical acrostic, beginning with the *tav*, the last letter of the Hebrew alphabet, and working back to *alef*. According to *Siddur Rashi*, *Machzor Vitry*, and *Sefer Hapardes* (eleventh- to twelfth-century works from the school of *Rashi*), this Shabbat acrostic hints at messianic redemption that will come through the merit of observing Shabbat—an idea *(p. 142)*

LANDES (HALAKHAH)

[5] *"There we will offer before You the offerings that are our obligation" Musaf* is recited immediately after *Shacharit* and the reading of Torah (*Shulchan Arukh*, O. Ch. 286:1). The *musaf* sacrifice was offered at the sixth halakhic hour (the day being divided from sunrise to sunset by twelve, rendering a variable halakhic hour), but the service on which it is based can be prayed earlier, as long as *Shacharit* and the Torah reading have been completed. Nonetheless it should be said before the

[Hebrew text:]

‪¹תִּכַּנְתָּ שַׁבָּת, רָצִיתָ קָרְבְּנוֹתֶיהָ. צִוִּיתָ פֵּרוּשֶׁיהָ עִם סִדּוּרֵי נְסָכֶיהָ. ²מְעַנְּגֶיהָ לְעוֹלָם כָּבוֹד יִנְחָלוּ; טוֹעֲמֶיהָ חַיִּים זָכוּ; וְגַם הָאוֹהֲבִים דְּבָרֶיהָ גְּדֻלָּה בָּחָרוּ. ³אָז מִסִּינַי נִצְטַוּוּ עָלֶיהָ. וַתְּצַוֵּנוּ, יְיָ אֱלֹהֵינוּ, לְהַקְרִיב בָּהּ קָרְבַּן מוּסַף שַׁבָּת כָּרָאוּי. ⁴יְהִי רָצוֹן מִלְּפָנֶיךָ, יְיָ אֱלֹהֵינוּ וֵאלֹהֵי אֲבוֹתֵינוּ, שֶׁתַּעֲלֵנוּ בְשִׂמְחָה לְאַרְצֵנוּ,‬

seventh halakhic hour is completed, for by then the *musaf* offering was over. Indeed, Jacob ben Asher (*Tur*, O. Ch. 620) recounts that if his father Rabbenu Asher bar Yechiel (the *Rosh*, 1250–1327, Germany, Spain) saw that the Yom Kippur service was dragging, he would pray *Musaf* on his own in order to finish on time.

The *Musaf Amidah* is intrinsically different from the others. The Talmud (Ber. 26b) reports the view of Rabbi Yose ben Rabbi Chanina that the three daily *Amidah* prayers were *(p. 143)*

L. HOFFMAN (HISTORY)

AS WITH THE MORNING AMIDAH, THE THIRTEEN MIDDLE BENEDICTIONS ARE REPLACED BY THE K'DUSHAT HAYOM, ("SANCTIFICATION OF THE DAY"), A SINGLE BLESSING THAT DECLARES THE SANCTITY OF HOLY TIME. FOR THE PARALLEL SHACHARIT BLESSING, SEE P. 105. FOR AN ALTERNATIVE MUSAF BLESSING (FOR ROSH CHODESH [THE NEW MOON]), SEE P. 146.

[1] *"You instituted Shabbat* [Tikanta Shabbat]" The opening twenty-two Hebrew words constitute a reverse alphabetic acrostic, ending in the *alef* word *az* ("then"). But in Sefardi prayer books the next few words, *(p. 144)*

J. HOFFMAN (TRANSLATION)

[4] *"Bring us back up"* Literally, "bring us up," or "re-bring us up." Because Hebrew has no prefix "re-," we frequently insert it (as in "rebuild the Temple") or otherwise paraphrase (as here) when necessary.

[4] *"Plant"* Or "replant."

[5] *"Tamid"* The "*tamid*,"—literally, "perpetual"—was a communal sacrifice offered twice daily, morning and afternoon.

[5] *"Musaf"* Literally, "additional," another kind of sacrifice, the name of which is also used to name the Shabbat afternoon additional prayer service.

[7] *"Lambs"* That is, a male *(p. 145)*

additional offering on it, as is appropriate. ⁴Adonai our God and our ancestors' God, may You find it favorable to bring us back up to our land in joy, and plant us within our borders. ⁵There we will offer before You the offerings that are our obligation, the *tamid* offerings in the right order and the *musaf* offerings in the right way. ⁶And we will perform and offer this Shabbat *musaf* before You in love, in accordance with your will and your commandment, as You wrote about us in your Torah, transcribed by Moses your servant and dictated by your very self:

⁷On the day of Shabbat, two perfect year-old lambs, two-tenths of a measure of choice flour, a meal-offering mixed with oil, and its libation. ⁸The Shabbat *olah* every Shabbat, and its libation on top of the *olah*.

⁹Those who keep Shabbat and who call it a delight will rejoice in your kingdom. A people who sanctifies the seventh day, they will all be satisfied and delight in your goodness. You loved the seventh day and sanctified it, calling it the favorite of days, in memory of acts of creation.

¹⁰Our God and our ancestors' God, accept our rest, sanctify us through your commandments, and grant us a share in your Torah. ¹¹Satisfy us with your goodness, and gladden us with your salvation. And purify our heart to

וְתִטָּעֵנוּ בִּגְבוּלֵנוּ; ⁵וְשָׁם נַעֲשֶׂה לְפָנֶיךָ, אֶת קָרְבְּנוֹת חוֹבוֹתֵינוּ, תְּמִידִים כְּסִדְרָם וּמוּסָפִים כְּהִלְכָתָם. ⁶וְאֶת מוּסַף יוֹם הַשַּׁבָּת הַזֶּה נַעֲשֶׂה וְנַקְרִיב לְפָנֶיךָ, בְּאַהֲבָה, כְּמִצְוַת רְצוֹנֶךָ, כְּמוֹ שֶׁכָּתַבְתָּ עָלֵינוּ בְּתוֹרָתֶךָ, עַל יְדֵי מֹשֶׁה עַבְדֶּךָ, מִפִּי כְבוֹדֶךָ, כָּאָמוּר:

⁷וּבְיוֹם הַשַּׁבָּת, שְׁנֵי כְבָשִׂים בְּנֵי שָׁנָה תְּמִימִם; וּשְׁנֵי עֶשְׂרֹנִים סֹלֶת, מִנְחָה בְּלוּלָה בַשֶּׁמֶן, וְנִסְכּוֹ. ⁸עֹלַת שַׁבָּת בְּשַׁבַּתּוֹ, עַל עֹלַת הַתָּמִיד וְנִסְכָּהּ.

⁹יִשְׂמְחוּ בְמַלְכוּתְךָ שׁוֹמְרֵי שַׁבָּת וְקוֹרְאֵי עֹנֶג, עַם מְקַדְּשֵׁי שְׁבִיעִי, כֻּלָּם יִשְׂבְּעוּ וְיִתְעַנְּגוּ מִטּוּבֶךָ; וּבַשְּׁבִיעִי רָצִיתָ בּוֹ וְקִדַּשְׁתּוֹ, חֶמְדַּת יָמִים אוֹתוֹ קָרָאתָ, זֵכֶר לְמַעֲשֵׂה בְרֵאשִׁית.

¹⁰אֱלֹהֵינוּ וֵאלֹהֵי אֲבוֹתֵינוּ, רְצֵה בִמְנוּחָתֵנוּ; קַדְּשֵׁנוּ בְּמִצְוֹתֶיךָ, וְתֵן חֶלְקֵנוּ בְּתוֹרָתֶךָ; ¹¹שַׂבְּעֵנוּ מִטּוּבֶךָ, וְשַׂמְּחֵנוּ בִּישׁוּעָתֶךָ; וְטַהֵר לִבֵּנוּ לְעָבְדְּךָ בֶּאֱמֶת; ¹²וְהַנְחִילֵנוּ, יְיָ אֱלֹהֵינוּ, בְּאַהֲבָה וּבְרָצוֹן שַׁבַּת קָדְשֶׁךָ, וְיָנוּחוּ בָהּ יִשְׂרָאֵל מְקַדְּשֵׁי שְׁמֶךָ. ¹³בָּרוּךְ אַתָּה, יְיָ, מְקַדֵּשׁ הַשַּׁבָּת.

serve You in truth. [12] And, Adonai our God, lovingly and adoringly grant us as our inheritance your holy Shabbat, that all of Israel, who sanctify your name, might rest on it. [13] Blessed are You, Adonai, who sanctifies Shabbat.

BRETTLER (BIBLE)

[4–5] *"Back up to our land.... we will offer before You ... "* The future restoration is imagined as the return from Babylonian exile, the Temple's reconstruction, and the restoration of sacrifices. Even though Psalm 51:19 proclaims, "True sacrifice to God is a contrite spirit," classical rabbinic Judaism typically anticipated a restoration of the Temple cult.

[7] *"On the day of Shabbat ... year-old lambs"* Numbers 28:9–10. That entire chapter deals with Tabernacle sacrifice, beginning with the most frequent, the daily offering (the *tamid*), then the Sabbath and New Moon offerings. The chapter then follows calendrical order, beginning with the Passover offering in the first month, later called Nisan (in the Bible, the month of Passover was Rosh Hashanah).

[9] *"Rejoice in your kingdom"* Following the first creation story in Genesis, which implicitly depicts God as king, this line commemorates God's kingship.

[9] *"Call it a delight ... will ... delight* [oneg ... v'yitangu]" The concept of *oneg* ("joy" or "delight" on Shabbat) appears twice, cleverly paralleling the pun in Isaiah 58:13–14:

> If you refrain from trampling Shabbat,
> From pursuing your affairs on my holy day;
> If you call Shabbat "delight [*oneg*],"
> Adonai's holy day "honored";
> And if you honor it and go not your ways
> Nor look to your affairs, nor strike bargains—
> Then you can seek the favor [*titangu*, from the root for *oneg*] of Adonai.

DORFF (THEOLOGY)

Eleazar (Ber. 32b), "is more efficacious than animal offerings, as it says, 'What need have I [God] of all your sacrifices?' [Isa. 1:11]; and then, 'When you lift up your hands [in prayer] ...' [Isa. 1:15]." Isaiah's primary point is that God accepts neither sacrifices nor prayer if people act immorally, but the fact that "prayer" is mentioned after "sacrifice" is taken to indicate that God regards prayer as more efficacious. (On the substitution of prayer for sacrifice, see Volume 6, *Tachanun and the Concluding Prayers*, p. 105.)

Maimonides goes even further: he maintains (*Guide for the Perplexed*, part 3, chap. 32) that God never wanted sacrifice to begin with; God went along with the practice only to let the Israelites worship the way other people in the ancient world did.

This notion of evolution informs the Conservative Movement's practice regarding the retention of *Musaf*. Rabbi Robert Gordis, who chaired its original Prayer Book Commission in 1945, explains that the prayer for the restoration of sacrifice exemplifies "passages in the traditional Prayer Book that no longer seem to express the convictions and hopes of our day.... [Still] the sacrificial system represents a legitimate stage in the evolution of Judaism and religion generally ... [so] neither the deletion of the *Musaf* nor its retention unchanged would satisfy the basic principles of a Jewish Prayer Book for the modern age" (*Sabbath and Festival Prayer Book*, pp. vi, ix–x). Complicating matters is the fact that Conservative Judaism has advocated Zionism ever since Solomon Schechter published an essay in its defense in 1906, just eight years after the First Zionist Congress. As a result, ever since its first prayer book (in 1945), Conservative liturgy has maintained this sentence asking God to restore our homeland, but transformed the request to restore the Temple into a historical recollection: "For there our ancestors offered the required sacrifices...." Mention of sacrifice becomes a reminder of our ancestors' devotion to God, and a stimulus for our own devotion, expressed through prayer.

[9] *"Those who keep Shabbat and who call it a delight will rejoice in your kingdom"* Shabbat is not a burden; it is a delight. But that very delight requires our refraining from many normal activities and engaging instead in acts that are special to the day: spending leisurely time with family and friends, eating specially prepared food, enjoying sexual relations with one's spouse, getting extra sleep, and renewing one's relationship to God and community. These experiences make Shabbat "a foretaste of the world-to-come [*novelet olam haba*]" (Gen. Rab. 17:5 [17:7 in some editions]; *Mechilta* to Exod. 31:13). In Abraham Joshua Heschel's memorable metaphor (*The Sabbath*, [New York: Farrar, Straus and Giroux, 1951], chap. 1), Shabbat is "a palace [or cathedral] in time." Expanding on that metaphor, I would depict the restrictions embedded in Shabbat legislation as the moat necessary to mark off Shabbat from the rest of week.

◆

ELLENSON (MODERN LITURGIES)

The issue was first raised officially at a rabbinic conference in mid-nineteenth-century Germany, when a motion to ban the traditional *Musaf* service altogether failed. A commission tried to hammer out an alternative, but that too did not attract universal approval, so the issue of *Musaf* was left to individual congregations to handle as each saw fit. There were as yet no denominations in European Judaism, but nowadays, especially in North America, where denominationalism has firmly taken root, most congregations allow their denominational prayer books to dictate how *Musaf* should be approached.

The Reconstructionist *Kol Haneshamah* (1996) succinctly and directly summarizes the rationale for rejecting, or at least altering, the traditional *Musaf* service:

> The *Musaf Amidah* corresponds to the additional sacrifice that was offered in the Temple on Shabbat and Festivals. Because Reconstructionists do not anticipate or hope for the rebuilding of the Temple, we do not feel a strong need to retain its liturgical rhythms or emphasis on animal sacrifice. This siddur therefore omits the *Musaf Amidah*.

Similarly, Rabbi Jules Harlow, editor of the 1985 Conservative *Siddur Sim Shalom*, explains, "Conservative liturgy continues to pray for the restoration of the Jewish people to the Land of Israel and for the experience of worship there, but the liturgy merely recalls with reverence the sacrificial ritual of our ancestors. It does not petition for its restoration."

In a variety of ways, non-Orthodox *Siddurim* from the nineteenth century through the present day have responded to the ideological dilemma this service poses. Modern American Reform, as evidenced by *Olath Tamid* (1856), *Union Prayer Book* (1895/6), *Gates of Prayer* (1975), and *Mishkan T'filah* (2006), omit the *Musaf* service altogether. The Liberal British *Lev Chadash* (1996) as well as the Reconstructionist *Kol Haneshamah* (1996) have followed suit.

Among other approaches is the modern Israeli Reform *Ha'avodah Shebalev* (1982), which adds a brief prayer entitled *Zecher L'musaf* ("A Remembrance of *Musaf*"), stating, in part:

> May the memory of our ancestors who came near to You in ancient days through their sacrifices of obligation be pleasing before You, O Lord our God and God of our ancestors, ... and since the destruction of our Sanctuary and the time that we were exiled from our land the offerings of our lips and the meditations of our hearts be as the sacrifices were that our ancestors offered before You.

In a similar vein the 1965 Reconstructionist *Sabbath Prayer Book* did retain *Musaf*, "An Additional Sabbath Service," and labeled its *K'dushat Hayom*, "In Remembrance of the Ancient Temple Service." The novel composition under this name states, among other points, "The Temple has long been destroyed, yet the remembrance of it lives in the heart of our people. Today ... our worship is one of prayer and praise."

In responding in this way, both *Ha'avodah Shebalev* and the 1965 Reconstructionist *Sabbath Prayer Book* follow the model established by most nineteenth-century Reform

Siddurim, which preserved the traditional structure of the worship service while simultaneously altering the manifest content of prayers that were deemed objectionable. The authors of these liberal liturgies, for whom attachment to Jewish historical tradition was great, aspired to lead whole Jewish communities and not merely "denominational" Reform groups. Indeed, these twin goals—fidelity to liturgical tradition as evidenced by retention of *K'dushat Hayom* and innovation in the actual content of the prayer in response to perceived theological problems—has led to some of the most interesting liberal liturgical creativity of the modern era, from Hamburg, Geiger, and Wise in the 1800s to American Conservative prayer books and Dutch, French, and German Liberal ones today.

1–4 *"You instituted Shabbat ... may You find it favorable"* The Hamburg Temple prayer books (1819, 1845) substituted the Sefardi "You commanded Moses" (see L. Hoffman, "You instituted Shabbat," p. 135). In this way, the Hamburg Temple created a distinct "reform" identity for itself apart from the established traditional community there and demonstrated its authenticity by borrowing a liturgical precedent from a Sefardi tradition that the Reformers lionized.

Nineteenth-century Abraham Geiger was of two minds. In his first prayer book (1854), which reflected his desire to appeal to more conservative worshipers, he rewrote these lines as follows:

> You instituted the Sabbath and commanded its specific obligations. Those that find delight in it shall inherit glory forever. Already from Sinai they were commanded concerning it. And we are holding the *Musaf* service of this Sabbath day before You in love, according to the commandment of Your will, even as you have written us in Your Torah through Your servant Moses, by the mouth of Your glory.

By 1870, with the need to appeal to tradition somewhat weakened (see "Give thanks to Adonai for He is good," p. 24), he removed his 1854 alternative altogether.

4 *"Bring us back up to our land in joy"* The 1985 Conservative *Siddur Sim Shalom* inserts the words, "Who restores His children to their land." This addition reflects the Conservative conviction that the "re-establishment of the Jewish State in the Land of Israel" represents a divine answer to the millennial-old prayers of the Jewish people for a genuine restoration of Jewish autonomy—a modern-day version of "ingathering of the exiles."

The 1998 Israeli Masorti movement's *Va'ani Tefillati* manifests an appropriately distinctive Israeli character where (in one version of the prayer) it replaces the traditional phraseology with, "May they [Jews of the Diaspora] willingly come up to the land which is the beloved of your dispersed." In a second version, it prays, "May our dispersed come up in joy to our land and may You plant them within our border." In both texts, the Israeli authors champion the centrality of Israel and affirm the concept of the "ingathering of the exiles."

5–6 *"There we will offer before You the offerings that are our obligation"* In keeping with the observation made by Jules Harlow, editor of the 1985 *Sim Shalom* (see p. 139, "*Musaf K'dushat Hayom*"), for "There we will offer You the offerings that are our obligation" (v. 5), all Conservative liturgy (1946 Conservative *Sabbath and Festival Prayerbook*, (1998) *Va'ani Tefillati*, and the 1985 and 1998 *Siddur Sim Shalom*) substitute, "There our ancestors sacrificed to You [*shesham asu avoteinu l'fanekha et korb'noteihem*] ...," thereby changing the prayer from a wish for the future to a historical remembrance. Similarly, where the traditional wording says, (v. 5), "And we will prepare and offer this Shabbat *musaf* before You in love [*na'aseh v'nakriv*]" (v. 6), all modern Conservative Siddurim substitute, "And the additional offering for the Sabbath Day they offered lovingly [*asu v'hikrivu*]"—again, not a hope for a time to come, but a recollection of the past.

[6] "*Transcribed by Moses*" The 1985 *Siddur Sim Shalom* adds, "Accept with compassion the prayer of Your people Israel wherever they dwell," thereby reflecting a distinctly American Zionist sensibility. While Israel enjoys sanctified status, the diaspora is proclaimed an equally fit venue for Jewish life. God hears the prayers of the People Israel everywhere. Interestingly, this line is removed in the 1998 edition of *Sim Shalom* because of criticisms that were lodged against the failure of the 1985 version to affirm an exclusive focus upon Israel.

[9] "*Calling it the favorite of days, in memory of acts of creation*" Isaac Mayer Wise inserted the Decalogue passage from Deuteronomy at this point in his *Musaf* service instead of calling for a return to Zion and the reestablishment of the Temple sacrifices. In perfect symmetry, his *Shacharit* service features the Exodus passage of the Ten Commandments in its *K'dushat Hayom* in lieu of the traditional prayer that speaks of how the gentiles (lit., "uncircumcised") did not enjoy Sabbath rest.

◆

FRANKEL (A WOMAN'S VOICE)

reinstatement of animal sacrifices in the messianic age; non-Orthodox texts (Conservative, Reform, Reconstructionist, Renewal, Feminist, Chavurot, et al.) have either historicized the sacrifices, changing the verbs to past tense; made the *Musaf Amidah* optional; offered alternatives, such as poems and meditation; or dropped the *Musaf Amidah* altogether.

Whether a worshiper looks backwards to a lost sacrificial system, looks forward to a restored one, or transforms the system into a metaphor, it's useful to explore how biblical and rabbinic literature regard women's roles within the context of Temple sacrifice, a matter not often discussed by most scholars, rabbis, or educators. Were women obligated to bring sacrifices to the Temple? Were they even allowed to do so?

As a matter of fact, Israelite women were required to perform a number of sacrifices, including one following childbirth (Lev. 12); a thanksgiving offering (*todah*) and a meal (*minchah*) offering following recovery from illness or danger; the paschal offering *(pesach)* on Passover; sin *(chatat)* and purification *(asham)* offerings to atone for unintentional transgressions; Nazirite offerings *(nazir)* to mark their fulfillment of a Nazirite vow; and *tazri'a*, *m'tsora*, and *zavah* offerings after being cured from certain diseases and unusual bodily discharges. In addition, women could choose to participate in certain other offerings even though they were not obligated to perform them, such as the first fruits offering *(bikurim)* on Shavuot; donating a half-shekel tax for the Temple *(sh'kalim)*; and voluntary donations such as peace offerings *(sh'lamim)* and other contributions. Furthermore, women were permitted to lay their hands upon sacrificial animals *(s'mikhah)* prior to their slaughter, even if these offerings were not obligatory (Ber. 19a).

Clarifying women's obligations vis-à-vis Temple sacrifices has helped support efforts to expand women's liturgical roles in today's traditional community. It has been consistently argued within Orthodoxy that women cannot lead services because as voluntary worshipers themselves, they cannot fulfill the role of representing men who are obliged to offer prayers. However, since biblical and rabbinic texts establish that women *were* obligated to bring certain sacrifices during Temple times, they should accordingly be allowed to play the same leadership role as men in leading services.

The Jewish Feminist Orthodox Alliance (JOFA) has applauded efforts among some modern Orthodox congregations to extend liturgical participation to women, referring to such synagogues as "partnership congregations." Generally, expanded roles for women include leading *Kabbalat Shabbat* and *P'sukei D'zimrah* (services added to the liturgy after the Talmud's completion, or seen as having lesser halakhic standing than the *Sh'ma* and the *Amidah*). They also read Torah and give *divrei torah*.

———◆———

GRAY (OUR TALMUDIC HERITAGE)

with talmudic roots. The Babylonian Talmud (Shab. 118b) promises redemption if all Jews observe Shabbat properly two weeks in a row (the Yerushalmi [Ta'an. 1:1, 64a] demands it only once). Our medieval sources connect the reverse acrostic to several biblical verses about redemption that also include a reverse counting-back of the Hebrew alphabet. For example, the reverse progression *mem-lamed-khaf* is indicated by Zechariah 14:9, "When Adonai becomes king [*MeLeKH*: M = mem, L = lamed, and KH = khaf] over all the earth." This connection between Shabbat and the messianic redemption is strengthened by an allusion to Isaiah 56, where those who observe Shabbat (vv. 4, 6) will be brought "to My holy Mountain" (v. 7).

[9] *"Those who keep Shabbat … will rejoice in your kingdom* [yism'chu v'malkhut'cha shomrei Shabbat]" The nominal form of *yism'chu* ("They shall rejoice") is *simchah* ("joy"). A third-century midrash connects *simchah* to Shabbat by pointing out that the biblical phrase "On the day of your *simchah*" (Num. 10:10) refers to Shabbat (Midrash Sifre to Numbers 77).

The Yerushalmi gives a halakhic spin to the notion that *simchah* is a mandatory feature of Shabbat. A tannaitic (second- to third-century source) states that if Purim falls on Shabbat, the required *s'udat Purim* (Purim festive meal) is put off until after Shabbat. Rabbi Abbahu explains this in light of the command in Esther 9:22 to "make these [days of Purim] days of partying and *simchah*." Rabbi Abbahu interprets that this Purim partying should be done on a day when the *simchah* of the day is instituted through an action of the *bet din* (the Jewish court), which is responsible for establishing holidays. But on Shabbat, when the *simchah* of the day already exists through the action of heaven, no other human-crafted *simchah*—even that of the Purim meal—can be permitted to intrude (PT Meg. 1:6, 70b).

---◆---

LANDES (HALAKHAH)

instituted by the patriarchs; Rabbi Joshua ben Levi held that they were instituted to parallel the daily sacrifices. In the end the argument is settled by compromise: "The patriarchs instituted the *Amidot* but the Rabbis found support for them in the [institution] of the sacrifices." The essence of the usual *Amidah* is one's personal cry for help in all of one's finitude, as demonstrated by the support verses showing the patriarchs' individual situations, as they instituted the prayers. The sacrificial element is mostly indicated in the precision and nuance of time and the grace—the choreography—of the actual performance.

This is not the case of *Musaf*, which is not attributed to any patriarch, and therefore is *completely* derived from its sacrificial roots not just as to form but also as to content. The *Musaf Amidah* is both the verbal evocation of the sacrifice and its virtual reenactment. The verse applied to it is *un'shalmah farim s'fateinu*, "[Instead of bulls] we will pay the offering of our lips" (Hosea 14:3). This means that the *kavvanah* (our "inner intent") should be that the words of the *Musaf Amidah* be indeed a sacrifice.

The sacrificial system is commonly derided. I have heard the scorn heaped on this so-called brutal and wasteful cultic rite—often at banqueting halls or fine restaurants where mounds of flesh are consumed by ravenous crowds and even greater mounds are discarded afterwards. How different was the sacrifice, a *KoRBaN* in Hebrew (from Hebrew *k.r.v/b*), meaning "to draw us near," and intended to bring us closer (*l'KaReV*) to God. The *korban* is an expression of life's finitude, an encounter with mortality, a forced admission of how fleeting life really is. The priests of old would lay hands upon the sacrifice, then (in some cases) say a *vidui* ("a confession," pronounced vee-DOO-ee), and then sprinkle or dash the blood on the altar, as if to say, "There but for the grace of God go I."

But even as sacrifice allows us to encounter human finitude, it also draws us near to infinity. The *korban* allows for transformation: the offering and the lifting up of the merely material into the spiritual. From the most base and mundane parts of existence, one brings a gift that finds its way to God.

It also connects us to another form of life. Judaism clearly embraces a hierarchy of life—it places animal existence below the human plane. But it demands a reverence for that life, as expressed by the way the laws of ritual slaughter (*sh'chitah*, pronounced sh'-khee-TAH, or, commonly, sh'-KHEE-tah), First, *sh'chitah* requires a blessing; second, it demands skill in using a specially sharpened blade that limits suffering because the animal dies instantly, without so much as an unnecessary nick in the neck.

Finally, pedagogically speaking, sacrifice enhances the sacrificer's dedication to others. Sacrifice is counter-egocentric—one offers up and gives. Eventually one is supposed to be able to give willingly in a wider and deeper sense. Sacrifice becomes a template for how life is to be lived.

Of course sacrifices are worse than useless if they are considered a magic-like way of "bribing" God. The prophets properly railed against such dishonesty and conceit. Understanding that tendency, the Rabbis responded to the demise of the sacrificial system by deepening Torah study, expanding the realm of the ethical, describing the home and table as the new altar, and seeing human interiority as a place of sacrifice. They reinterpreted the verse *zove'ach todah y'khabdan'ni*, "One who offers up the thanksgiving sacrifice honors Me [God]" (Ps. 50:23), to mean, "If you sacrifice your inner [evil] desire and confess upon the sacrifice, you honor Me" (San. 43b). They saw the sacrificial model as the ethical basis for communal life, intellectual honesty, and complete and full personal morality. Toward that end, they retained verbal evocation of sacrifice in the glorious and joyous *Musaf Amidah*. Such is the way of Halakhah: the preservation of a core facticity of observance, which, upon expansion and deepening, provides blessings.

———◆———

L. HOFFMAN (HISTORY)

Misinai NiTStavu P'olekha K'ra'u'i, add to the acrostic by providing the combination *M[em][.N[un].TS[adi].P[eh].K[uf]*—the letters in the Hebrew alphabet that are shaped differently when they occur as a word's final letter. Not only every letter, but every shape of every letter is represented.

Nowadays both Sefardi and Ashkenazi rites have *Tikanta Shabbat*, but classical observers of the Sefardi service (like twelfth-century Maimonides and fourteenth-century David Abudarham) said instead just, "You taught Moses on Mount Sinai the commandment of keeping and remembering Shabbat, and on it, You commanded us to offer the *musaf* sacrifice, as appropriate."

3–4 "An additional [musaf] offering on it [Shabbat] … bring us back up to our land in joy" The hope for a restoration of the sacrificial system is intrinsically connected to the further idea of an ultimate return to the Land of Israel. Newly emancipated nineteenth-century Jews objected to both notions. In 1812, the year Prussian Jews were freed from their pariah status, one of its leaders, David Friedlander, expressed the concern clearly:

"As long as the Jews were actually persecuted," he maintained, "and told that they were only tolerated and that they really belonged in Palestine, so long was there neither cause nor reason to change the contents and language of the prayers." But now, with emancipation, Jews should pray for "success for my king, for my fellow citizens, for myself and for my family—and not for the return to Jerusalem nor for the restoration of the Temple and the sacrifices." Even modern Orthodox leader Samson Raphael Hirsch no longer preached a return from "exile," except at the end of days, perhaps, when the messianic coming would change all the rules, including those associated with modern nationalism and its citizenship obligations. Unlike Reform rabbis, Hirsch could not change the prayer book, but he also did not have to worry about praying in the vernacular—the normative Reform model, in which congregants discovered (to their horror) what they were saying and objected to it.

Modern Jews who advocate *aliyah* (migration to Israel) face the problem of disentangling the twin notions of restoration of sacrifices on one hand and the return of world Jewry on the other. They reject the former, but (at least, in large part) advocate the latter. Those who question the latter as well (since they, personally, do not yearn for a return) want at least to *support* and even *encourage aliyah*, without, however, *advocating* it, and they confront the same difficulty with this passage. Both groups are likely to reject the medieval notion that diaspora Jews are in "exile," and they by no means associate a return to Zion with a parallel return to sacrifice.

⁵ *"The offerings that are our obligation* [korb'not chovoteinu]" The liturgical inclusion of the biblical citations that demand sacrifices *(korbanot)* are themselves called *korbanot*. Some prominent medieval authorities (most notably Maimonides) objected to them, but they remain nonetheless.

———◆———

J. HOFFMAN (TRANSLATION)

ram. The "perfect" attribution may indicate "uncastrated," in which case the animal would be called in English a "heeder." (A castrated male lamb is a "wether lamb.") The translation of animal terms is always a problem because the ancients were so much more familiar with animals than we are. To a modern reader, the immediate images of a "male lamb" and a "female lamb" are probably identical.

⁸ *"Olah"* Another kind of sacrifice, literally, "rising," and commonly translated "burnt offering."

⁹ *"Seventh day"* See "Seventh day," p. 118.

⁹ *"In memory"* See "In memory," p. 118.

———◆ ◆ ◆———

III. K'DUSHAT HAYOM ("SANCTIFICATION OF THE DAY") IF SHABBAT FALLS ON ROSH CHODESH (THE NEW MOON)

[1] You created your world long ago. You finished your work on the seventh day. You loved us and favored us, and exalted us beyond all the other nations, and You sanctified us with your commandments and drew us near to your service, our King, and You called us by your great and holy name, [2] and, Adonai our God, in love You gave us Sabbaths for rest and New Months for atonement. [3] And as we have sinned before You, we and our ancestors, our city was destroyed, and our Temple laid waste, and our wealth departed and the house of our lives is left without glory, and we cannot fulfill our obligations in the house of your choosing, in the great and holy house that bears your name, because of the hand turned against your Temple.

[4] Adonai our God and our ancestors' God, may You find it favorable to bring us back up to our land in joy, and plant us within our borders. [5] There we will offer before You the offerings that are our obligation, the *tamid* offerings in the right order and the *musaf* offerings in the right way. [6] And we will perform and offer this Shabbat's *musafs* before You in love, in accordance with your will and your commandment, as You wrote about us in your Torah, transcribed by Moses your servant and dictated by your very self:

[7] On the day of Shabbat, two perfect year-old lambs, two-tenths of a measure of choice flour, a meal-offering mixed with oil, and its libation. [8] The Shabbat *olah* every Shabbat, and its libation on top of the *olah*.

[9] And on the New Months offer an *olah* to

אַ[1] תָּה יָצַרְתָּ עוֹלָמְךָ מִקֶּדֶם; כִּלִּיתָ מְלַאכְתְּךָ בַּיּוֹם הַשְּׁבִיעִי. אָהַבְתָּ אוֹתָנוּ וְרָצִיתָ בָּנוּ, וְרוֹמַמְתָּנוּ מִכָּל הַלְּשׁוֹנוֹת, וְקִדַּשְׁתָּנוּ בְּמִצְוֹתֶיךָ, וְקֵרַבְתָּנוּ מַלְכֵּנוּ לַעֲבוֹדָתֶךָ, וְשִׁמְךָ הַגָּדוֹל וְהַקָּדוֹשׁ עָלֵינוּ קָרָאתָ: [2]וַתִּתֶּן־ לָנוּ, יְיָ אֱלֹהֵינוּ, בְּאַהֲבָה, שַׁבָּתוֹת לִמְנוּחָה וְרָאשֵׁי חֳדָשִׁים לְכַפָּרָה. [3]וּלְפִי שֶׁחָטָאנוּ לְפָנֶיךָ, אֲנַחְנוּ וַאֲבוֹתֵינוּ, חָרְבָה עִירֵנוּ, וְשָׁמֵם בֵּית מִקְדָּשֵׁנוּ, וְגָלָה יְקָרֵנוּ, וְנִטַּל כָּבוֹד מִבֵּית חַיֵּינוּ, וְאֵין אֲנַחְנוּ יְכוֹלִים לַעֲשׂוֹת חוֹבוֹתֵינוּ בְּבֵית בְּחִירָתֶךָ, בַּבַּיִת הַגָּדוֹל וְהַקָּדוֹשׁ שֶׁנִּקְרָא שִׁמְךָ עָלָיו, מִפְּנֵי הַיָּד שֶׁנִּשְׁתַּלְּחָה בְּמִקְדָּשֶׁךָ.

[4]יְהִי רָצוֹן מִלְּפָנֶיךָ, יְיָ אֱלֹהֵינוּ וֵאלֹהֵי אֲבוֹתֵינוּ, שֶׁתַּעֲלֵנוּ בְשִׂמְחָה לְאַרְצֵנוּ, וְתִטָּעֵנוּ בִּגְבוּלֵנוּ; [5]וְשָׁם נַעֲשֶׂה לְפָנֶיךָ, אֶת קָרְבְּנוֹת חוֹבוֹתֵינוּ, תְּמִידִים כְּסִדְרָם וּמוּסָפִים כְּהִלְכָתָם. [6]וְאֶת מוּסְפֵי יוֹם הַשַּׁבָּת הַזֶּה וְיוֹם רֹאשׁ הַחֹדֶשׁ הַזֶּה נַעֲשֶׂה וְנַקְרִיב לְפָנֶיךָ, בְּאַהֲבָה, כְּמִצְוַת רְצוֹנֶךָ, כְּמוֹ שֶׁכָּתַבְתָּ עָלֵינוּ בְּתוֹרָתֶךָ, עַל יְדֵי מֹשֶׁה עַבְדֶּךָ, מִפִּי כְבוֹדֶךָ, כָּאָמוּר:

Adonai, two young bulls, one ram and seven perfect year-old lambs.

10 Their meal-offering and their libations are as recorded: Three-tenths per bull, and two-tenths per ram, and one-tenth per lamb, and wine for its libation, and a goat for atonement, and two *tamid* offerings as usual.

7וּבְיוֹם הַשַּׁבָּת, שְׁנֵי כְבָשִׂים בְּנֵי שָׁנָה תְּמִימִם: וּשְׁנֵי עֶשְׂרֹנִים סְלֶת, מִנְחָה בְּלוּלָה בַשֶּׁמֶן, וְנִסְכּוֹ. 8עֹלַת שַׁבַּת בְּשַׁבַּתּוֹ, עַל עֹלַת הַתָּמִיד וְנִסְכָּהּ.

9וּבְרָאשֵׁי חָדְשֵׁיכֶם תַּקְרִיבוּ עֹלָה לַיְיָ: פָּרִים בְּנֵי בָקָר שְׁנַיִם, וְאַיִל אֶחָד, כְּבָשִׂים בְּנֵי שָׁנָה שִׁבְעָה, תְּמִימִם.

10וּמִנְחָתָם וְנִסְכֵּיהֶם, כִּמְדֻבָּר: שְׁלֹשָׁה עֶשְׂרֹנִים לַפָּר, וּשְׁנֵי עֶשְׂרֹנִים לָאַיִל, וְעִשָּׂרוֹן לַכֶּבֶשׂ. וְיַיִן כְּנִסְכּוֹ, וְשָׂעִיר לְכַפֵּר, וּשְׁנֵי תְמִידִים כְּהִלְכָתָם.

BRETTLER (BIBLE)

[2] *"New Months"* The new moon that marked the arrival of a new month was a significant festival in biblical Israel. It is often mentioned together with Shabbat. Amos 8:5 accuses everyday Israelites of wishing, "If only the New Moon were over, so that we could sell grain; the Sabbath, so that we could offer wheat for sale, using an *ephah* that is too small, and a shekel that is too big, tilting a dishonest scale." Apparently, no less than Shabbat, work was prohibited on the New Moon (even though no Torah text actually says this).

[2] *"For atonement"* The idea of the New Moon offering atonement has no biblical basis; for the Rabbis, however, it was imagined as a mini–Rosh *(p. 151)*

DORFF (THEOLOGY)

[2] *"New Months for atonement"* The New Moon is considered a mini–Rosh Hashanah, with creation renewed through the reappearance of the moon. It is an opportunity to renew our lives through atonement and making a new beginning. *(p. 151)*

ELLENSON (MODERN LITURGIES)

[1] *"You loved us and favored us, and exalted us beyond all the other nations"* Abraham Geiger would not retain this phrase, but here in America, Isaac Mayer Wise did. Clearly, nineteenth-century Reform leaders were not agreed on this important point. *(p. 152)*

FRANKEL (A WOMAN'S VOICE)

[3] *"As we have sinned before You"* Like the "Blessing of the New Moon" recited near the end of the Torah Service the week prior to the new month (see Volume 4, *Seder K'riat Hatorah [The Torah Service]*, p. 169), this special section of the *Amidah* recited on the actual Sabbath of the New Moon touches on the themes of sin and redemption. We confess our collective sins that have led to destruction and exile, and appeal to God to restore us to favor. *(p. 152)*

III. *K'DUSHAT HAYOM* ("SANCTIFICATION OF THE DAY") IF SHABBAT FALLS ON ROSH CHODESH (THE NEW MOON)

[1] You created your world long ago. You finished your work on the seventh day. You loved us and favored us, and exalted us beyond all the other nations, and You sanctified us with your commandments and drew us near to your service, our King, and You called us by your great and holy name, [2] and, Adonai our God, in love You gave us Sabbaths for rest and

GRAY (OUR TALMUDIC HERITAGE)

Rosh Chodesh K'dushat Hayom Here we have nothing less than a theological mini-review, from the classic rabbinic perspective, of past and future sacred history: (1) creation (v. 1); and in the same verse, (2) God's love for and election of Israel; then (3) God's gracing of Israel with *Shabbatot* and *Roshei Chodashim* (v. 2); (4) Israel's sin, the destruction of the Temple, and the attendant inability to offer the proper requisite sacrifices (v. 3); instead we can offer (5) prayer for restoration *(p. 153)*

KUSHNER & POLEN (CHASIDISM)

[2] *"Sabbaths for rest and New Months for atonement"* The solar (or Gregorian) calendar has a year of 365¼ days. The lunar calendar (or Hebrew) has a year of about 354 days (twelve lunar months, each approximately 29½ days). Instead of a leap year every four years, it requires the addition of a leap month (Adar Sheni) seven years out of every nineteen-year cycle. The reason Jewish holidays fall "differently" every year in our English "solar" calendar is that they are reckoned by (Jewish) lunar months

אַתָּה יָצַרְתָּ עוֹלָמְךָ מִקֶּדֶם: כִּלִּיתָ מְלַאכְתְּךָ בַּיּוֹם הַשְּׁבִיעִי. אָהַבְתָּ אוֹתָנוּ וְרָצִיתָ בָּנוּ, וְרוֹמַמְתָּנוּ מִכָּל הַלְּשׁוֹנוֹת, וְקִדַּשְׁתָּנוּ בְּמִצְוֹתֶיךָ, וְקֵרַבְתָּנוּ מַלְכֵּנוּ לַעֲבוֹדָתֶךָ, וְשִׁמְךָ הַגָּדוֹל וְהַקָּדוֹשׁ עָלֵינוּ קָרָאתָ: [2]וַתִּתֶּן־לָנוּ, יְיָ אֱלֹהֵינוּ, בְּאַהֲבָה, שַׁבָּתוֹת לִמְנוּחָה

within a (secular) solar year. The lunar and solar cycles realign every nineteen years, however, at which time we start all over again.

So Jewish holidays are reckoned by their place in the lunar months. But Shabbat is different! It is exclusively a solar calendrical event. The setting of its time has nothing whatsoever to do with the moon: you count six sunsets, and the seventh is Shabbat.

Shabbat Rosh Chodesh (when the Sabbath coincides with the appearance of the new moon) occurs on *(p. 153)*

L. HOFFMAN (HISTORY)

AS WITH THE MORNING AMIDAH, THE THIRTEEN MIDDLE BENEDICTIONS ARE REPLACED BY THE K'DUSHAT HAYOM, ("SANCTIFICATION OF THE DAY"), A SINGLE BLESSING THAT DECLARES THE SANCTITY OF HOLY TIME. WHEN SHABBAT FALLS ON ROSH CHODESH (THE NEW MOON) THE LITURGY CELEBRATES BOTH OCCASIONS WITH A UNIQUE FORM OF THE K'DUSHAT HAYOM. FOR THE USUAL MUSAF BENEDICTION, SEE P. 132–133. FOR THE SHACHARIT VERSION, SEE P. 105.

[3] *"The hand turned against your Temple [hayad shenishtalchah b'mikdashekha]"* The late Jakob J. Petuchowski pointed out that the *Musaf* version of the *(p. 153)*

J. HOFFMAN (TRANSLATION)

[1] *"Long ago"* The Hebrew word *kedem* denoted "long ago" in time, but "the east" in space—in particular, the place where the Garden of Eden was located. See Volume 8, *Kabbalat Shabbat*, p. 136.

[1] *"All the other"* Literally, just "all."

[1] *"Nations"* Literally, "tongues," clearly used metonymically.

[2] *"New Months"* That is, the first of the month, akin to "New Year" for the first day of the year. Some prefer to call this the "New Moon."

[3] *"Laid waste"* Following Birnbaum.

[3] *"Wealth [y'kareinu, from (p. 154)*

New Months for atonement. ³And as we have sinned before You, we and our ancestors, our city was destroyed, and our Temple laid waste, and our wealth departed and the house of our lives is left without glory, and we cannot fulfill our obligations in the house of your choosing, in the great and holy house that bears your name, because of the hand turned against your Temple.

⁴Adonai our God and our ancestors' God, may You find it favorable to bring us back up to our land in joy, and plant us within our borders. ⁵There we will offer before You the offerings that are our obligation, the *tamid* offerings in the right order and the *musaf* offerings in the right way. ⁶And we will perform and offer this Shabbat's *musafs* before You in love, in accordance with your will and your commandment, as You wrote about us in your Torah, transcribed by Moses your servant and dictated by your very self:

⁷On the day of Shabbat, two perfect year-old lambs, two-tenths of a measure of choice flour, a meal-offering mixed with oil, and its libation. ⁸The Shabbat *olah* every Shabbat, and its libation on top of the *olah*.

⁹And on the New Months offer an *olah* to Adonai, two young bulls, one ram and seven perfect year-old lambs.

¹⁰Their meal-offering and their libations are as recorded: Three-

וְרָאשֵׁי חֳדָשִׁים לְכַפָּרָה. ³וּלְפִי שֶׁחָטָאנוּ לְפָנֶיךָ, אֲנַחְנוּ וַאֲבוֹתֵינוּ, חָרְבָה עִירֵנוּ, וְשָׁמֵם בֵּית מִקְדָּשֵׁנוּ, וְגָלָה יְקָרֵנוּ, וְנֻטַּל כָּבוֹד מִבֵּית חַיֵּינוּ, וְאֵין אֲנַחְנוּ יְכוֹלִים לַעֲשׂוֹת חוֹבוֹתֵינוּ בְּבֵית בְּחִירָתֶךָ, בַּבַּיִת הַגָּדוֹל וְהַקָּדוֹשׁ שֶׁנִּקְרָא שִׁמְךָ עָלָיו, מִפְּנֵי הַיָּד שֶׁנִּשְׁתַּלְּחָה בְּמִקְדָּשֶׁךָ.

⁴יְהִי רָצוֹן מִלְּפָנֶיךָ, יְיָ אֱלֹהֵינוּ וֵאלֹהֵי אֲבוֹתֵינוּ, שֶׁתַּעֲלֵנוּ בְשִׂמְחָה לְאַרְצֵנוּ, וְתִטָּעֵנוּ בִּגְבוּלֵנוּ; ⁵וְשָׁם נַעֲשֶׂה לְפָנֶיךָ, אֶת קָרְבְּנוֹת חוֹבוֹתֵינוּ, תְּמִידִים כְּסִדְרָם וּמוּסָפִים כְּהִלְכָתָם. ⁶וְאֶת מוּסְפֵי יוֹם הַשַּׁבָּת הַזֶּה וְיוֹם רֹאשׁ הַחֹדֶשׁ הַזֶּה נַעֲשֶׂה וְנַקְרִיב לְפָנֶיךָ, בְּאַהֲבָה, כְּמִצְוַת רְצוֹנֶךָ, כְּמוֹ שֶׁכָּתַבְתָּ עָלֵינוּ בְּתוֹרָתֶךָ, עַל יְדֵי מֹשֶׁה עַבְדֶּךָ, מִפִּי כְבוֹדֶךָ, כָּאָמוּר:

⁷וּבְיוֹם הַשַּׁבָּת, שְׁנֵי כְבָשִׂים בְּנֵי שָׁנָה תְמִימִם; וּשְׁנֵי עֶשְׂרֹנִים סֹלֶת, מִנְחָה בְּלוּלָה בַשֶּׁמֶן, וְנִסְכּוֹ. ⁸עֹלַת שַׁבַּת בְּשַׁבַּתּוֹ, עַל עֹלַת הַתָּמִיד וְנִסְכָּהּ.

⁹וּבְרָאשֵׁי חָדְשֵׁיכֶם תַּקְרִיבוּ עֹלָה לַיְיָ: פָּרִים בְּנֵי בָקָר שְׁנַיִם, וְאַיִל אֶחָד, כְּבָשִׂים בְּנֵי שָׁנָה שִׁבְעָה, תְּמִימִם.

¹⁰וּמִנְחָתָם וְנִסְכֵּיהֶם, כִּמְדֻבָּר: שְׁלֹשָׁה עֶשְׂרֹנִים לַפָּר, וּשְׁנֵי עֶשְׂרֹנִים לָאַיִל, וְעִשָּׂרוֹן לַכֶּבֶשׂ, וְיַיִן כְּנִסְכּוֹ, וְשָׂעִיר לְכַפֵּר, וּשְׁנֵי תְמִידִים כְּהִלְכָתָם.

tenths per bull, and two-tenths per ram, and one-tenth per lamb, and wine for its libation, and a goat for atonement, and two *tamid* offerings as usual.

BRETTLER (BIBLE)

Hashanah and Yom Kippur.

[3] *"As we have sinned"* Following the standard, but not the only, biblical view that destruction is the result of sin (e.g., Lam. 1); a smaller number of texts suggest that it results from irrational divine anger (e.g., Lam. 2).

[9] *"On the New Months offer"* These offerings are enumerated in Numbers 28:11–15. Given that the New Moon was less frequent than Shabbat, it is not surprising that its offerings were more extensive.

———◆———

DORFF (THEOLOGY)

[3] *"And as we have sinned before You, we and our ancestors, our city was destroyed, and our Temple laid waste"* As in *Musaf* for the Festivals, we find here the doctrine that our sins caused the destruction of the two Temples, the end of Jewish sovereignty in Israel, and subsequent exile and dispersion—an idea going back to Jeremiah. In the ancient world, the fall of a temple meant that its god was too weak to defend it. Jeremiah (chap. 7) claims that God Himself destroyed the Temple in response to Israel's sins. Ultimately, though, God will bring the people back to Israel, as the Torah (Lev. 26:44–45) and Second Isaiah (Isa. 40ff.) promise.

That explanation fit the First Temple's destruction in 586 B.C.E.—indeed, the prophets had predicted it—but the reasons behind the fall of the Second Temple in 70 C.E. were less clear. The Rabbis claim that idolatry had ceased among Jews by that time (Song of Songs Rab. 7:8; Yoma 69b). Unable to attribute idolatry to the Jews of their time, the Rabbis cited two other sins: baseless hatred *(sin'at chinam)* of some Jews toward others (Yoma 9b) and the failure to act morally beyond the letter of the law (B.M. 30b, 88a). (See my commentary in Volume 6, *Tachanun and Concluding Prayers,* pp. 40, 48–50.)

Conservative, Reform, and Reconstructionist Jews have no trouble praying for a Jewish homeland in Israel. They do not, however, request the restoration of sacrifices (see "May you find it favorable," p. 134), and do not share the traditional liturgy's negative view of the diaspora. To begin with, we now live in modern countries with more favorable conditions than our ancestors faced, when this and similar prayers were written. In addition, much of Jewish creativity occurred in the diaspora—the Babylonian Talmud, for instance, and the work of Maimonides. Jews have certainly suffered in many places and times in the diaspora, with the Holocaust the ultimate example; but if Jewish history teaches us anything, it is that we dare not "put all our eggs in the same basket," even if that basket is our homeland. Minimally, the simple theology expressed here—that living diasporan existence is a result of our sins and that redemption will occur only when we all live in Israel—is doubted greatly by most Jews living outside Israel and even by many who do live there.

Ellenson (Modern Liturgies)

Contemporary North American thinkers differ as well. The founder of Reconstructionism, Mordecai Kaplan, especially, objected to the "chosen people" concept. Rabbi Lawrence Hoffman recollects that when North American Reform rabbis composed their High Holy Day liturgy (*Gates of Repentance*, 1978), the subcommittee charged with the final manuscript was divided on whether to say, in a newly composed reading, "You [God] chose us [Israel]" or "We [Israel] chose You [God]." In the end, the prayer book contains both, one after the other.

[3] *"And as we have sinned before You"* The Israeli Masorti *Va'ani Tefillati* (1998) omits "we." Its editors believe that the contemporary Jewish condition of life on the soil of the State of Israel makes it inappropriate for modern-day Jews to accept the responsibility our ancestors assumed for expulsion from the Land of Israel.

[5] *"There we will offer before You the offerings that are our obligation"* As in the *Musaf K'dushat Hayom* for Shabbat (but not Rosh Chodesh), the North American Conservative *Sim Shalom* (1985) here substitutes, "There our ancestors sacrificed to you [*shesham asu avoteinu l'fanekha et korb'noteihem*]," to convert a hope for sacrifice in the future to a recollection of its existence in the past.

Frankel (A Woman's Voice)

For Jewish women in particular, Rosh Chodesh represents a special occasion. Women's menses mirror the cyclical waxing and waning of the moon. According to the Midrash (*Pirkei D'rabbi Eliezer*, chap. 45), because the Israelite women refused to give Aaron their jewelry to make the golden calf, God rewarded them with *rosh chodesh*, the first day of the new month, as their special holiday. And so for centuries, Rosh Chodesh has been observed as a women's holiday, a time for women to gather together and to refrain from housework, especially spinning, weaving, and sewing, because, according to the eleventh-century commentary of *Rashi*, Israelite women so enthusiastically contributed these skills to the building of the *Mishkan* (Tabernacle). Some Sefardi sources even describe women gathering together to share gossip and coffee (what they shared is not just gossip and coffee, of course, but community). In our own time, Jewish women have renewed and expanded these customs by forming Rosh Chodesh groups, as a sacred time for celebration, study, and fellowship.

———◆———

GRAY (OUR TALMUDIC HERITAGE)

to the Land of Israel, where the appropriate observances will be restored (vv. 4–6). Rabbi Barukh Halevi Epstein glosses the thematic transition from creation (1) to God's love for Israel (2). The Torah's account of creation (alluded to here in the prayer with "You finished your work on the seventh day") ends badly, with Adam and Eve's disobedience and exile from Eden. But despite that difficult beginning, God always loved us and continues to do so *(v'ahavta otanu)*.

———◆———

KUSHNER & POLEN (CHASIDISM)

average only twice a year and represents a rare confluence of both calendars, the solar and the lunar. That is why it is given its own liturgical text.

———◆———

L. HOFFMAN (HISTORY)

middle blessing *(K'dushat Hayom)* presents a particularly bold theological claim. It applies biblical reasoning to explain the Temple's fall. Prophets saw the marauding Babylonians as only the proximate cause of the destruction. Behind the Babylonians was God, who used the Babylonian army to punish Israel. Here, too, with the Second Temple, our prayer does not single out Rome, but God, whose "hand turned against your Temple." The hand in question is both the controlling hand of God and the Roman army that plays the earthly role of doing God's will.

———◆———

J. HOFFMAN (TRANSLATION)

yakar]" Or, perhaps, "glory days," the idea being that our glorious past has left us.

³ *"Departed"* More literally, "was exiled," an interesting choice of words in Hebrew. 1 Samuel 4:22 uses the word in the same sense to describe Israel's losses, but specifically the capture of the ark of the covenant—probably because the author considered the ark to be the forerunner of the Temple. In both cases, the loss is described as an "exile."

We think of exile as our being sent out of our Land. The author seems to think of it simply as separation from our holy source (the ark or the Temple), not just when we leave it behind, but when it, as it were, leaves us behind.

³ *"House of our lives"* Birnbaum: "source of our life." We assume this is poetic imagery deliberately intended in the Hebrew. We therefore translate it literally, so as to remain faithful to the imagery (whatever it may be) in English.

⁴ *"Adonai our God"* For notes on this paragraph and the next, see pp. 135, 145.

¹⁰ *"Recorded"* Literally, "spoken."

¹⁰ *"Goat"* Others, "he-goat." Better would be "male goat" or, more technically, "billy goat" or "buckling." As with lambs (see "Lambs," p. 145), most modern readers don't distinguish between male and female goats.

◆ ◆ ◆

3 Concluding Prayers

A. EIN KELOHEINU ("THERE IS NONE LIKE OUR GOD")

[1] There is none like our God. There is none like our Lord. There is none like our King. There is none like our Redeemer.

[2] Who is like our God? Who is like our Lord? Who is like our King? Who is like our Redeemer?

[3] Let us gratefully acknowledge our God. Let us gratefully acknowledge our Lord. Let us gratefully acknowledge our King. Let us gratefully acknowledge our Redeemer.

[4] Blessed be our God. Blessed be our Lord. Blessed be our King. Blessed be our Redeemer.

[5] You are our God. You are our Lord. You are our King. You are our Redeemer.

[6] You are the One before whom our ancestors offered fragrant incense.

¹אֵין כֵּאלֹהֵֽינוּ, אֵין כַּאדוֹנֵֽינוּ, אֵין כְּמַלְכֵּֽנוּ, אֵין כְּמוֹשִׁיעֵֽנוּ.

²מִי כֵאלֹהֵֽינוּ, מִי כַאדוֹנֵֽינוּ, מִי כְמַלְכֵּֽנוּ, מִי כְמוֹשִׁיעֵֽנוּ.

³נוֹדֶה לֵאלֹהֵֽינוּ, נוֹדֶה לַאדוֹנֵֽינוּ, נוֹדֶה לְמַלְכֵּֽנוּ, נוֹדֶה לְמוֹשִׁיעֵֽנוּ.

⁴בָּרוּךְ אֱלֹהֵֽינוּ, בָּרוּךְ אֲדוֹנֵֽינוּ, בָּרוּךְ מַלְכֵּֽנוּ, בָּרוּךְ מוֹשִׁיעֵֽנוּ.

⁵אַתָּה הוּא אֱלֹהֵֽינוּ, אַתָּה הוּא אֲדוֹנֵֽינוּ, אַתָּה הוּא מַלְכֵּֽנוּ, אַתָּה הוּא מוֹשִׁיעֵֽנוּ.

⁶אַתָּה הוּא שֶׁהִקְטִֽירוּ אֲבוֹתֵֽינוּ לְפָנֶֽיךָ, אֶת קְטֹֽרֶת הַסַּמִּים.

BRETTLER (BIBLE)

[1] *"There is none … [ein keloheinu]"* No biblical composition displays the poetic style of *Ein Keloheinu*. The composition is best divided into three parts:

1. The first two lines, *ein* and *mi*, are a word pair in the Bible.
2. The next two lines, *nodeh* and *barukh*, are a post-biblical word pair.
3. The final two lines open with *Atah hu*. The last line breaks the earlier poetic pattern. In the first four lines, the initial words get longer and longer (one syllable, one syl-

DORFF (THEOLOGY)

[1] *"There is none like our God [ein keloheinu]"* The words of *Ein Keloheinu* seem almost trivial, especially because the same four names for God recur in each line, with just a different modifier (*ein*, *mi*, and so on). The very simplicity of the structure leads us to believe that the substance is also simple. *(p. 158)*

ELLENSON (MODERN LITURGIES)

[6] *"You are the One before whom our ancestors offered fragrant incense [in the Temple]"* This final line is omitted in a number of non-Orthodox prayer books of all denominations. The Reconstructionist *Kol Haneshamah* (1996) succinctly summarizes the

rationale for this deletion when it notes its "nostalgic reference to Temple worship [that] implies a longing for the reinstitution of sacrifices that we do not share." Already in 1965, the Reconstructionist *Sabbath Prayer Book* had omitted it. The liturgy of American Reform (from the 1895/6 *Union Prayer Book* to the 2006 *Mishkan T'filah*) and the (1982) Israeli Reform *(Ha'avodah Shebalev)* also excise this passage, as does the Israeli Masorti *Va'ani Tefillati* (1998).

Interestingly, both the 1965 *(p. 159)*

A. EIN KELOHEINU ("THERE IS NONE LIKE OUR GOD")

[1] There is none like our God. There is none like our Lord. There is none like our King. There is none like our Redeemer.

[2] Who is like our God? Who is like our Lord? Who is like our King? Who is like our Redeemer?

[3] Let us gratefully acknowledge our God. Let us gratefully acknowledge our Lord. Let us gratefully

GRAY (OUR TALMUDIC HERITAGE)

Ein Keloheinu Siddur Rashi and *Machzor Vitry* point out that we recite *ein* ("there is not") 4 times, *mi* ("who") 4 times, and *nodeh* ("we thank") 4 times, for a total of 12. When this number is added to the 7 *b'rachot* of the Shabbat *Amidah*, the total is 19—the number of blessings in the daily *Amidah*. Since on Shabbat we "lose" the recitation of 12 blessings (the middle ones that are not said on Shabbat), these 12 are, as it were, "added back in."

WITH THE SERVICE COMING TO A CLOSE, WE TURN TO THE CONCLUDING PRAYERS. THE USUAL PRAYERS (MOST NOTABLY, ALENU AND KADDISH) ARE AUGMENTED IN SEVERAL WAYS:

1. A well-known song that asserts the oneness of God, *Ein Keloheinu* ("There is none like our God"), included here.
2. A list of Levitical Psalms, the psalms that the Levites sung in the Temple (see p. 162).
3. Lessons on Study and Peace (see pp. 162–163)
4. *Shir Hakavod* ("The Song of Glory") (see p. 177).

(p. 159)

¹אֵין כֵּאלֹהֵינוּ, אֵין כַּאדוֹנֵינוּ, אֵין כְּמַלְכֵּנוּ, אֵין כְּמוֹשִׁיעֵנוּ.

²מִי כֵאלֹהֵינוּ, מִי כַאדוֹנֵינוּ, מִי כְמַלְכֵּנוּ, מִי כְמוֹשִׁיעֵנוּ.

³נוֹדֶה לֵאלֹהֵינוּ, נוֹדֶה לַאדוֹנֵינוּ, נוֹדֶה לְמַלְכֵּנוּ, נוֹדֶה לְמוֹשִׁיעֵנוּ.

J. HOFFMAN (TRANSLATION)

¹ *"None"* Once again (see "Adonai is the most holy," p. 71), we have a choice among "no one," "nothing," and "none." The last option sounds awkward in a way that the Hebrew does not, but it is the only one that approximates the breadth of the Hebrew *ein.*

¹ *"Lord"* Again (see "Master," p. 81), we have a choice between "our lord" and "our Lord." We somewhat arbitrarily chose the latter. See also "King" below.

¹ *"King ... Redeemer"* We capitalize "King" and "Redeemer" to preserve the strong parallel structure among all four phrases in each stanza.

² *"Who is like our God?"* (p. 161)

acknowledge our King. Let us gratefully acknowledge our Redeemer.

⁴Blessed be our God. Blessed be our Lord. Blessed be our King. Blessed be our Redeemer.

⁵You are our God. You are our Lord. You are our King. You are our Redeemer.

⁶You are the One before whom our ancestors offered fragrant incense.

⁴בָּרוּךְ אֱלֹהֵינוּ, בָּרוּךְ אֲדוֹנֵינוּ, בָּרוּךְ מַלְכֵּנוּ, בָּרוּךְ מוֹשִׁיעֵנוּ.

⁵אַתָּה הוּא אֱלֹהֵינוּ, אַתָּה הוּא אֲדוֹנֵינוּ, אַתָּה הוּא מַלְכֵּנוּ, אַתָּה הוּא מוֹשִׁיעֵנוּ.

⁶אַתָּה הוּא שֶׁהִקְטִירוּ אֲבוֹתֵינוּ לְפָנֶיךָ, אֶת קְטֹרֶת הַסַּמִּים.

BRETTLER (BIBLE)

lable, two syllables, two words/three syllables), following the "law of increasing members."

⁶*"Incense"* Incense was an especially important part of the sacrificial service. It served the utilitarian purpose of masking the odors of preparing animals for sacrifice, but was seen also as a valuable offering in and of itself (see Ps. 141:2, "Take my prayer as an offering of incense").

DORFF (THEOLOGY)

For many people, this hymn, often sung to a bouncy tune, means only that the end of the long Shabbat morning service is finally here.

Rashi explains that this prayer is recited only on Shabbats and the Festivals because the *Amidah* on those days consists of seven blessings instead of the normal nineteen of weekdays. The initial letters of the introductory words in the first three stanzas (*ein*, *mi*, and *nodeh*) make up the word *amen*, which we normally say after a blessing. Each of the three letters of *amen* is repeated four times, for a total of twelve, in order to represent enough extra blessings to make up the usual nineteen. (The words beginning the last two stanzas spell out *barukh atah*, "Blessed are You," which also adds blessings for the day.)

Actually *Ein Keloheinu* asserts important themes of Jewish belief appropriate for the end of the service as something we should take away with us. These include: There is no God (Lord, King, Redeemer) but ours, for who could be like Him? Therefore we thank and bless God, as we should, given his exclusive claim to being God (Lord, King, Redeemer).

———◆———

ELLENSON (MODERN LITURGIES)

Reconstructionist *Sabbath Prayer Book* and *Va'ani Tefillati* follow Sefardi tradition in replacing it with Psalm 102:14, "You will surely arise and take pity on Zion, for it is time to be gracious to her; the appointed time has come." Such an addition not only has the merit of strong Jewish liturgical precedent; its manifest content is also very much in accord with a pro-Israel sensibility.

———◆———

L. HOFFMAN (HISTORY)

[1] *"There is none like our God* [ein keloheinu]*" Ein Keloheinu* is a simple poem, composed of five lines, each one divisible into four identical parts except for the last word, which moves progressively from "God" to "Lord" to "King" to "Redeemer."

> There is none like our God ... Lord ... King ... Redeemer.
> Who is like our God ... Lord ... King ... Redeemer?
> Let us gratefully acknowledge our God ... Lord ... King ... Redeemer.
> Blessed be our God ... Lord ... King ... Redeemer.
> You are our God ... Lord ... King ... Redeemer.

The first two lines are out of order. Logically, the poem ought to ask, "Who is like...?" and then answer, "There is none like...." There then follows the commitment to acknowledge this unique God ("Let us gratefully acknowledge") and the acknowledgment itself, in the form of the last two lines, which begin *barukh* ("blessed") and *atah* ("You"), alluding to the standard opening for rabbinic blessings (*Barukh atah* = "Blessed [are] You").

> Who [*mi*] is like ...
> There is none [*ein*] like ...
> Let us [therefore] gratefully acknowledge [*nodeh*] ...
> [That grateful acknowledgement that we give is] Blessed [*barukh*] ...
> Are You [*atah*] ...

The poem first appears in our earliest comprehensive prayer book, *Seder Rav Amram* (c. 860 C.E., Babylonia)—but as a conclusion for the weekday service and in proper logical order. To understand how the order got changed, we need an exercise in "the arithmetic of prayer."

Roughly 200 years after Amram, rabbis raised an issue dependent on a second-century dictum of Rabbi Meir to the effect that everyone should say 100 blessings daily. Meir was probably speaking figuratively—100 was just a round number implying "a lot." But medieval Jews who read him literally struggled to make sure the daily liturgy contained at least 100 blessings. On weekdays that sum was easy to arrive at since the 3 daily recitations of the *Amidah* (*Shacharit, Minchah,* and *Ma'ariv*) alone contain 19 blessings each. On Shabbat, however, the 13 middle petitionary blessings of the *Amidah* are replaced with a single blessing (the *K'dushat Hayom*—see pp. 105–106) announcing the sanctity of the day, thus producing 7, instead of the usual 19, blessings—losing 12 blessings per *Amidah*. The total Shabbat loss would be 36 (12 per *Amidah*; 3 *Amidah* recitations per day).

But the original Palestinian tradition included only 18 (not 19) blessings in this prayer (which was called *Sh'moneh Esreh*, "The Eighteen," after all). Using the original Palestinian count, the net loss was only 11 blessings 3 times a day (11 x 3) for a total shortage of 33.

Medieval rabbis thus turned their attention to making up 33 blessings. The extra *Musaf Amidah* gave them 7. The extra Shabbat meal (*s'udah sh'lishit*—see Volume 7, *Shabbat at Home*, pp. 30–36) provided another 6 (the blessing for washing before eating, the blessing over bread [*Motsi*], and the four blessings that make up the Grace after Meals [*Birkat Hamazon*]). That left a deficit of 20. Here, *Ein Keloheinu* came in. Its last two lines *(barukh atah)* suggest that it should count as a blessing. But any given blessing need mention God's name only once, and here we have five lines, each one containing four names of God ("God ... Lord ... King ... Redeemer"), so that each line can be assumed to reflect not just one but four: 5 x 4 = 20!

At this point, people noticed that if they reversed the first two lines, starting with *ein* and then *mi*, and following them with the third line, *nodeh*, they had yet another acrostic. The first letter of each opening word *(alef, mem, nun)* spelled *amen*—precisely the response that blessings evoke. The final acrostic, assumed to apply 20 times, read: *amen barukh atah.*

Finally, as we saw, *Ein Keloheinu* appears in *Seder Rav Amram* but for weekdays. As the prayer became increasingly known as a means to make up missing Shabbat blessings, it tended to be limited to Shabbat. Such is the Ashkenazi (though not the Sefardi) custom to this day, although both Sefardim and Ashkenazim reverse the first two lines to produce the acrostic *amen*.

It is hard to say when or where this arithmetical solution arose. It is but one of many such equations used in medieval times (other comments here reproduce some of the others). The one discussed here already appears in early Ashkenazi and Sefardi sources: *Machzor Vitry* and *Siddur Rashi* (eleventh- to twelfth-century France) and Abudarham (fourteenth-century Spain). So it is relatively early. It is not, however, Babylonian—the pioneering Babylonian Siddur by Rav Amram *(Seder Rav Amram)* still retains the original order of verses. Since the count of missing verses assumes the Palestinian version of the *Amidah*, it may go back to a Palestinian tradition prior to the Crusades.

When Christian armies arrived during the First Crusade, Jews of Eretz Yisrael fled and settled in the diaspora. From there, their custom regarding *Ein Keloheinu* entered the practice of both Ashkenazim and Sefardim.

———◆———

J. HOFFMAN (TRANSLATION)

Frequently we choose to punctuate "who is ..." with an exclamation point (e.g., "who is like you!") because usually in our liturgy *mi* ("who") introduces an exclamation, not a question. But here we do have a question—and an answer (see L. Hoffman, "There is none like our God," p. 159).

◆ ◆ ◆

B. List of Levitical Psalms and Lessons on Study and Peace

I. List of Levitical Psalms

[1] This is the poetry that the Levites used to sing in the Temple:

[2] On Sunday they would sing: The earth and all that fills it—the world and all who dwell there—are Adonai's....

[3] On Monday they would sing: Great is Adonai and highly praised, in our God's city, his holy mountain....

[4] On Tuesday they would sing: God stands in the divine assembly judging among gods....

[5] On Wednesday they would sing: Adonai is a God of vengeance. Appear, O God of vengeance....

[6] On Thursday they would sing: Sing in joy to God, our strength. Sing in celebration to Jacob's God....

[7] On Friday they would sing: Adonai is king, majestically robed, robed is Adonai, girded in strength. The world was made firm, unshakable....

[8] On Shabbat they would sing: A musical psalm for the Sabbath day.... It is a musical psalm for time to come, for the day that is all Shabbat and rest for eternal life.

II. Lessons on Study and Peace

[9] It was taught in the school of Elijah: whoever studies Halakhah every day is guaranteed a place in the world-to-come, for it says: "The world's ways are his." [10] Do not read this word as "ways," but rather as "Halakhah."

שִׁיר שֶׁהָיוּ הַלְוִיִּם אוֹמְרִים בְּבֵית הַמִּקְדָּשׁ. [1]

בַּיּוֹם הָרִאשׁוֹן הָיוּ אוֹמְרִים: לַיְיָ הָאָרֶץ וּמְלוֹאָהּ, תֵּבֵל וְיֹשְׁבֵי בָהּ. [2]

בַּשֵּׁנִי הָיוּ אוֹמְרִים: גָּדוֹל יְיָ וּמְהֻלָּל מְאֹד, בְּעִיר אֱלֹהֵינוּ, הַר קָדְשׁוֹ. [3]

בַּשְּׁלִישִׁי הָיוּ אוֹמְרִים: אֱלֹהִים נִצָּב בַּעֲדַת אֵל, בְּקֶרֶב אֱלֹהִים יִשְׁפֹּט. [4]

בָּרְבִיעִי הָיוּ אוֹמְרִים: אֵל נְקָמוֹת יְיָ, אֵל נְקָמוֹת הוֹפִיעַ. [5]

בַּחֲמִישִׁי הָיוּ אוֹמְרִים: הַרְנִינוּ לֵאלֹהִים עוּזֵּנוּ, הָרִיעוּ לֵאלֹהֵי יַעֲקֹב. [6]

בַּשִּׁשִּׁי הָיוּ אוֹמְרִים: יְיָ מָלָךְ, גֵּאוּת לָבֵשׁ; לָבֵשׁ יְיָ, עֹז הִתְאַזָּר; אַף תִּכּוֹן תֵּבֵל, בַּל תִּמּוֹט. [7]

בַּשַּׁבָּת הָיוּ אוֹמְרִים: מִזְמוֹר שִׁיר לְיוֹם הַשַּׁבָּת. מִזְמוֹר שִׁיר לֶעָתִיד לָבֹא, לְיוֹם שֶׁכֻּלּוֹ שַׁבָּת וּמְנוּחָה, לְחַיֵּי הָעוֹלָמִים. [8]

תָּנָא דְבֵי אֵלִיָּהוּ: כָּל הַשּׁוֹנֶה הֲלָכוֹת בְּכָל יוֹם, מֻבְטָח לוֹ שֶׁהוּא בֶן עוֹלָם הַבָּא, שֶׁנֶּאֱמַר: הֲלִיכוֹת עוֹלָם לוֹ. [10] אַל תִּקְרָא הֲלִיכוֹת אֶלָּא הֲלָכוֹת. [9]

11 Rabbi Elazar said that Rabbi Chanina said: Scholars increase peace in the world, as it is said, "All of your children are disciples of Adonai; great is the peace among your children." 12 Do not read this word as "children" but rather as "builders." 13 Let there be great peace for those who love your Torah; let them know no obstacle. 14 May there be peace within your walls, tranquility in your palaces. 15 For the sake of my fellows and friends, I hope that you find peace. 16 For the sake of the house of Adonai our God, I ask that you know goodness. 17 May Adonai give strength to his people. May Adonai bless his people with peace.

11אָמַר רַבִּי אֶלְעָזָר, אָמַר רַבִּי חֲנִינָא: תַּלְמִידֵי חֲכָמִים מַרְבִּים שָׁלוֹם בָּעוֹלָם, שֶׁנֶּאֱמַר: וְכָל בָּנַיִךְ לִמּוּדֵי יְיָ, וְרַב שָׁלוֹם בָּנָיִךְ. 12אַל תִּקְרָא בָּנַיִךְ, אֶלָּא בּוֹנָיִךְ. 13שָׁלוֹם רָב לְאֹהֲבֵי תוֹרָתֶךְ, וְאֵין לָמוֹ מִכְשׁוֹל. 14יְהִי שָׁלוֹם בְּחֵילֵךְ, שַׁלְוָה בְּאַרְמְנוֹתָיִךְ. 15לְמַעַן אַחַי וְרֵעָי, אֲדַבְּרָה נָּא שָׁלוֹם בָּךְ. 16לְמַעַן בֵּית יְיָ אֱלֹהֵינוּ, אֲבַקְשָׁה טוֹב לָךְ. 17יְיָ עֹז לְעַמּוֹ יִתֵּן, יְיָ יְבָרֵךְ אֶת עַמּוֹ בַשָּׁלוֹם.

BRETTLER (BIBLE)

[1] *"The poetry"* As far as we know, except for festivals and Shabbat, the Temple ritual as described in the Bible was identical each day—there was no special Tuesday or Friday ritual. Of the seven songs found here, only the Sabbath song (Psalm 92) is specifically assigned to its own particular day. A separate psalm for every day is therefore post-biblical, but not altogether unsurprising, since the Dead Sea Scrolls indicate distinct liturgies for each day of the week.

Psalm 93 (which deals with creation) is appropriate for Friday, when creation ended. Psalm 24 (which can be read as describing the beginning of creation) fits Sunday. It is *(p. 167)*

DORFF (THEOLOGY)

[1] *"This is the poetry ... "* This choice of psalms reflects practice from Temple times. The Talmud (R.H. 31a) justifies Psalm 24 for Sunday (day one of a new week) on the grounds of its first line, "The earth and all that fills it—the world and all who dwell there—are Adonai's." *(p. 168)*

ELLENSON (MODERN LITURGIES)

List of Levitical Psalms Associated solely with the Temple cult, and probably considered a meaningless addition that only lengthens the service, this is omitted from all non-Orthodox Siddurim.

[12] *"Do not read this word* *(p. 168)*

FRANKEL (A WOMAN'S VOICE)

[10–12] *"'Halakhah' ... 'builders'"* What wonderful punsters the Rabbis were! Because of Hebrew's remarkable permutability and the customary absence of vowels in the texts that the Rabbis studied, they were able to transform one word into another with the flick of a jot and tittle. In the two *mishnayot* contained in this service—Megillah 28b, which playfully misreads *halikhot* ("ways") as *halakhot* ("laws"); and Berakhot 64a, which similarly misreads *banayikh* ("your *(p. 168)*

I. LIST OF LEVITICAL PSALMS

[1] This is the poetry that the Levites used to sing in the Temple:

[2] On Sunday they would sing: The earth and all that fills it—the world and all who dwell there—are Adonai's....

[3] On Monday they would sing: Great is Adonai and highly praised, in our God's city, his holy mountain....

GRAY (OUR TALMUDIC HERITAGE)

[1] *"This is the poetry [from Mishnah Tamid 7:4]* This final text in tractate Tamid deals with the Temple's daily sacrifices. As the Rabbis saw it (e.g., Ber. 26b), prayer replaced sacrifice so, quite appropriately, we close the *Musaf* service (*Musaf* is especially reminiscent of the sacrificial system) by recalling this final mishnah in the tractate that details the daily Temple offerings.

Typical of rabbinic literature, this report exists in several similar yet different versions: this one *(p. 169)*

KUSHNER & POLEN (CHASIDISM)

[9] "*The world's ways are his* [halikhot olam lo]' [*from Megillah 28b*]" This innocuous phrase from Habbakuk 3:6 is translated in the 1985 Jewish Publication Society's *Tanakh* as, "His [i.e., God's] are the ancient routes." A footnote, however, advises us that the meaning of the Hebrew is uncertain. The old (1917) *JPS* renders the phrase, "His goings are as of old."

The talmudic passage that quotes Habakkuk 3:6—the way the verse is cited here in the prayer   *(p. 172)*

¹הַשִּׁיר שֶׁהָיוּ הַלְוִיִּם אוֹמְרִים בְּבֵית הַמִּקְדָּשׁ.

²בַּיּוֹם הָרִאשׁוֹן הָיוּ אוֹמְרִים: לַיָי הָאָרֶץ וּמְלוֹאָהּ, תֵּבֵל וְיֹשְׁבֵי בָהּ.

³בַּשֵּׁנִי הָיוּ אוֹמְרִים: גָּדוֹל יְיָ וּמְהֻלָּל מְאֹד, בְּעִיר אֱלֹהֵינוּ, הַר קָדְשׁוֹ.

LANDES (HALAKHAH)

[11] "*Scholars increase peace*" Rabbi Abraham Isaac Kook was the signal rabbinic thinker, mystic, and personality of the early twentieth century (1865–1935, Latvia and Land of Israel). He thought long, hard, and creatively regarding Torah study, those who study it, and the place of both within the world. He applied these thoughts to his commentary on *Berakhot, Ayin Ay-ah* (which I cite here). In advance, it should be admitted that translating Rav Kook's   *(p. 173)*

L. HOFFMAN (HISTORY)

THE FIRST OF OUR CONCLUDING PRAYERS INTENDED FOR SHABBAT (EIN KELOHEINU)—*SEE P. 155 IS FOLLOWED BY:*

1. A list of the daily psalms sung by the Levites
2. Rabbinic lessons on study and peace
3. *Shir Hakavod* ("The Song of Glory") (see p. 177).

THE PSALMS WERE SUNG IN THE TEMPLE AS PART OF THE SACRIFICIAL CULT. THE LESSONS ON STUDY AND PEACE SUMMARIZE ESPECIALLY PROMINENT THEMES IN JUDAISM. THEY ARE BOTH CONNECTED TO THE END OF TIME, IN THAT STUDY BRINGS ABOUT THAT FINAL AGE OF PEACE FOR WHICH WE YEARN.

— ◆ —

J. HOFFMAN (TRANSLATION)

[1] "*Poetry*" The "poetry" is all taken from Psalms, which is probably why Birnbaum translates "psalms" here. But the Hebrew is singular when it could have been plural, suggesting that the passages are being considered jointly.

[1] "*Sing*" Or "recite." The Hebrew verb allows both possibilities, while in English we have to choose.

[2] "*Sunday*" Literally, "the first day." The Jewish week starts with Sunday. The Greek translation of some of these psalms in the Septuagint (or LXX, dated from the third century   *(p. 174)*

⁴ On Tuesday they would sing: God stands in the divine assembly judging among gods....

⁵ On Wednesday they would sing: Adonai is a God of vengeance. Appear, O God of vengeance....

⁶ On Thursday they would sing: Sing in joy to God, our strength. Sing in celebration to Jacob's God....

⁷ On Friday they would sing: Adonai is king, majestically robed, robed is Adonai, girded in strength. The world was made firm, unshakable....

⁸ On Shabbat they would sing: A musical psalm for the Sabbath day.... It is a musical psalm for time to come, for the day that is all Shabbat and rest for eternal life.

II. LESSONS ON STUDY AND PEACE

⁹ It was taught in the school of Elijah: whoever studies Halakhah every day is guaranteed a place in the world-to-come, for it says: "The world's ways are his." ¹⁰ Do not read this word as "ways," but rather as "Halakhah."

¹¹ Rabbi Elazar said that Rabbi Chanina said: Scholars increase peace in the world, as it is said, "All of your children are disciples of Adonai; great is the peace among your children." ¹² Do not read this word as "children" but rather as "builders." ¹³ Let there be great peace for those who love your Torah; let them know no obstacle.

בַּשְּׁלִישִׁי הָיוּ אוֹמְרִים: אֱלֹהִים נִצָּב בַּעֲדַת אֵל, בְּקֶרֶב אֱלֹהִים יִשְׁפֹּט. ⁴

בָּרְבִיעִי הָיוּ אוֹמְרִים: אֵל נְקָמוֹת יְיָ, אֵל נְקָמוֹת הוֹפִיעַ. ⁵

בַּחֲמִישִׁי הָיוּ אוֹמְרִים: הַרְנִינוּ לֵאלֹהִים עוּזֵּנוּ, הָרִיעוּ לֵאלֹהֵי יַעֲקֹב. ⁶

בַּשִּׁשִּׁי הָיוּ אוֹמְרִים: יְיָ מָלָךְ, גֵּאוּת לָבֵשׁ: לָבֵשׁ יְיָ, עֹז הִתְאַזָּר; אַף תִּכּוֹן תֵּבֵל, בַּל תִּמּוֹט. ⁷

בַּשַּׁבָּת הָיוּ אוֹמְרִים: מִזְמוֹר שִׁיר לְיוֹם הַשַּׁבָּת. מִזְמוֹר שִׁיר לֶעָתִיד לָבֹא, לְיוֹם שֶׁכֻּלּוֹ שַׁבָּת וּמְנוּחָה, לְחַיֵּי הָעוֹלָמִים. ⁸

תָּנָא דְבֵי אֵלִיָּהוּ: כָּל הַשּׁוֹנֶה הֲלָכוֹת בְּכָל יוֹם, מֻבְטָח לוֹ שֶׁהוּא בֶּן עוֹלָם הַבָּא, שֶׁנֶּאֱמַר: הֲלִיכוֹת עוֹלָם לוֹ. אַל ¹⁰. ⁹ תִּקְרָא הֲלִיכוֹת אֶלָּא הֲלָכוֹת.

אָמַר רַבִּי אֶלְעָזָר, אָמַר רַבִּי חֲנִינָא: ¹¹ תַּלְמִידֵי חֲכָמִים מַרְבִּים שָׁלוֹם בָּעוֹלָם, שֶׁנֶּאֱמַר: וְכָל בָּנַיִךְ לִמּוּדֵי יְיָ, וְרַב שְׁלוֹם בָּנָיִךְ. אַל תִּקְרָא בָּנַיִךְ, אֶלָּא בּוֹנָיִךְ. ¹² שָׁלוֹם רָב לְאֹהֲבֵי תוֹרָתֶךָ, וְאֵין לָמוֹ ¹³ מִכְשׁוֹל. יְהִי שָׁלוֹם בְּחֵילֵךְ, שַׁלְוָה ¹⁴ בְּאַרְמְנוֹתָיִךְ. לְמַעַן אַחַי וְרֵעָי, אֲדַבְּרָה ¹⁵

14 May there be peace within your walls, tranquility in your palaces. 15 For the sake of my fellows and friends, I hope that you find peace. 16 the sake of the house of Adonai our God, I ask that you know goodness. 17 May Adonai give strength to his people. May Adonai bless his people with peace.

נָא שָׁלוֹם בָּךְ. 16 לְמַעַן בֵּית יְיָ אֱלֹהֵינוּ, אֲבַקְשָׁה טוֹב לָךְ. 17 יְיָ עֹז לְעַמּוֹ יִתֵּן, יְיָ יְבָרֵךְ אֶת עַמּוֹ בַשָּׁלוֹם.

BRETTLER (BIBLE)

unknown how and exactly when the other psalms were connected to their respective days (48 for Monday; 82 for Tuesday; 94 for Wednesday; 81 for Thursday).

8 *"The day that is all Shabbat"* Equating Shabbat with the eschaton (the final days)—a post-biblical concept.

9 *"Whoever studies"* Based loosely on Psalm 1 (for example), where Torah study in general rather than specific study of halakhot (a post-biblical word) lengthens life.

12 *"Do not read this word as 'children' [banayikh] but rather as 'builders' [bonayikh]"* The reading *bonayikh* ("your builders") is found in the Dead Sea Scrolls, where, however, it reads without the *vav*. The *vav* is suspended, the way corrections are often written on this scroll.

To create midrashic play on words, the Rabbis often cite scripture by saying, "Do not read [*al tikra*] it as ... but, rather, as ...." But given the correction in Dead Sea Scrolls, it may be that, in some cases, *al tikra* midrashim are actually based on variant textual traditions.

13–15 *"Peace ... peace ... peace"* From Psalms 119:165, 122:7–9, and 29:11, all of which mention "peace" *(shalom)*. They build upwards, starting with the peace that the Torah scholar experiences and ending with shalom for the entire community.

◆

DORFF (THEOLOGY)

As the creator of all, God owns everything. Psalm 92 fits Shabbat because Shabbat is a foretaste of the world-to-come (see "Those who keep Shabbat and who call it a delight will rejoice in your kingdom," p. 138). The Talmud's explanation for the other psalms, however, is forced. Clearly the ancient practice was either arbitrary or its rationale had been forgotten.

[9] *"Guaranteed a place in the world-to-come"* The last sentence of the Mishnah just recited describes Shabbat as a foretaste of the world-to-come. It prompts citation of another source to spell out how we gain a portion in that world—namely, by studying traditional laws each day. It need not be Shabbat for us to taste the joys of the world-to-come. The midrash assures us that we may do so throughout the week by devoting time to study. This teaching is attributed to Elijah, the harbinger of messianic times (see Mal. 3:23–24; M. Sot. 9:15 [end]; and M. Edu. 8:7). The centrality of Elijah is seen liturgically in *Birkat Hamazon* (Grace after Meals); the third benediction after reading the *Haftarah* (see Volume 4, *Seder K'riat Hatorah [The Torah Service]*, p. 144); and the popular song *Eliyahu Hanavi* ("Elijah the Prophet") sung at *Havdalah* (see Volume 7, *Shabbat at Home*, pp. 185–190).

[11] *"Scholars increase peace in the world"* Study of Torah brings peace to this world. Professor Saul Lieberman, arguably the world's greatest talmudist in the middle of the last century, who himself was familiar with jealousy and backbiting among scholars, used to tell us rabbinical students that this was the one joke in the Talmud!

———◆———

ELLENSON (MODERN LITURGIES)

as 'children' but rather as 'builders'" All present-day Conservative prayer books—*Sim Shalom* (1985 and 1998) and *Va'ani Tefillati* (1998)—contain this passage. *Sim Shalom* explains, "This ancient rabbinic lesson emphasizes that our future rests upon our children and their disciples."

———◆———

FRANKEL (A WOMAN'S VOICE)

children") as *bonayikh* ("your builders"), interpreted here as "scholars, the true builders of peace"—the talmudic authors enlist word play in the service of quite serious ends: to prove that traditional study and observance bring the rewards of eternal life and peace.

This kind of "homiletic punning"—that is, playing with words in order to teach ethical and spiritual lessons—is a familiar ploy among the Sages. What was much less familiar to them was the display of such verbal wit by a woman, the only woman in the folios of the Talmud who teaches both ethics and Jewish law. I refer, of course, to Beruriah, the wife of Rabbi Meir, who was renowned for her sharp mind and razor tongue. Here is one of her teachings employing the same form of word play as our two *mishnayot*:

> There were once some thieves in the neighborhood of Rabbi Meir who caused him a great deal of trouble. Rabbi Meir used to pray that they should die. His wife Beruriah said to him: How do you reason [that such a prayer should be permitted]? Is it written, "[Let] *chot'im* (sinners) [cease]"? Is it not written, "Let *chata'im* (sins) cease"? [Indeed] it is written *chata'im* (sins)! And further, look at the end of the verse: "And let the wicked be no more" (Ps. 104:35). When the sins cease, there will be no more wicked people! Therefore, pray for them that they should repent, and [then] "the wicked will be no more." He did pray for them and they repented. (Ber. 10a)

Unlike the authors cited in the *Musaf* liturgy who praise the virtues of scholarship and law as ends in themselves, Beruriah uses learning and legal knowledge to overrule halakhah in the interests of compassion. For without the repentance of sinners, scholars will never know true peace.

———◆———

GRAY (OUR TALMUDIC HERITAGE)

(from the Mishnah); two others (from the Talmud, R.H. 31a), one attributed to Rabbi Yehudah in the name of Rabbi Akiba, and a second attributed to Rabbi Nehemiah; and finally, an anonymous version (from a late midrash, *Avot D'rabbi Natan* 1). These multiple versions remind us of the rich oral culture in which Jewish thought circulated. Scholarly circles transmitted versions similar enough to testify to a common origin, but differentiated according to contending views on ideology, theology, or, sometimes, just the vagaries of memory.

The Siddur version (taken from the Mishnah) simply matches the days of the week and the psalms the Levites recited, breaking this pattern only to comment on the psalm for Shabbat. (For other versions, see R.H. 31a and *Avot D'rabbi Natan*.)

Psalm 24, for Sunday (the first day of the week), begins, "The earth and all that fills it—the world and all who dwell there—are Adonai's." It fits the day when God began creating a world, thereby becoming its owner.

Psalm 48 ("Great is Adonai and highly praised"), the psalm for Monday, paints the picture of God dwelling on high, distinct from the world below. This calls to mind the second day of creation, when God divided the waters of the upper firmament from the lower waters on earth.

Psalm 82 ("God stands in the divine assembly") is the appropriate psalm for Tuesday, when dry land, necessary for human habitation, God's "assembly," appeared. *Rambam* (Maimonides, Spain and Egypt, 1135/8–1204) offers a different explanation however: since the latter part of verse 1 of the psalm refers to God's judgment, the

Levites recited it on Tuesday, when dry land appeared and a system of justice had a place to be established.

Psalm 94 ("Adonai is a God of vengeance. Appear, O God of vengeance") on Wednesday alludes to the creation of the sun, moon, and stars and the punishment God will eventually mete out to pagans who worship those heavenly bodies.

Psalm 81 ("Sing in joy to God, our strength") acknowledges the fifth-day creation of birds and fish, who (like us humans) are said to praise God (*Avot D'rabbi Natan*). What an idea: *all* life forms respond as best they can to God's love in creating them. The Talmud is more ambiguous, however, saying simply that the creation of these creatures on the fifth day is "to praise God." It remains unclear whether the animals themselves praise God (as in *Avot D'rabbi Natan*) or whether human beings praise God for the creation of these animals. *Rashi* explains the Talmud in the latter sense. He says that when human beings see the wide variety of species, they will offer praise to the single God who created biodiversity. *Rambam* (the scientist, after all) takes this notion further: when humans observe the varieties inherent in such things as the animals' modes of locomotion and ways of handling the environment, they will praise God for creativity.

Psalm 93 refers to God as "king" (*melekh*) so is appropriate for Friday, when the active work of creation was finished and God began to reign as universal divine monarch. Again, *Rambam* goes deeper, adding the idea that humanity is the sole species that "understands the exaltedness of God." Since human beings were created on the sixth day, the Levites recited a psalm celebrating the way in which a discerning humanity makes God king.

Finally we come to the psalm for Shabbat, Psalm 92 ("A musical psalm for the Sabbath day"). Mishnah Tamid 7:4 sees here not just any Shabbat, but the final Shabbat of history; and not just a single day of the week, but the "coming future" that "is all Shabbat" and when the entire world may finally rest. *Avot D'rabbi Natan* describes it as a time in which there is neither eating nor drinking, nor physical pleasures: only the righteous sitting with crowns on their heads, basking in the divine presence.

⁹ "*Whoever studies* [*from Megillah 28b*]" This teaching attributed to *Tanna D'vei Eliyahu* also appears in the Talmud (Nid. 73a)—the last words of that tractate, and the final lesson of the Babylonian Talmud as a whole. Our medieval commentary Tosafot (Ber. 31a) naturally wonders at the choice of this particular teaching to end the Talmud, a question complicated by the fact that certain manuscripts of the Talmud omit it entirely! Tosafot affirms its right to be there: it comes at the end to affirm the spiritual value of learning Jewish law and to finish our most elaborate literary work on an upbeat note, as the prophets had, when they ended their teachings "with words of praise and comfort." This teaching's placement as a "sign-off" to the Talmud may well be part of why it appears as a "sign-off" to our service, which thus also ends "with words of praise and comfort."

As to the teaching itself, *Tanna D'vei Eliyahu* states that whoever recites (*shoneh*, from the same root as Mishnah) halakhot every day is guaranteed a place in the world-to-come. *Rashi* defines the halakhot as only the Mishnah and the "laws to Moses from Sinai," a subset of classical Jewish law that is so extremely limited that it excludes most of the Talmud (let alone post-talmudic Jewish law). Why would *Rashi* limit the term in this way? Part of the reason is undoubtedly *Rashi's* awareness of the limited range of meanings that the words *halakhah* and *halakhot* had in the talmudic period. At that time, these words tended to denote relatively short, declarative statements of decided law with which no one disagreed (unless they could quote yet other similar statements of decided law). As an example of such "decided law" *(halakhah p'sukah)*, the Talmud (Ber. 31a) provides a simply stated legal formulation pertaining to Jewish women's alleged decision to be stringent in their observance of the laws of menstruation.

Apropos of this point, Maharsha (Rabbi Samuel Edels, Poland, 1555–1631) cites *Pirkei Avot* 3:18, where the laws of menstruation are classified as "essential halakhot" *(gufei halakhot)*. *Rashi* comments there that the laws of the menstruant should be studied with extreme care *because of the intellectual and spiritual depth they contain.* *Tanna D'vei Eliyahu* is telling us that "whoever recites halakhot," referring in part to these "essential halakhot" of menstruation, is guaranteed a place in the world-to-come because of the religious insights that such study will yield.

Tanna D'vei Eliyahu's teaching is based on a creative misreading of Habakkuk 3:6, *halikhot* ("ways," based on the root meaning of *h.l.kh*, to "walk" or "go") as *halakhot*, "laws." The beginning of the verse reads, "[God] saw and uprooted [*vayater*] the nations." The Rabbis interpreted *vayater* as *mutar*, a similar-sounding word, meaning "permitted"—as if to say, "God permitted the nations...." The interpretation pictures God looking out on the world and seeing its inhabitants not living up to the standards of the seven universal laws of civilization called the Noahide laws, and then declaring these basic laws invalid, presumably so that the nations can escape punishment.

Other Rabbis found this notion outrageous: how could God reward law breaking by suspending the laws?! Rather, the verse must mean that the laws are "suspended" to the extent that those who obey them receive a lesser reward than they otherwise would have (A.Z. 2b–3a). It follows that *Tanna D'vei Eliyahu* is teaching the following: unlike the Jewish People, other nations of the world have had an indifferent relationship to their covenant with God (the Noahide laws). As to us, however, *halikhot olam lo*, "the eternal laws" (reading *halikhot* as *halakhot*) are with us (the *lo*, meaning "to him" in the verse being taken as a reference to the Jewish people). By reciting this teaching attributed to *Tanna D'vei Eliyahu* at the end of services daily, we are guaranteed a share in the world-to-come.

[11] *"Scholars increase peace [from Berakhot 64a]"* This very passage, or at least portions of it, concludes a number of talmudic tractates (see Volume 8, *Kabbalat Shabbat*, pp. 165–166). Rabbi Barukh Halevi Epstein offers an interesting and original explanation for this. Someone who studies much Talmud may conclude, upon completing a new tractate, that the Rabbis are simply all about arguing: Rabbi X says this and Rabbi Y says that, the point being simply to amplify disagreement. So we conclude talmudic tractates with the guarantee that Torah scholars (and their arguments) actually increase

peace in the world: their intense disagreements are not ends in themselves, but efforts to arrive at whatever truth humans are capable of. By means of these intense struggles for truth, we, who follow the Rabbis, will be better able to establish justice, righteousness, and (someday) universal peace.

———◆———

KUSHNER & POLEN (CHASIDISM)

book—is fascinated with a pun on the word *halikhot*. While the word seems to have the superficial meaning of "walking, ways, goings, routes," it also sounds very much like *halakhot*, our religious "laws." So now our verse speaks not of God, but of the religious behavior of people and, by implication, of an instructive and fundamental difference between prophetic and rabbinic encounters with God.

For the prophets, God was encountered directly, personally, and therefore unequivocally. The prophetic message is one of apocalyptic certainty. They say, "Thus says Adonai"—a phrase never uttered by subsequent rabbinic teachers. For the Rabbis, the source of religious illumination is less apodictic. For them, the mechanism for attaining religious truth is not an encounter with the divine but sustained questioning and argumentation. This kind of truth is painstakingly distilled, one drop at a time. To put it another way, deprived of the direct experience of God's will, the Rabbis resort to intellect. This same theme is echoed by the great twentieth-century scholar and mystical poet Rabbi Abraham Isaac Hakohen Kook (1865–1935), the first Ashkenazi chief rabbi of Israel.

In his essay "The Sage Is More Important than the Prophet," Kook teaches: "And what prophecy [through its direct perception of the divine] ... could not accomplish ... was accomplished by the sages [Rabbis] through the expanded development of the Torah, by raising many disciples and by the assiduous study of the particular laws and their derivative applications." Kook read our verse (Habbakuk 3:6) as, "The eternal paths lead to Him," and concluded, "'Paths,' *halikhot*, may also be read as *halakhot*, and the text would then mean that the laws lead to Him (Nid. 73a)" (*Abraham Isaac Kook*, trans. Ben Zion Bokser [New York: Paulist Press, 1978], p. 254).

Rav Kook thus teaches that the attempts of us non-prophets to comprehend prophetically only leads to apocalyptic errors. Instead, we who inherit the rabbinic tradition must rely upon the often punctilious, often tedious and incremental, interpretation of Jewish laws *(halakhot)*. Indeed, for us, the only way we can heal creation comes one tiny bit at a time. God showed the prophets his *halikhot*, God's eternal ways. We must rely instead upon the *halakhot*, the minutiae of legal detail.

[12] *"Do not read not this word as 'children' [banayikh], but rather as 'builders'* [bonayikh]" The usual translation here of *bonayikh* (your "builders," from the Hebrew verb *livnot*, "to build") feels somewhat forced. What does "building" have to do with increasing peace? The clue to a more appropriate translation appears in the commentary

Etz Yosef (Hanokh Zundel ben Yosef) on Shir Hashirim (Song of Songs) Rabbah. The midrash there explores the meanings of Song of Songs 1:5, "I am dark, but comely, O daughters [*b'not*] of Jerusalem...." The *Etz Yosef* counsels us not to read the Hebrew as *b'not*, "daughters," but as *beenot*, "discerners," from the Hebrew verb *l'havin*, "to discern." Similarly, for our prayer: instead of "builders," we might read "discerners." For, indeed, this is the real task of a scholar: to increase our understanding, our insight, our wisdom. Those who increase discernment give us greater peace.

———◆———

LANDES (HALAKHAH)

evocative style is not simple, because his creative thought did not always distinguish among midrash, Halakhah, mysticism, and contemporary life. The translation will therefore sound stilted, in my attempt to retain Rav Kook's genius.

> Those who think that universal peace will only be built by adopting one form of ideas and of qualities—they err. Indeed, when they observe a Torah scholar analyzing a text and thereby creating an increase of theories and nuances, they think this to cause division and the very opposite of peace. This is not so. True peace [*shalom ha'amiti*] can only come to the world through an increase [*ribu'i*] of peace. Increase of peace occurs when all nuances and theories of wisdom are brought into view, when it is made clear that all have a place respective to their value, their situation, and their content. Contrary to what you might think: There are matters that seem irrelevant or contradictory; nonetheless, when their true wisdom is fully revealed— it will then be understood that only through assembling all parts and details and all seemingly diverse and conflicting opinions and ideas can one come through them to see the light of truth and of justice, the knowledge, fear, and love of God, and the light of the Torah of truth.

"Scholars increase [marbim] *peace in the world"* in that they widen, explain, (and) birth new words and interpretations of Torah, which contains a *ribu'i*, increase of content, so that they [the scholars] increase peace—as it says, "And all thy children should be learned of God" (Isaiah 54:13). All shall recognize that even people seemingly completely opposite in direction and orientation are learned of God. Each one has a [divine] aspect that shall be revealed through knowledge of God and the light of truth.

[11] *"Great* [rav] *is the peace* [shalom] *among your children"* It does not say *gadol*, which would mean "great" in the sense of there being a single great design in which all sections must conform. That would mean that *shalom* necessitates unified thought. Such a concept actually detracts from the power of wisdom and the expansion of knowledge. For the light of knowledge must expand from every dimension of light that it contains. *Ribu'i* ["increase"] is what is meant by the phrase *"rav* is the peace among your children" [both *rav* and *rivu'i* come from the same Hebrew root].

[12] *"Do not read this word as 'children' but rather as 'builders'"* The edifice shall be built from different pieces. The true light of the universe shall be constructed from differing elements, different orientations, for "these and those [*elu v'elu*] are the words

of the living God" (Eruv. 13b). It shall be built from differing ways of service, instruction, and education—each one occupying its own place of value. This is the rule: It is not fitting to waste any talent or any wholeness; rather, one must expand each one and find its place. And if one observes a contradiction between concepts, from that itself shall wisdom construct its house. One must closely analyze the pieces in order to discover the innermost content of each concept, and through this process shall the differing pieces eventually be brought into alignment, so that they do not contradict each other. But it is specifically the increase of opinions that originates from differing souls and education that enriches wisdom and causes its expansion. In the end it is that increase that will build all in a fitting manner. In the end it shall be realized that it is impossible for the edifice of *Shalom* to be erected, except through analyzing all those contrary forces that seemingly desire to vanquish each other…

[17] *"May Adonai give strength* [oz] *to his people"* [*Ps. 29:11*] He shall give them life filled with meaning, which is peace. And when life is filled with meaning, it is filled with many dimensions and it is built by the grafting together of many forces. This is the true blessing of peace that comes from strength.

[17] *"May Adonai bless his people with peace* [shalom]*"* The blessing of peace that comes from strength is the *shalom* of unifying all the opposites. But it is necessary to discover all the opposites in order for there to be that which can be unified. Then the blessing [of peace] shall be recognized through the principle of "these and those are the words of the living God." Therefore *Shalom* is the name of God (Lev. Rab. 9:9). For He is the master of all forces, the omnipotent who includes all. May his name be blessed from here to eternity!

Rav Kook's rabbinic/mystical explanation of how Torah is to be studied emphasizes the dialectic of *ribu'i* (increase or plurality) and *yichud* (unity). The process is achieved through a radicalization of *ribu'i* so that every opinion is developed and expanded to reach its fullest potential. At that point the movement toward unity has already begun. As one who has participated in these ten volumes, I believe that Rav Kook's analysis pertains to this very work. These pages contain very different commentaries—radically so. Ultimate unity resides in God alone, but it is my confident hope that it can be achieved on a human plane in the hearts of those who study these pages and who are inspired to utter these prayers.

---◆---

J. HOFFMAN (TRANSLATION)

B.C.E.) reflects this numbering system of days within a week: "A Psalm for David on the first of the Shabbat," with "Shabbat" being used generically to mean "week." The pairing of psalms with specific days apparently came after the psalms were numbered, because the psalms for the days do not appear one after the other.

[2] *"Sing"* Again, "recite" is another possibility. (See above, v. 1, p. 165, and below, v. 6.)

[3] *"Monday"* According to the Septuagint, for the second day of the week.

[4] *"Tuesday"* The Septuagint does not mention Tuesday here.

[4] *"Divine assembly"* Or "assembly of God," but the word for "god" here *(el)* is not the one we just saw in this verse. Particularly in light of the continuation of the line, it's not clear if the assembly belongs to the one God, or if it is an assembly of gods.

[4] *"Gods"* Birnbaum's "judges" reflects an old tradition and is probably an attempt to remove any mention of other gods from the liturgy.

[5] *"Wednesday"* According to the Septuagint, for the fourth day of the week.

[6] *"Sing in joy"* Here and above, and v. 1, p. 165, we would prefer synonyms for "sing."

[7] *"Friday"* "The sixth day," in Hebrew. The Septuagint tells us that this psalm was "for the day before the Sabbath," adding, "when the land was first inhabited," a reference, perhaps, to the creation of human beings.

[7] *"Adonai is king"* The Hebrew phrase here, *Adonai malakh*, literally means "Adonai was king," but it was probably a common expression for "Adonai is king." We translate the phrase here as we have elsewhere, but also note the likelihood that this psalm may describe the process by which Adonai became king. If so, a better translation here would be "Adonai became king."

[7] *"Majestically robed"* More literally, "robed in majesty."

[7] *"Strength"* Or "glory." *Oz* is another word (see "Songs of glory" p. 103) that seems to refer at times to godly matters and at other times to military matters.

[8] *"A musical psalm"* Or "A psalm. A song."

[9] *"Studies"* More accurately, studies through repetition.

[9] *"[The] world's [ways]"* This literal translation from the prophet Habakkuk is misleading, for the point there is "ancient ways." Hebrew uses the word "world" to express eternity. Here we translate "world" to help preserve the midrashic pun that follows.

[9] *"Halakhah"* The words for "way" and "Halakhah" in Hebrew are identical except for the vowels. (The Hebrew equates "ways" and *halakhot*. We use the collective singular to make it more accessible to English readers.) So this is a much more reasonable midrash in Hebrew than it is in English, akin to taking an English story about "lead" (the metal) and reading it as "lead" ("make others follow"). As it happens, etymologically both "ways" and Halakhah derive from the root meaning "to walk." "Ways" are paths for literal walking, and Halakhah is a path for spiritual walking.

[11] *"Scholars"* Or "wise students."

[12] *"Builders"* The words for "children" and "builders" in Hebrew are identical except for the vowels. Like the preceding midrash, this makes much more sense in Hebrew than it does in English.

[15] *"Hope that you find peace"* Literally, "I ask for/speak good for you." Here and immediately below, we find poetic first-person verbs ("ask for/speak" and "request"). We translate the phrases to preserve the Hebrew parallel structure.

[17] *"May Adonai"* We translate this phrase elsewhere as "Adonai will…." Hebrew is often ambiguous in this regard, using the same language both for a hope for the future and a description of it. In this context, we think the hope-meaning is better.

◆ ◆ ◆

C. *Shir Hakavod* ("Song of Glory")

I sing hymns and compose songs because my soul longs for You.

² My soul desired [*ChiMDah*] the protective shade [*tsel*] of your hand, to know all your mystery.

³ When I speak of your Glory [*biKHVoDekha*], my heart yearns after You [i.e., the upper (*KaVoD*'s) love].

⁴ And so I speak about your glories [*niKHBaDot*] and glorify [*aKHaBeD*] your name in love songs.

⁵ I talk about your Glory [*K'VoD'kha*]) though I have not seen you; I describe You, though I have not known You.

⁶ Mediated to your prophets and the circle of those who serve You, You compared [Yourself] to the splendor of your *KaVoD*'s power.

⁷ Your greatness and power they traced to your mighty acts.

⁸ They imagined You, not as You are in reality; they described You only by your acts.

⁹ They depicted You in countless visions; despite all comparisons You are One.

¹⁰ They looked at You as both aged and youthful, with the hair of your *head* [*R'oSH'kha*] now gray, now black.

¹¹ Aged in judgment day, youthful in time of war, as a warrior whose hands fight for Him.

¹² He donned his helmet of salvation on his *head* [*R'oSHo*], his holy right arm made Him victorious.

¹³ As though his *head* is drenched with dew of light, and his locks are filled with drops of the night.

¹ אָ נְעִים זְמִירוֹת וְשִׁירִים אֶאֱרֹג, כִּי אֵלֶיךָ נַפְשִׁי תַעֲרֹג.

² נַפְשִׁי חִמְּדָה בְּצֵל יָדֶךָ, לָדַעַת כָּל רָז סוֹדֶךָ.

³ מִדֵּי דַבְּרִי בִּכְבוֹדֶךָ, הוֹמֶה לִבִּי אֶל דּוֹדֶיךָ.

⁴ עַל כֵּן אֲדַבֵּר בְּךָ נִכְבָּדוֹת, וְשִׁמְךָ אֲכַבֵּד בְּשִׁירֵי יְדִידוֹת.

⁵ אֲסַפְּרָה כְבוֹדְךָ וְלֹא רְאִיתִיךָ, אֲדַמְּךָ אֲכַנְּךָ וְלֹא יְדַעְתִּיךָ.

⁶ בְּיַד נְבִיאֶיךָ בְּסוֹד עֲבָדֶיךָ, דִּמִּיתָ הֲדַר כְּבוֹד הוֹדֶךָ.

⁷ גְּדֻלָּתְךָ וּגְבוּרָתֶךָ, כִּנּוּ לְתֹקֶף פְּעֻלָּתֶךָ.

⁸ דִּמּוּ אוֹתְךָ וְלֹא כְּפִי יֶשְׁךָ, וַיְשַׁוּוּךָ לְפִי מַעֲשֶׂיךָ.

⁹ הִמְשִׁילוּךָ בְּרֹב חֶזְיוֹנוֹת, הִנְּךָ אֶחָד בְּכָל דִּמְיוֹנוֹת.

¹⁰ וַיֶּחֱזוּ בְךָ זִקְנָה וּבַחֲרוּת, וּשְׂעַר רֹאשְׁךָ בְּשֵׂיבָה וְשַׁחֲרוּת.

¹¹ זִקְנָה בְּיוֹם דִּין וּבַחֲרוּת בְּיוֹם קְרָב, כְּאִישׁ מִלְחָמוֹת יָדָיו לוֹ רָב.

¹² חָבַשׁ כּוֹבַע יְשׁוּעָה בְּרֹאשׁוֹ, הוֹשִׁיעָה לּוֹ יְמִינוֹ וּזְרוֹעַ קָדְשׁוֹ.

¹³ טַלְלֵי אוֹרוֹת רֹאשׁוֹ נִמְלָא, וּקְוֻצּוֹתָיו רְסִיסֵי לָיְלָה.

¹⁴He beautifies Himself [yitPa'eR] through me [bi] because He delights in me; my *crown* of beauty He shall ever be.

¹⁵His *head* [R'oSHo] is like pure gold; on the *forehead (metsach)* he engraved his glorious holy name.

¹⁶For grace and glory [KaVoD], beauty and splendor, his own people has made a *crown* for Him.

¹⁷The locks of his *head* [R'oSHo] are those of a youth; his locks are curled and black.

¹⁸May his splendid Temple of righteousness [tif'aRto] be prized by Him above his highest [R'oSH] joy.

¹⁹May his treasured people be a *crown* in his hand, a royal diadem of great beauty [tiF'eRet].

²⁰Borne by Him, He uplifted and *crowned* them; being precious to Him, He honored [KiBDam] them.

²¹His adornment [P'eRo] rests on me, and mine on Him: He is near to me when I call to Him.

²²Dazzling is He and ruddy, his clothes, red, when from treating Edom's winepress He comes.

²³He showed the *t'fillin* knot to humble Moses, when Adonai's image was before his eyes.

²⁴Pleased with his people, He adorns [y'Fa'eR] them; enthroned in praise He adorns Himself [l'hitPa'eR].

²⁵Your chief [R'oSH] word is truth, caller into existence in the beginning [meR'oSH] of everything; seek out [d'RoSH] your people who seek You [doReSH'kha].

²⁶Set my many songs before You; may my piercing cry approach You.

¹⁴יִתְפָּאֵר בִּי כִּי חָפֵץ בִּי, וְהוּא יִהְיֶה לִי לַעֲטֶרֶת צְבִי.

¹⁵כֶּתֶם טָהוֹר פָּז דְּמוּת רֹאשׁוֹ, וְחַק עַל מֵצַח כְּבוֹד שֵׁם קָדְשׁוֹ.

¹⁶לְחֵן וּלְכָבוֹד צְבִי תִפְאָרָה, אֻמָּתוֹ לוֹ עִטְּרָה עֲטָרָה.

¹⁷מַחְלְפוֹת רֹאשׁוֹ כְּבִימֵי בְחֻרוֹת, קְוֻצּוֹתָיו תַּלְתַּלִּים שְׁחוֹרוֹת.

¹⁸נְוֵה הַצֶּדֶק צְבִי תִפְאַרְתּוֹ, יַעֲלֶה נָּא עַל רֹאשׁ שִׂמְחָתוֹ.

¹⁹סְגֻלָּתוֹ תְּהִי בְיָדוֹ עֲטֶרֶת, וּצְנִיף מְלוּכָה צְבִי תִפְאָרֶת.

²⁰עֲמוּסִים נְשָׂאָם עֲטֶרֶת עִנְּדָם, מֵאֲשֶׁר יָקְרוּ בְעֵינָיו כִּבְּדָם.

²¹פְּאֵרוֹ עָלַי וּפְאֵרִי עָלָיו, וְקָרוֹב אֵלַי בְּקָרְאִי אֵלָיו.

²²צַח וְאָדוֹם לִלְבוּשׁוֹ אָדֹם, פּוּרָה בְּדָרְכוֹ בְּבוֹאוֹ מֵאֱדוֹם.

²³קֶשֶׁר תְּפִלִּין הֶרְאָה לֶעָנָו, תְּמוּנַת יְיָ לְנֶגֶד עֵינָיו.

²⁴רוֹצֶה בְעַמּוֹ עֲנָוִים יְפָאֵר, יוֹשֵׁב תְּהִלּוֹת בָּם לְהִתְפָּאֵר.

²⁵רֹאשׁ דְּבָרְךָ אֱמֶת, קוֹרֵא מֵרֹאשׁ דּוֹר וָדוֹר, עַם דּוֹרֶשְׁךָ דְּרוֹשׁ.

²⁶שִׁית הֲמוֹן שִׁירַי נָא עָלֶיךָ, וְרִנָּתִי תִּקְרַב אֵלֶיךָ.

27 May my praise be like a *crown* for your *head*; let my prayer rise like incense before You.

28 Let a poor man's [*RaSH*] song be precious to You like the song that was sung at the sacrifices.

29 May my blessings rise to the *head* of the One who sustains, creates and brings forth, the just, the mighty.

30 As for my prayer, nod your *head* in approval, and accept it as the choicest incense.

31 May my meditation be sweet [*ye'eRaV*] to You, for all my being is yearning [*ta'aRoG*] for You.

‏²⁷תְּהִלָּתִי תְּהִי לְרֹאשְׁךָ עֲטֶרֶת, וּתְפִלָּתִי תִּכּוֹן קְטֹרֶת.

‏²⁸תִּיקַר שִׁירַת רָשׁ בְּעֵינֶיךָ, כַּשִּׁיר יוּשַׁר עַל קָרְבָּנֶיךָ.

‏²⁹בִּרְכָתִי תַעֲלֶה לְרֹאשׁ מַשְׁבִּיר, מְחוֹלֵל וּמוֹלִיד צַדִּיק כַּבִּיר.

‏³⁰וּבְבִרְכָתִי תְּנַעֲנַע לִי רֹאשׁ, וְאוֹתָהּ קַח לְךָ כִּבְשָׂמִים רֹאשׁ.

‏³¹יֶעֱרַב נָא שִׂיחִי עָלֶיךָ, כִּי נַפְשִׁי תַעֲרֹג אֵלֶיךָ.

Shir Hakavod ("Song of Glory") Writing during a time of relative security in the medieval German towns of Speyer (on the Rhine) and Regensburg (in Bavaria), German-Jewish pietist and mystical rabbis known as *Chasidei Ashkenaz* pioneered the deep meaning of every word and letter in their prayers. To the consternation of neighbors in the synagogue, they prayed in slow motion, so that they could think about numerical associations of word-letter clusters in the prayers (each Hebrew letter has a numerical value) and enhance the experience accordingly.

They also wrote new prayers. One of these is still recited in traditional Ashkenazi synagogues on Shabbat near the end of the service. It's formal title, *Shir Hakavod* ("Song of Glory"), reflective, as we shall see, of its theology, is attributed to Rabbi Judah the Pietist (Yehudah Hechasid), who died in 1217. It is also known by its opening phrase, *Anim z'mirot* (pronounced ah-NEEM z'-mee-ROHT), "I sing hymns."

Judah was a religious judge but also an eccentric and charismatic descendant of one of the founding families of German Jewry. His religious fervor and ascetic behavior attracted notice among a small group of followers. Among the theological conflicts that concerned him—and it underlies this prayer—is that God is, in essence, unknowable, so can be understood only by reference to divine actions—on the analogy of the way we judge people by what they do. Yet, when we pray, we want to connect to a personal God who can hear us, not to a remote abstraction.

The first major Jewish philosopher, Rabbi Saadiah ben Joseph Gaon (d. 942) of Baghdad, had provided a partial solution to the problem. His *Book of Beliefs and Opinions* distinguished between God as an unqualified and unknowable Oneness, on the one hand, and all of the humanlike attributes that we find in the Bible and rabbinic

C. *Shir Hakavod* ("Song of Glory")

¹ I sing hymns and compose songs because my soul longs for You.

² My soul desired [*ChiMDah*] the protective shade [*tsel*] of your hand, to know all your mystery.

³ When I speak of your Glory [*biKHVoDekha*], my heart yearns after You [i.e., the upper (*KaVoD*'s) love].

⁴ And so I speak about your glories [*niKHBaDot*] and

literature, such as God's face or back (Exodus 33), on the other. Saadiah argued that God reveals these humanlike or anthropomorphic images to the prophets by creating a separate angelic being who is not God but a created being that the Bible sometimes refers to as the Glory or divine presence *(kavod)*. This is what Ezekiel (chap. 1) and the other prophets (for example, Isa. 6) saw when they thought they were seeing images of God; they really were seeing images of the created *kavod* or Glory.

Judah appreciated this intellectual solution, which preserved a pure idea of a non-anthropomorphic God while also explaining how God reveals images to the prophets. But it did not satisfy him. His concern was not with the purely academic idea of revelation but with a practical religious problem: to what does a Jew pray when thinking of God? One can hardly pray to the abstraction of the divine Oneness that cannot be seen or imagined. But equally, one cannot pray to Saadiah's idea of the *kavod* (the subject of divine images in

1 אַנְעִים זְמִירוֹת וְשִׁירִים אֶאֱרֹג, כִּי אֵלֶיךָ נַפְשִׁי תַעֲרֹג.

2 נַפְשִׁי חִמְּדָה בְּצֵל יָדֶךָ, לָדַעַת כָּל רָז סוֹדֶךָ.

3 מִדֵּי דַבְּרִי בִּכְבוֹדֶךָ, הוֹמֶה לִבִּי אֶל דּוֹדֶיךָ.

4 עַל כֵּן אֲדַבֵּר בְּךָ נִכְבָּדוֹת, וְשִׁמְךָ אֲכַבֵּד בְּשִׁירֵי יְדִידוֹת.

the Bible), since, for Saadiah, the *kavod* is a separate created being, and praying to a created being would be a form of idolatry.

To arrive at his own solution about what is the proper object of prayer, Rabbi Judah refers to the teaching in the Talmud that says, "One should pray with eyes directed below [to the Temple] and heart upward toward [the heavens]" (Yev. 105b). How can one pray upward but not to a created *kavod*?

Judah's brilliant solution depended on making a distinction   *(p. 184)*

L. HOFFMAN (History)

SHIR HAKAVOD ("SONG OF GLORY") WAS COMPOSED BY JUDAH THE PIETIST (YEHUDAH HECHASID) OF GERMANY (D. 1217). AS A MYSTICAL POEM, ITS OSTENSIVE MEANING IS SECOND TO ITS UNDERLYING MESSAGE, WHICH CAN BE UNDERSTOOD ONLY BY APPRECIATING THE HEBREW WORD PLAYS THAT POINT TOWARD ITS ESOTERIC DOCTRINE OF AN ESSENTIALLY UNKNOWABLE DEITY WHO, HOWEVER, BECOMES KNOWN TO US BY A DIVINE ASPECT KNOWN AS KAVOD ("GLORY"). READERS SHOULD APPROACH THE POEM ONLY AFTER READING THE TRANSLATOR'S INTRODUCTION (SEE MARCUS, SHIR HAKAVOD ["SONG OF GLORY"]), WHICH SUMMARIZES THE DOCTRINE IN QUESTION. IN ADDITION, EACH LINE MUST BE READ ALONGSIDE HIS ACCOMPANYING COMMENTARY.

To appreciate the poem's brilliance, we provide [in brackets] the key Hebrew words—those with esoteric meaning, because they come from a Hebrew root, or puns on that root, that suggest the poet's mystical doctrine. Readers must also keep in mind some characteristics of the Hebrew language.

1. Hebrew is essentially consonantal—the vowels are added to the more or less fixed consonants that make up a Hebrew root (usually a three-letter root). *Kavod* ("glory") is from the root *k.v.d*; or, since the Hebrew *v* can appear as *b* (see 4, below), from the root *k.b.d*.   *(p. 191)*

glorify [aKHaBeD] your name in love songs.

5 I talk about your Glory [K'VoD'kha]) though I have not seen you; I describe You, though I have not known You.

6 Mediated to your prophets and the circle of those who serve You, You compared [Yourself] to the splendor of your KaVoD's power.

7 Your greatness and power they traced to your mighty acts.

8 They imagined You, not as You are in reality; they described You only by your acts.

9 They depicted You in countless visions; despite all comparisons You are One.

10 They looked at You as both aged and youthful, with the hair of your head [R'oSH'kha] now gray, now black.

11 Aged in judgment day, youthful in time of war, as a warrior whose hands fight for Him.

12 He donned his helmet of salvation on his head [R'oSHo], his holy right arm made Him victorious.

13 As though his head is drenched with dew of light, and his locks are filled with drops of the night.

14 He beautifies Himself [yitPa'eR] through me [bi] because He delights in me; my crown of beauty He shall ever be.

אֶסְפְּרָה כְּבוֹדְךָ וְלֹא רְאִיתִיךָ, אֲדַמְּךָ אֲכַנְּךָ וְלֹא יְדַעְתִּיךָ. 5

בְּיַד נְבִיאֶיךָ בְּסוֹד עֲבָדֶיךָ, דִּמִּיתָ הֲדַר כְּבוֹד הוֹדֶךָ. 6

גְּדֻלָּתְךָ וּגְבוּרָתֶךָ, כִּנּוּ לְתֹקֶף פְּעֻלָּתֶךָ. 7

דִּמּוּ אוֹתְךָ וְלֹא כְּפִי יֶשְׁךָ, וַיְשַׁוּוּךָ לְפִי מַעֲשֶׂיךָ. 8

הִמְשִׁילוּךָ בְּרֹב חֶזְיוֹנוֹת, הִנְּךָ אֶחָד בְּכָל דִּמְיוֹנוֹת. 9

וַיֶּחֱזוּ בְךָ זִקְנָה וּבַחֲרוּת, וּשְׂעַר רֹאשְׁךָ בְּשֵׂיבָה וְשַׁחֲרוּת. 10

זִקְנָה בְּיוֹם דִּין וּבַחֲרוּת בְּיוֹם קְרָב, כְּאִישׁ מִלְחָמוֹת יָדָיו לוֹ רָב. 11

חָבַשׁ כּוֹבַע יְשׁוּעָה בְּרֹאשׁוֹ, הוֹשִׁיעָה לוֹ יְמִינוֹ וּזְרוֹעַ קָדְשׁוֹ. 12

טַלְלֵי אוֹרוֹת רֹאשׁוֹ נִמְלָא, וּקְוֻצּוֹתָיו רְסִיסֵי לָיְלָה. 13

יִתְפָּאֵר בִּי כִּי חָפֵץ בִּי, וְהוּא יִהְיֶה לִי לַעֲטֶרֶת צְבִי. 14

כֶּתֶם טָהוֹר פָּז דְּמוּת רֹאשׁוֹ, וְחַק עַל מֵצַח כְּבוֹד שֵׁם קָדְשׁוֹ. 15

לְחֵן וּלְכָבוֹד צְבִי תִּפְאָרָה, אֻמָּתוֹ לוֹ עִטְּרָה עֲטָרָה. 16

מַחְלְפוֹת רֹאשׁוֹ כְּבִימֵי בְחֻרוֹת, קְוֻצּוֹתָיו תַּלְתַּלִּים שְׁחוֹרוֹת. 17

¹⁵ His *head* [*R'oSHo*] is like pure gold; on the *forehead (metsach)* he engraved his glorious holy name.

¹⁶ For grace and glory [*KaVoD*], beauty and splendor, his own people has made a *crown* for Him.

¹⁷ The locks of his *head* are those of a youth; his locks are curled and black.

¹⁸ May his splendid Temple of righteousness [*tiF'aRto*] be prized by Him above his highest [*R'oSH*] joy.

¹⁹ May his treasured people be a *crown* in his hand, a royal diadem of great beauty [*tiF'eRet*].

²⁰ Borne by Him, He uplifted and *crowned* them; being precious to Him, He honored [*KiBDam*] them.

²¹ His adornment [*P'eRo*] rests on me, and mine on Him: He is near to me when I call to Him.

²² Dazzling is He and ruddy, his clothes, red, when from treating Edom's winepress He comes.

²³ He showed the *t'fillin* knot to humble Moses, when Adonai's image was before his eyes.

²⁴ Pleased with his people, He adorns [*y'Fa'eR*] them; enthroned in praise He adorns Himself [*l'hitPa'eR*].

²⁵ Your chief [*R'oSH*] word is truth, caller into existence in the beginning [*meR'oSH*] of everything; seek out [*d'RoSH*] your people who seek You

¹⁸נְוֵה הַצֶּדֶק צְבִי תִפְאַרְתּוֹ, יַעֲלֶה נָּא עַל רֹאשׁ שִׂמְחָתוֹ.

¹⁹סְגֻלָּתוֹ תְּהִי בְּיָדוֹ עֲטֶרֶת, וּצְנִיף מְלוּכָה צְבִי תִפְאָרֶת.

²⁰עֲמוּסִים נְשָׂאָם עֲטֶרֶת עִנְּדָם, מֵאֲשֶׁר יָקְרוּ בְעֵינָיו כִּבְּדָם.

²¹פְּאֵרוֹ עָלַי וּפְאֵרִי עָלָיו, וְקָרוֹב אֵלַי בְּקָרְאִי אֵלָיו.

²²צַח וְאָדוֹם לִלְבוּשׁוֹ אָדֹם, פּוּרָה בְדָרְכוֹ בְּבוֹאוֹ מֵאֱדוֹם.

²³קֶשֶׁר תְּפִלִּין הֶרְאָה לֶעָנָו, תְּמוּנַת יְיָ לְנֶגֶד עֵינָיו.

²⁴רוֹצֶה בְּעַמּוֹ עֲנָוִים יְפָאֵר, יוֹשֵׁב תְּהִלּוֹת בָּם לְהִתְפָּאֵר.

²⁵רֹאשׁ דְּבָרְךָ אֱמֶת, קוֹרֵא מֵרֹאשׁ דּוֹר וָדוֹר, עַם דּוֹרֶשְׁךָ דְּרוֹשׁ.

²⁶שִׁית הֲמוֹן שִׁירַי נָא עָלֶיךָ, וְרִנָּתִי תִּקְרַב אֵלֶיךָ.

²⁷תְּהִלָּתִי תְּהִי לְרֹאשְׁךָ עֲטֶרֶת, וּתְפִלָּתִי תִּכּוֹן קְטֹרֶת.

²⁸תִּיקַר שִׁירַת רָשׁ בְּעֵינֶיךָ, כַּשִּׁיר יוּשַׁר עַל קָרְבָּנֶיךָ.

²⁹בִּרְכָתִי תַעֲלֶה לְרֹאשׁ מַשְׁבִּיר, מְחוֹלֵל וּמוֹלִיד צַדִּיק כַּבִּיר.

[doReSH'kha].

26 Set my many songs before You; may my piercing cry approach You.

27 May my praise be like a *crown* for your *head*; let my prayer rise like incense before You.

28 Let a poor man's [RaSH] song be precious to You like the song that was sung at the sacrifices.

29 May my blessings rise to the *head* of the One who sustains, creates and brings forth, the just, the mighty.

30 As for my prayer, nod your *head* in approval, and accept it as the choicest incense.

31 May my meditation be sweet [ye'eRaV] to You, for all my being is yearning [ta'aRoG] for You.

30וּבְרַכְתִּי תְנַעֲנַע לִי רֹאשׁ, וְאוֹתָהּ קַח לָךְ כִּבְשָׂמִים רֹאשׁ.

31יֶעֱרַב נָא שִׂיחִי עָלֶיךָ, כִּי נַפְשִׁי תַעֲרֹג אֵלֶיךָ.

MARCUS (MEDIEVAL PIETY)

within God. On the one hand, God, the pure Oneness, is *borei* (pronounced boh-RAY), "the creator." The *borei* has no particular location. On the other hand, there is indeed a *kavod*, but far from being a created entity separate from God, the *kavod* is part of God—and it has two aspects facing in different directions. The part that is turned away from humanity, "God's face," considered the upper *kavod*, is the inaccessible part of God that one cannot apprehend and is high up. The lower *kavod*, on the other hand, "God's back," is like a screen onto which God projects various images for the benefit of the prophets and other mortals. When one prays, it is either to the creator or, to follow the talmudic teaching to pray upward, to the upper *kavod*. When the poet addresses a divine "You," this should be understood either as the *borei* ("creator") or as the upper *kavod*.

The quest to see God has deep roots in Judaism. Long before the German pietists, biblical and rabbinic sources wrestled with the problem of how to make contact with the invisible. In the Bible (Exod. 33:18), Moses importunes God, "Let me behold your presence [*k'vodekha*]," but God refuses. "You cannot see my face," God cautions, "for man may not see Me and live.... you will see my back; but my face must not be seen" (Exod. 33:20, 33:23).

The distinction between God's "face" and "back," which could here mean "back of the head," acknowledges the human quest for face-to-face contact with God, but settles for far less—something partial and ultimately unsatisfactory. In German pietist thinking, the distinction is expressed as the upper and lower *kavod*. The former is God's unknowable "face," the latter, God's imaginable back. *Anim z'mirot* tells us from its very first verses that we must struggle to penetrate beyond the visible lower *kavod* to try and catch a glimpse of the hidden upper *kavod*, God's face. But the only way to do this is by engaging with the visible *kavod*. *Anim z'mirot* makes its point by being filled with biblical and (to some extent) rabbinic allusions or quotations. Key to the range of images is the idea already discussed (from Exod. 33): seeing God's back, and with it, at least an aspect of God's "head."

As the Rabbis read it, Song of Songs 5:10–16a had already pictured God in graphic detail. They considered it not just a romantic song referring to human lovers, but an allegory symbolizing God's relationship to the Jewish People. Nonetheless, they could hardly fail to admit the erotic power of its poetry, which, transferred to *Anim z'mirot*, charges the prayer with passion.

Only some of that biblical passage describing God as a virile young male lover is used: the images that describe the head—supplemented by passages in Isaiah and Psalms that refer to God's crown, again an image building on God's head. Still other quotations come from the Talmud in which Moses is said to see the knot of the *t'fillin* tied at the back of the head. And at the end, the poet compares his prayer to the sacrificial incense offered on the Temple altar, the rising smoke again pointing upward to the crowned head and the point of contact between the lower *kavod* and the upper *kavod* that the poet tries to reach. And so, if composing the prayer is thought of as making a crown for God's head, and as equivalent to the incense sacrifice offered "up" to God, perhaps the act of reciting it today is also a way of trying to reach up and touch God's face.

The emphasis on "head" is evident in the poetry. The prayer is written as a Hebrew alphabetic acrostic, each verse beginning with a successive letter of the Hebrew alphabet. But the Hebrew letter *resh*, which begins the Hebrew word for "head" *(rosh)*, receives an extra verse. In addition, as Arthur Green has noted, the Hebrew word *rosh* or its sound or homophone (words meaning something else but also pronounced *rosh*) appears several times in the poem. The focus on *rosh* echoes the talmudic idea, quoted in the prayer, that Moses was granted a glimpse of the back of God's head, but there is still a tension between the image of seeing the back of God's head and of wanting to see God's actual face.

By understanding the two-part *kavod* as part of God's being, the German pietists present their version of what would later become a key tenet of Kabbalah, the most famous Jewish system of mysticism: the existence of a plurality within the godhead.

Like Kabbalah's tenfold understanding of God, writes Elliot Wolfson, the idea of the *kavod* too has both male and female associations. Both Kabbalah and the pietists believed as well that a Jew's performance of the commandments can effect a divine union. Judah and his student Eleazar of Worms (d. 1230) view the lower *kavod* as female and the upper *kavod* as male. The former is associated with making a crown for God; the latter is thought of as God's hidden head. The process of composing or reciting the prayer, then, is pictured as a coronation ceremony in which the poet's/Jew's prayer places the crown on God's head, thereby achieving a kind of unification within God and between God and the one seeking Him.

Although often recited by rote, this prayer can be a source of spiritual sustenance as one faces the limits of human-divine contact even while thirsting for it.

(For background to this Introduction, see Elliott R. Wolfson, "The Image of Jacob Engraved upon the Throne: Further Reflection on the Esoteric Doctrine of the German Pietists," in his *Along the Path: Studies in Kabbalistic Myth, Symbolism, and Hermeneutics* [Albany: SUNY Press, 1995], pp. 1–62, 111–187; and Arthur Green, *Keter: The Crown of God in Early Jewish Mysticism* [Princeton, NJ: Princeton University Press, 1997], pp. 106–120.)

[*Editor's Note:* Appreciation of the poem depends on an understanding of Hebrew word plays, described in this commentary. But the word plays require some basic knowledge of the way Hebrew words are formed out of (usually) three-letter roots. This information is provided in the Editor's Note to the Liturgy, pp. 185, 191.]

[1] *"I sing hymns and compose songs* [e'eRoG] *because my soul longs for You"* Echoing Psalm 42:2, "Like a hart panting [*ta'aRoG*] by the wadis of water, so my being yearns for You." The verse contains the word play "I will compose" (*e'eRoG* spelled with an *alef*) and the verb used in Psalm 42:2 (*ta'aRoG* spelled with an *ayin*) in order to connect the poet's act of composition to the personal experience of longing or panting for God. The simile suggests the poet's understanding of the role he plays as a composer of prayer. More than just writing to express feelings about God, he is trying to overcome the distance that separates him from God.

The opening phrase, "I sing hymns" (*anim z'mirot*), alludes to David, who is called *n'im z'mirot* (2 Sam. 23:1), thus lending the longing a possible messianic flavor as well as a personal one.

The poet implicitly compares himself to David, the traditional author of Psalms—the book of the Hebrew Bible most often quoted in the prayer book generally, and in this prayer specifically. Another great medieval Hebrew poet, Rabbi Samuel Ibn Nagrella of Granada (d. 1056), explicitly justified writing his poetry by saying, "I am the David of my generation" (*ani david b'dori*).

The prayer may be divided into several sections that express different sets of relationships. First, we have "I-You," in which "I" is the one who composes or prays and "You" is God the upper *kavod*. But we also have "they," referring to others' relationship with the divine "You." And sometimes we find no personal relationship at all, but just a third-person description of *kavod*.

These sections can be outlined as follows:

Verses 1–5: I-You
Verses 6–10: they-You
Verses 11–13: *kavod* is described in the third person
Verse 14: Interruption of third-person description to reassert the I-You relationship
Verses 15–20: *kavod* is described in the third person
Verse 21: Interruption (as in v. 14) to reassert I-You relationship
Verses 22–24: *kavod* is again described in the third person
Verse 25: A return to God as You
Verses 26–31: I-You

The last verse (31) reprises the themes of the first. Structurally, too, the I-You pattern opens the prayer and closes it. See specifically the parallelism in the beginning of verse 1, "I sing hymns and compose songs [*e'eRoG*]," to the end of verse 31, "all my being is yearning [*ta'aRoG*] for You."

[2] *"My soul desired* [CHiMDah] *the protective shade* [tsel] *of your hand, to know all your mystery"* The first part echoes Song of Songs 2:3, "I desired [*ChiMaD'ti*] and sat in his shade." It requests a place of intimacy with God. But the accent on "mystery" in the second part expresses dissatisfaction—we cannot really know God's essence.

There also is an allusion here to the Moses episode: "As my presence [*K'VoDi*] passes by, I will … shield you with my hand…. Then I will take my hand away and you will see my back; but my face must not be seen" (Exod. 33:22–23). See, too, Isaiah 51:16, "sheltered you with my hand." The desire to know or see God completely remains frustrated.

[4] *"I speak about your glories* [niKHBaDot] *and glorify* [aKHaBeD] *your name in love songs"* See Psalm 87:3 ("Glorious things [*niKHBaDot*] are spoken of you," applied to Jerusalem) and 45:1 ("A love song").

The poet uses the root for *kavod (k.v.d)* as a plural noun, "glories" *(niKHBaDot)*, and as a verb, "glorify" *(aKHaBeD)*. The repetition rubs in the frustration of wanting the unknowable upper *kavod* and having to settle for the available lower *kavod* that alone can be described in human terms.

[5] *"I talk about your Glory* [K'VoD'kha], *though I have not seen You* [the creator]; *I describe You, though I have not known You* [the creator]*"* The writer's prayers properly describe the knowable lower *kavod*, but cannot reach beyond that to the upper *kavod* and surely not to the utterly unknowable creator-God, who fashions both.

[6] *"Mediated to your prophets and the circle of those who serve You"* The author's effort to reach God through descriptions of God's lower *kavod* is a well-trod path, going back to God's self-description provided to prophets. Verse 7 will shift to the third person "they-You," how the prophets learned about God only from divine descriptions of the *kavod*.

[6] *"You compared [Yourself] to the splendor of your* kavod's *power"* This verse sets the stage for a series of images about the lower *kavod* that will begin in verse 10. They reflect ways of knowing *about* the upper *kavod* through the actions of the lower *kavod*, that is, only indirectly.

[7-8] *"Traced to your mighty acts ... not as You are in reality; they described You only by your acts"* See Psalm 145:3-4 (part of *Ashre*—see Volume 3, *P'sukei D'zimrah [Morning Psalms]*, pp. 107–108): "Great is Adonai…. Generation upon generation will praise your deeds and tell of your mighty acts."

[9] *"They depicted You in countless visions; despite all comparisons You are One"* A return to the theme of verse 6, indirect knowledge of God. The prophets had no access to the upper *kavod* but only to its visible acts in the form of the lower *kavod* that work in history. In reality, God is One, that is, the upper *kavod*; but the prophets saw a multiplicity of divine acts that they describe based on the lower *kavod*.

[10] *"Both aged and youthful, with the hair of your* head [R'oSH'kha] *now gray, now black"* The poet makes a transition from prophetic images based on divine acts to God as a young and vigorous man (from Song of Songs 5:10–16a). He will then focus on Song of Songs 5:10, which pictures God's head. The image and sound of the Hebrew word for head *(rosh)* and the complementary image of crown will be central motifs from here on.

[11] *"Aged in judgment day, youthful in time of war, as a warrior"* Based on a rabbinic comment on Exodus 15:3, where God appears like a war hero at the crossing of the Sea (*Mekhilta, Bachodesh* 5, *Shirta* 4; Chag. 14a and *Rashi* on the Exodus verse).

[11] *"Whose hands fight for Him"* Echoing Moses's blessing of Judah "though his own hands fight for him" (Deut. 33:7).

[13] *"His* head [R'oSHo] *is drenched with dew of light* [orot], *and his locks are filled with drops of the night"* See Isaiah 26:19, "For your dew is like the dew on fresh growth [orot]"; and Song of Songs 5:2, "For my head is drenched with dew, my locks with the damp of night."

[14] *"He beautifies Himself* [yitPa'eR] *through me* [bi] *because He delights in me"* Interrupting the physical metaphors about the lower *kavod* and God's mighty acts reported in the third person, the author inserts himself in a parenthetical first-person/third-person verse that anticipates the culminating section of I-You union with the upper *kavod* at the end of the prayer.

[14] *"He beautifies Himself* [yitPa'eR] *through me* [bi] *... my crown of beauty He shall ever be"* This verse and verse 21 (see next page) extend the theme of the divine head and crown as vehicles of mutual bonding and adornment between God and Israel; related too is the image of the boxes and straps of the head *t'fillin*. The verb *yitPa'eR* ("beautifies") is used in rabbinic literature to refer to the *t'fillin* that surround the head

(and arm) to adorn the daily morning worshiper. On the end of the line, see Isaiah 28:5, "On that day Adonai of hosts shall become a crown of beauty."

This poet thinks that the upper *kavod* desires the one who prays and expresses this yearning by adorning its head with the speaker's prayers ("He beautifies Himself with me"), as it were. The line continues with the hope that the upper *kavod* will reciprocally become the poet's crown. After expressing this hope about mutual bonding or union, the author will return to prophetic images emphasizing the head.

¹⁵ *"His head [R'oSHo] is like pure gold"* See Song of Songs 5:11, "His head is finest gold"; and Psalm 21:4, "You have set upon his head a crown of fine gold."

¹⁶ *"His own people has made a crown for Him"* Compare Song of Songs 3:11, "wearing the crown that his mother gave him."

¹⁷ *"The locks of his head are those of a youth; his locks are curled and black"* For the second part, see Song of Songs 5:11, "His locks are curled and black as a raven."

¹⁸ *"May his splendid Temple of righteousness [tiF'aRto] be prized by Him above his highest [R'oSH] joy"* See Jeremiah 31:23, "Abode of righteousness, O holy mountain" (referring to the Temple); and Psalm 137:6, "If I do not keep Jerusalem in memory above [R'oSH] my greatest hour of joy."

The author now expresses another wish, still about God in the third person.

¹⁹ *"May his treasured people be a crown in his hand, a royal diadem of great beauty [tiF'eRet]"* See Isaiah 62:3, "You shall be a glorious crown in the hand of Adonai, and a royal diadem in the palm of your God."

²⁰ *"Borne by Him, He uplifted and crowned them; being precious to Him, He honored [KiBDam] them"* See Isaiah 46:3, "Who have been borne since birth, uplifted since leaving the womb"; and Isaiah 43:4, "Because you are precious to Me, and honored, and I love you."

²¹ *"His adornment [P'eRo] rests on me, and mine on Him: He is near to me when I call to Him"* Once again (as in v. 14, above), the descriptions of the lower *kavod* are interrupted with a first-person/third-person statement about communion between the poet and God, the upper *kavod*:

Once again, too (as in v. 14), we find "beautification" *(P'eR)* alluding to the leather boxes and straps of the *t'fillin* worn on the forehead and arm. The Rabbis interpret the phrase, "Wrap your turban around your head" (Ezek. 24:17) to refer to the *t'fillin* worn on the head (Ber. 11a). The poet imagines that God's *t'fillin* box is worn on, and its straps wrapped around, the author's/Israel's head; reciprocally the author's/Israel's *t'fillin* (or crown consisting of his prayers) are worn on God's head (see vv. 27, 29, and 30).

For the second part of the line, see Psalm 145:18, another line from the *Ashre*, "Adonai is near to all who call upon Him, to all who call Him in truth."

²² *"Dazzling is He and ruddy, his clothes, red, when from treating Edom's winepress He*

comes" The poet now returns to third-person descriptions of images of the lower *kavod* as a vigorous male. See Song of Songs 5:10, "My beloved is clear-skinned and ruddy"; Isaiah 63:2, "Why is your clothing so red?"; Isaiah 63:3, "I trod out a vintage alone"; and Isaiah 63:1, "Who is this coming from Edom?"

²³ *"He showed the* t'fillin *knot to humble Moses, when Adonai's image was before his eyes"* Exodus 33:23 ("Then I will take my hand away and you will see my back") teaches that God showed Moses the knot of his *t'fillin* (Ber. 7a). For the end of the line, see Numbers 12:8, "And he beholds the image of Adonai."

²⁴ *"Pleased with his people, He adorns* [y'Fa'eR] *them; enthroned in praise He adorns himself* [l'hitPa'eR]*"* See Psalm 149:4, "For Adonai delights in his people; He adorns the lowly with salvation."

²⁵ *"Your chief* [R'oSH] *word is truth, caller into existence in the beginning* [meR'oSH] *of everything; seek out* [d'R'oSH] *your people who seek You* [doReSH'kha]*"* Instead of continuing with the next letter in the alphabet acrostic *(shin)*, the prior one *(resh)* is repeated via the word *R'oSH* ("head"). Through word plays on the root *r.'.sh*, the poet turns to God and refers to God's people and to God in the third and second person.

See Psalm 119:160, "Truth is the essence of your word." The Hebrew word for "truth" *(e'MeT)* is found in the last letters of the first three Hebrew words of the Torah: *bereishiT bara' elohiM* ("In the beginning of God's creating"). This exegetical technique was popular among the German pietists and was called interpreting by "final letters of words" *(sofei teivot)*.

²⁶ *"Set my many songs before You; may my piercing cry approach You"* See Amos 5:23, "Spare me the sound of your songs," which the poet has reversed, asking God to accept his prayer; and see Psalm 119:169, "May my piercing cry reach You, O Adonai."

The poem concludes by returning to the I-You pattern. The poet hopes that composing the prayer and placing it on God's head as a crown will be comparable to the ancient sacrifices offered to God. He hopes that God will accept them and see that they are worthy.

²⁷ *"May my praise be like a* crown *for your* head; *let my prayer rise like incense before You"* The idea that prayers can become God's crown is found in the Talmud (Chag. 13b): "An angel named Sandelphon ... makes crowns for his maker." On this, the Tosafot (commentators of northern France, twelfth century) add, "From the prayers of the righteous he makes a crown."

For the end of the line, see Psalm 141:2, "Take my prayer as an offering of incense."

²⁸ *"Let a poor man's* [RaSH] *song be precious to You like the song that was sung at the sacrifices"* Again, the sound *R'oSH* ("head") is emphasized, this time by the homophone for "poor man" *(RaSH)*, which is similar to "head" *(R'oSH)* but lacks the middle *alef.*

²⁹ *"May my blessings rise to the* head *of the One who sustains, creates and brings forth,*

the just, the mighty" See Proverbs 11:26, "But blessings are on the head of one who dispenses it"; and Proverbs 10:6, "Blessings light upon the head of the righteous." For the end, see Job 34:17, "the just mighty One."

30 *"As for my prayer, nod your* head *in approval, and accept it as the choicest incense"* "It was taught: Rabbi Ishmael son of Elisha says: I once entered into the innermost part (of the Temple) to offer incense and saw Akatriel Yah, Adonai of Hosts, seated upon a high and exalted throne. He said to me: Ishmael, my son, bless Me! I replied: May it be your will that your mercy may suppress your anger and your mercy prevail over your other attributes, so that You may deal with your children according to the attribute of mercy and, on their behalf, stop short of the limit of strict justice! He [God] nodded to me with his head" (Ber. 7a).

The reference to God as AKaTRiel contains in it the word for "crown" *(KeTeR)*, and the context is entering the Temple to offer incense, an act our poet associates with composing this prayer. He hopes God will favor his efforts as much as Akatriel did Rabbi Ishmael's. For the end of the line, see Exodus 30:23, "Take choice [*R'oSH*] spices."

31 *"May my meditation be sweet* [ye'eRaV] *to You, for all my being is yearning* [ta'aRoG] *for You"* See Psalm 104:34, "May my prayer be sweet to Him"—but changed here to the second person, so as to end with the I-You relationship.

———◆———

L. HOFFMAN (HISTORY)

2. Sometimes one of the consonants is a silent *alef* or *ayin*, in which case there is no English transliteration. When the presence of such a letter must be recognized in order to appreciate the poem, we provide an apostrophe. Thus, *p'er* ("beauty") is from the three-letter root *p.'.r.*

3. Since Hebrew is consonantal, it is the consonants that provide the word plays. The relevant consonants (usually those of the three-letter root) are provided in capitals. Thus, the Hebrew *kavod* ("glory") appears here as *KaVoD*—the root being (as we saw) *k.v.d.*

4. Some Hebrew consonants change pronunciation, depending on the letter that they follow. To understand the word plays, it is necessary to know that the Hebrew *k* can sometimes appear as *kh*; *b* can be *v*; *p* can be *f*. Thus, for example, a variant word for "beauty" *(tiferet)* is written here *tiF'eRet*—denoting a word from the root *f.'.r* = *p.'.r.* Similarly, the Hebrew for "in your glory" appears as *biKHVoDekha*—since the root letters are *k.v.d*, with the *k* becoming *kh*.]

Shir Hakavod ("Song of Glory") A uniquely colorful song, attributed to Judah the Pietist (Yehudah Hechasid), founder of the medieval school of Ashkenazi pietists known as the *Chasidei Ashkenaz*. Medieval German Jewry had come into being with the migration of Italian Jews over the Alps into the Rhineland by the tenth century (and possibly earlier). By the eleventh century, its rabbis (like Rabbenu Gershom, nicknamed *M'or Hagolah*, "Light of the Diaspora") were becoming famous; among the students who journeyed to the Rhineland for study was Rabbi Shlomo bar Yitzchak—better known as *Rashi*. This glory came crashing down during the First Crusade (1096), when a populist army (constituting what is called the People's Crusade) bivouacked in Germany and massacred much of Rhineland Jewry. Thereafter, the center of Ashkenaz shifted to *Rashi's* France, which had remained untouched by the Crusader devastation.

After the Crusade, German Jews attempted to come to terms with their trauma. Among them were the *Chasidei Ashkenaz*, who, among other things, wrote liturgy pleading for divine vengeance on their persecutors and extolling Jewish martyrdom—surely, they held, their loved ones had died only *al kiddush hashem*, "to sanctify God's name." This pietist minority even adopted a regimen of bodily asceticism, some of them sitting barefoot in the snow, for example. Consumed with sin, they reshaped the age-old notion of repentance into penitence, a system of demanding certain penitential acts chosen to fit specific sins.

The *Chasidei Ashkenaz* were influenced not just by a post-Crusade mentality, but by their environment, the burgeoning of medieval cities. A population increase a century earlier, alongside the inability of existing landed estates to provide farming property for the next generation, had sent many young men outside the established feudal system into alternative ways to get ahead. One was the church; another, brigandage—highway robbers (romanticized by stories of Robin Hood); a third, the growing armies demanded by feudal lords, who fought each other and eventually joined together for the Crusades; and last, moving to the cities to form a nascent artisan class. Returning Crusaders often brought the wealth gained as warriors back to the cities, where they spent it on castles and cathedrals, both of which demanded artisans.

A casualty of city growth was medieval religion based in a rural class and its attendant feudal system of fealty to tradition. Christianity responded with new monastic orders called "mendicants," first and foremost the Dominicans and Franciscans, who differed from their monastic predecessors in that they were commissioned to work in cities, spreading the gospel to the new urban class that had become independent of old ties to tradition. These new monks walked city streets preaching a puritanical moral order in lieu of the old feudal rules that city dwellers had abandoned. At some point the close proximity of the *Chasidei Ashkenaz* to these urban mendicants only underscored the validity of their practice. In their asceticism and their accent on penitence (among other things), the *Chasidei Ashkenaz* became the Jewish equivalent of these urban monks.

Although they remained a minority, their influence spread horizontally across geographical borders and vertically ahead through time. Eliezer of Worms (1160–1238), for example, merged the pietists' values with established Halakhah. His disciple, Isaac Or Zaru'a (1160–1238), brought that amalgam east as far as Vienna. Isaac influenced Meir of Rothenberg (called also the *Maharam*), arguably the most influential Ashkenazi rabbi of all, who in turn determined the impact of a whole array of significant students, including Rabbenu Asher ben Yechi'el (called the *Rosh*). Rabbenu Asher's son, Jacob ben Asher, composed the most influential law code of its time, the *Tur*.

The actual liturgical impact of the *Chasidei Ashkenaz* is relatively minor compared to its subtle influence upon Jewish attitudes as a whole. But among the liturgical masterpieces that remain is *Anim z'mirot*, known technically as *Shir Hakavod*, significant as an index of the mystical system these pietists pioneered.

◆ ◆ ◆

About the Contributors

MARC BRETTLER
Marc Brettler, PhD, is Dora Golding Professor of Biblical Studies in the Department of Near Eastern and Judaic Studies at Brandeis University. His major areas of research are biblical historical texts, religious metaphors, and gender issues in the Bible. Brettler is author of *God Is King: Understanding an Israelite Metaphor* (Sheffield Academic Press), *The Creation of History in Ancient Israel* (Routledge), *The Book of Judges* (Routledge), *How to Read the Bible* (Jewish Publication Society), and *How to Read the Jewish Bible* (Oxford University Press), as well as a variety of articles on the Bible. He is also associate editor of the new edition of the *Oxford Annotated Bible* and coeditor of the *Jewish Study Bible* (Oxford University Press).

ELLIOT N. DORFF
Elliot N. Dorff, PhD, is rector and Sol and Anne Dorff Distinguished Professor of Philosophy at American Jewish University (formerly the University of Judaism) in Los Angeles. His book *Knowing God: Jewish Journeys to the Unknowable* (Rowman and Littlefield) includes an extensive analysis of the nature of prayer. Ordained a rabbi at The Jewish Theological Seminary of America, Dorff is vice-chair of the Conservative Movement's Committee on Jewish Law and Standards, and he contributed to the Conservative Movement's Torah commentary, *Etz Hayim*. He has chaired the Jewish Law Association, the Society of Jewish Ethics, and the Academy of Jewish Philosophy, and he is immediate past president of Jewish Family Service of Los Angeles. He has served on several federal and California government commissions on issues in bioethics. Winner of the National Jewish Book Award for *To Do the Right and the Good: A Jewish Approach to Modern Social Ethics*, he has written numerous books and more than 150 articles on Jewish thought, law, and ethics. His latest books are *The Way Into* Tikkun Olam *(Repairing the World)*, a finalist for the National Jewish Book Award; *The Jewish Approach to Repairing the World* (Tikkun Olam)*: A Brief Introduction for Christians* (both Jewish Lights); and *The Unfolding Tradition: Jewish Law After Sinai* (Aviv Press of the Rabbinical Assembly).

DAVID ELLENSON

David Ellenson, PhD, is president of Hebrew Union College–Jewish Institute of Religion. He holds the Gus Waterman Herrman Presidential Chair and is the I. H. and Anna Grancell Professor of Jewish Religious Thought. Ordained a rabbi by Hebrew Union College–Jewish Institute of Religion, he has served as a visiting professor at Hebrew University in Jerusalem, at The Jewish Theological Seminary in New York, and at the University of California at Los Angeles. Ellenson has also taught at the Pardes Institute of Jewish Studies and at the Shalom Hartman Institute, both in Jerusalem. Ellenson has published and lectured extensively on diverse topics in modern Jewish thought, history, and ethics. His book *After Emancipation* (HUC Press) won the National Jewish Book Award in the category of Modern Jewish Thought and Experience.

ELLEN FRANKEL

Dr. Ellen Frankel is editor emerita of and a consultant to The Jewish Publication Society. A scholar of Jewish folklore, Frankel has published several books, including *The Classic Tales; The Encyclopedia of Jewish Symbols,* coauthored with artist Betsy Teutsch; *The Five Books of Miriam: A Woman's Commentary on the Torah; The Jewish Spirit;* and *The Illustrated Hebrew Bible.* Frankel travels widely as a storyteller and lecturer, speaking at synagogues, summer study institutes, Hillels, Jewish women's groups, Jewish community centers, museums, schools, retirement communities, and nursing homes, and to radio audiences.

ALYSSA GRAY

Alyssa Gray, PhD, JD, is associate professor of codes and responsa literature at Hebrew Union College–Jewish Institute of Religion in New York. She has also taught at The Jewish Theological Seminary in New York. She has written on the topics of martyrdom and sexuality in rabbinic literature, as well as on talmudic redaction, talmudic *aggadah,* liturgy, and women and *tzedakah* in medieval Jewish law. Her first book, *A Talmud in Exile: The Influence of Yerushalmi Avodah Zarah on the Formation of Bavli Avodah Zarah,* was published by Brown Judaic Studies. Her current research focuses on wealth and poverty in classical rabbinic literature.

JOEL M. HOFFMAN

Dr. Joel M. Hoffman lectures around the globe on popular and scholarly topics spanning history, Hebrew, prayer, and Jewish continuity. He has served on the faculties of Brandeis University, the Academy for Jewish Religion, and Hebrew Union College–Jewish Institute of Religion in New York. Hoffman writes about Hebrew for the international *Jerusalem Post,* and is the author of *In the Beginning: A Short History of the Hebrew Language* and *And God Said: How Translations Conceal the Bible's Original Meaning.* He contributed to *My People's Passover Haggadah: Traditional Texts, Modern Commentaries* (Jewish Lights). He lives in Westchester, New York.

LAWRENCE A. HOFFMAN

Lawrence A. Hoffman, PhD, was ordained by and received his doctorate from Hebrew Union College–Jewish Institute of Religion. He has served in its New York campus for more than three decades, most recently as the Barbara and Stephen Friedman Professor of Liturgy, Worship and Ritual. Widely recognized for his scholarship and classroom teaching, Hoffman has combined research with a passion for the spiritual renewal of contemporary Judaism. He has written and edited over thirty books, including *Who by Fire, Who by Water*—Un'taneh Tokef and *All These Vows*—Kol Nidre, the first two volumes in the Prayers of Awe series; *My People's Passover Haggadah: Traditional Texts, Modern Commentaries*, in two volumes (all Jewish Lights), a finalist for the National Jewish Book Award; *The Art of Public Prayer: Not for Clergy Only* (SkyLight Paths, Jewish Lights' sister imprint), now used nationally by Jews and Christians as a handbook for liturgical planners in church and synagogue; as well as a revision of *What Is a Jew?*, the best-selling classic that remains the most widely read introduction to Judaism ever written in any language. He is also the author of *Israel—A Spiritual Travel Guide: A Companion for the Modern Jewish Pilgrim* and *The Way Into Jewish Prayer* (both Jewish Lights). Hoffman is a founder of Synagogue 2000 (now renamed Synagogue 3000), a transdenominational project designed to transform synagogues into the moral and spiritual centers of the twenty-first century. His book *Rethinking Synagogues: A New Vocabulary for Congregational Life* (Jewish Lights), an outgrowth of that project, was a finalist for the National Jewish Book Award.

LAWRENCE KUSHNER

Lawrence Kushner is the Emanu-El scholar at Congregation Emanu-El in San Francisco, an adjunct faculty member at Hebrew Union College–Jewish Institute of Religion, and a visiting professor of Jewish spirituality at the Graduate Theological Union in Berkeley, California. He served as spiritual leader of Congregation Beth El in Sudbury, Massachusetts, for twenty-eight years and is widely regarded as one of the most creative religious writers in America. Ordained a rabbi by Hebrew Union College–Jewish Institute of Religion, Kushner led his congregants in publishing their own prayer book, *V'taher Libenu* (Purify Our Hearts), the first gender-neutral liturgy ever written. Through his lectures and many books, including *Filling Words with Light: Hasidic and Mystical Reflections on Jewish Prayer* (with Nehemia Polen); *The Way Into Jewish Mystical Tradition; Invisible Lines of Connection: Sacred Stories of the Ordinary; The Book of Letters: A Mystical Hebrew Alphabet; Honey from the Rock: An Introduction to Jewish Mysticism; God Was in This Place and I, i Did Not Know: Finding Self, Spirituality, and Ultimate Meaning; Eyes Remade for Wonder: A Lawrence Kushner Reader; Jewish Spirituality: A Brief Introduction for Christians;* and *I'm God; You're Not: Observations on Organized Religion and other Disguises of the Ego*, all published by Jewish Lights, he has helped shape the Jewish community's present focus on personal and institutional spiritual renewal. He has also published a novel, *Kabbalah: A Love Story*.

DANIEL LANDES

Daniel Landes is director and Rosh HaYeshivah of the Pardes Institute of Jewish Studies in Jerusalem and was an adjunct professor of Jewish law at Loyola University Law School in Los Angeles. Ordained a rabbi by Rabbi Isaac Elchanan Theological Seminary, Landes was a founding faculty member of the Simon Wiesenthal Center and the Yeshiva of Los Angeles, and served as a judge in the Los Angeles Orthodox Beith Din. He has lectured and written various popular and scholarly articles on the subjects of Jewish thought, social ethics, and spirituality.

IVAN G. MARCUS

Ivan G. Marcus, PhD, is Frederick P. Rose Professor of Jewish History, professor of history and religious studies, and chair of the Program in Judaic Studies at Yale University. Marcus earned his bachelor's degree at Yale College, his master's degree at Columbia University, and he received his rabbinical ordination and PhD from The Jewish Theological Seminary in New York, where he taught for twenty years. His most recent book, *The Jewish Life Cycle: Rites of Passage from Biblical to Modern Times*, is based on the 1998 Samuel and Althea Stroum Lectures in Jewish Studies. He is also author of *Piety and Society: The Jewish Pietists of Medieval Germany*, a National Jewish Book Award finalist; and *Rituals of Childhood: Jewish Acculturation in Medieval Europe*. He is currently working on a translation of the medieval Hebrew classic *Sefer Hasidim* (Book of the Pietists) and writing *The Story of the Jews*, a new one-volume history.

NEHEMIA POLEN

Nehemia Polen is professor of Jewish thought and director of the Hasidic Text Institute at Boston's Hebrew College. He is the author of *The Holy Fire: The Teachings of Rabbi Kalonymus Shapira, the Rebbe of the Warsaw Ghetto* (Jason Aronson) as well as many academic and popular articles on Chasidism and Jewish spirituality, and coauthor of *Filling Words with Light: Hasidic and Mystical Reflections on Jewish Prayer* (Jewish Lights). He received his PhD from Boston University, where he studied with and served as teaching fellow for Nobel laureate Elie Wiesel. In 1994 he was Daniel Jeremy Silver Fellow at Harvard University, and he has also been a visiting scholar at the Hebrew University in Jerusalem. He was ordained a rabbi at the Ner Israel Rabbinical College in Baltimore, Maryland, and served as a congregational rabbi for twenty-three years. In 1998–1999 he was a National Endowment for the Humanities Fellow, working on the writings of Malkah Shapiro (1894–1971), the daughter of a noted Chasidic master, whose Hebrew memoirs focus on the spiritual lives of women in the context of prewar Chasidism in Poland. This work is documented in his book *The Rebbe's Daughter* (Jewish Publication Society), winner of the National Jewish Book Award.

GORDON TUCKER

Gordon Tucker is senior rabbi at Temple Israel Center in White Plains, New York, and adjunct assistant professor of Jewish philosophy at The Jewish Theological Seminary of America, where he was ordained. He also holds a PhD in philosophy from Princeton University. Tucker was dean of the Rabbinical School at The Jewish Theological Seminary from 1984 to 1992, a member of the Rabbinical Assembly Committee on Jewish Law and Standards from 1982 to 2007, and chairman of the Masorti Foundation for Conservative Judaism in Israel from 1997 to 2005. He has authored many articles on a wide range of subjects in Jewish thought, and is editor of *Heavenly Torah*, a translation of, and commentary on, Abraham Joshua Heschel's monumental work on Rabbinic theology. Tucker was also a White House Fellow in the Carter administration, during which he served in the U.S. Justice Department.

List of Abbreviations

Artscroll	*Siddur Kol Ya'akov,* 1984.
Birnbaum	*Daily Prayer Book: Hasiddur Hashalem,* 1949.
FOP	*Forms of Prayer,* 1997.
Fox	Everett Fox, *The Five Books of Moses* (New York: Schocken Books, 1995).
GOP	*Gates of Prayer,* 1975.
HS	*Ha'avodah Shebalev,* 1982.
KH	*Kol Haneshamah,* 1996.
King James	*King James Bible,* 1611/1769.
JPS	*Jewish Publication Society Bible* (Philadelphia: Jewish Publication Society, 1985).
NRSV	*New Revised Standard Bible,* 1989.
SLC	*Siddur Lev Chadash,* 1995.
SOH	*Service of the Heart,* 1967.
SSS	*Siddur Sim Shalom,* 1985; revised, 1998.
SVT	*Siddur Va'ani T'fillati,* 1998.
UPB	*Union Prayer Book,* 1894–1895.

Glossary

The following glossary presents names and Hebrew words used regularly throughout this volume and provides the way they are pronounced. Sometimes two pronunciations are common, in which case the first is the way the word is sounded in Hebrew, and the second is the way it is sometimes heard in common speech, under the influence of Yiddish, the folk language of Jews in northern and eastern Europe (a combination, mostly, of Hebrew and German). Our goal is to provide the way that many Jews actually use these words, not just the technically correct version.

- The pronunciations are divided into syllables by dashes.

- The accented syllable is written in capital letters.

- "Kh" represents a guttural sound, similar to the German (as in "sprach").

- The most common vowel is "a" as in "father," which appears here as "ah."

- The short "e" (as in "get") is written as either "e" (when it is in the middle of a syllable) or "eh" (when it ends a syllable).

- Similarly, the short "i" (as in "tin") is written as either "i" (when it is in the middle of a syllable) or "ih" (when it ends a syllable).

- A long "o" (as in Moses") is written as "oe" (as in the word "toe") or "oh" (as in the word "Oh!").

Abudarham: David ben Joseph Abudarham, fourteenth-century Spanish commentator on the liturgy. His *Sefer Abudarham* (completed in 1340) is our primary account of Spanish (Sefardi) practice of the time.

Acharonim (pronounced ah-khah-roh-NEEM or, commonly, akh-ROH-nim): The name given to Jewish legal authorities from the middle of the sixteenth century on. The word means, literally, "later ones," as opposed to the "earlier ones," authorities prior to that time who are held in higher regard and are called *Rishonim* (pronounced ree-shoh-NEEM or, commonly, ree-SHOH-nim). Singular: *Acharon* (pronounced ah-khah-ROHN) and *Rishon* (pronounced ree-SHOHN).

Alenu (pronounced ah-LAY-noo): The first word and, therefore, the title of a major prayer compiled in the second or third century as part of the New Year (Rosh Hashanah) service, but from about the fourteenth century on, used also as part of the concluding section of every daily service. *Alenu* means "it is incumbent upon us …" and introduces the prayer's theme: our duty to praise God.

Amidah (pronounced either ah-me-DAH or, commonly, ah-MEE-dah): One of three commonly used titles for the second of two central units in the worship service, the first being the *Sh'ma* and Its Blessings. It is composed of a series of blessings, many of which are petitionary, except on Sabbaths and holidays, when the petitions are removed out of deference to the holiness of the day. Also called **T'fillah** and **Sh'moneh Esreh**. *Amidah* means "standing," and refers to the fact that the prayer is said standing up.

Anim z'mirot (pronounced ah-NEEM z'-mee-ROHT): Literally, "I will sing melodies," the first words and, hence, the name of a prayer otherwise known as *Shir Hakavod*. See **Shir Hakavod**.

Arvit (pronounced ahr-VEET or, commonly, AHR-veet): From the Hebrew word *erev* (pronounced EH-rev), meaning "evening." One of two titles used for the evening worship service (also called **Ma'ariv**).

Ashkenazi (pronounced ahsh-k'-nah-ZEE or, commonly, ahsh'k'-NAH-zee): From the Hebrew word *Ashkenaz*, meaning the geographic area of northern and eastern Europe. Ashkenazi is the adjective, describing the liturgical rituals and customs practiced there, as opposed to Sefardi, meaning the liturgical rituals and customs that are derived from *Sefarad*, Spain (see **Sefardi**).

Bar'khu (pronounced bah-r'-KHOO or, commonly, BAH-r'-khoo): The first word and, therefore, the title of the formal Call to Prayer with which the section called the *Sh'ma* and Its Blessings begins. *Bar'khu* means "praise," and it introduces the invitation to the assembled congregation to praise God.

Benediction (also called a "blessing"): One of two terms used for the Rabbis' favorite prose formula for composing prayers. The worship service is composed of many different literary genres, but most of it is benedictions. Long benedictions end with a summary line that begins *Barukh atah Adonai* …, "Blessed are You, Adonai…." Short blessings have the summary line alone.

Bet Yosef (pronounced BAYT yoh-SAYF): Literally, "House of Joseph," title for sixteenth-century commentary to the *Tur*, by Joseph Caro.

Birkat (pronounced beer-KAHT): Literally, "Blessing of...." The titles of many blessings are known as "Blessing of ...," for example, "Blessing of Torah" and "Blessing of Jerusalem." Some titles are commonly shortened so that only the qualifying last words are used (such as "Jerusalem" instead of "Blessing of Jerusalem"), and they are listed in the glossary by the last words, e.g., *Y'rushalayim* instead of *Birkat Y'rushalayim* ("Jerusalem" instead of "Blessing of Jerusalem"). Those blessings that are more generally cited with the full title appear under *Birkat*.

Birkat Hashir (pronounced beer-KAHT hah-SHEER): Literally, "Blessing of song," and the title, therefore, of the final blessing to the *P'sukei D'zimrah*, the "warm-up" section to the morning service composed mainly of biblical material (chiefly psalms) that were intended to be sung as praise of God. Technically, a *Birkat Hashir* concludes any *Hallel* (see ***Hallel***), in this case, the Daily *Hallel*, which is the central component of the *P'sukei D'zimrah*.

Birkhot Hashachar (pronounced beer-KHOT hah-SHAH-khar): Literally, "Morning Blessings," the title of the first large section in the morning prayer regimen of Judaism; originally said privately upon arising in the morning, but now customarily recited immediately upon arriving at the synagogue. It is composed primarily of benedictions thanking God for the everyday gifts of health and wholeness, as well as study sections taken from the Bible and rabbinic literature.

B'rakhah (pronounced b'-rah-KHAH): The Hebrew word for "benediction" or "blessing." See ***Benediction***. Plural ("benedictions") is *b'rakhot* (pronounced b'-rah-KHOT).

Chasidei Ashkenaz (pronounced khah-see-DAY ahsh-k'-NAHZ or, commonly, khah-SEE-day AHSH-k'-nahz): Literally, "The pious of Germany," a loosely knit philosophical school of thought from twelfth- to thirteenth-century Germany that pioneered a mystical understanding of the liturgy and emphasized an ascetic way of life and a negative view of humanity. See ***Kavod***.

Chasidic: Pertaining to Chasidism, as "a chasidic custom, or interpretation." See ***Chasidism***.

Chasidism (pronounced KHAH-sih-dizm): The doctrine generally traced to an eighteenth-century Polish Jewish mystic and spiritual leader known as the Ba'al Shem Tov (called also the BeSHT, an acronym composed of the initials of his name B, SH, and T). Followers are called *Chasidim* (pronounced khah-see-DEEM or khah-SIH-dim; singular, *Chasid*, pronounced khah-SEED or, commonly, KHA-sid), from the Hebrew word *chesed* (pronounced KHEH-sed), meaning "loving-kindness" or "piety."

Chatimah (pronounced khah-tee-MAH): The final summary line of a benediction (see ***Benediction***).

Chazarat hashats (pronounced khah-zah-RAHT hah-SHATS): Repetition of the *Amidah* by the prayer leader.

Daily Hallel (pronounced hah-LAYL or, commonly, HAH-layl): English for *Hallel Sheb'khol Yom*. See ***Hallel***.

D'ora'ita (pronounced d'-oh-RYE-tah): Aramaic for "from Torah," a category of mitzvah said to spring directly from the Torah, rather than by rabbinic fiat (see its opposite, ***D'rabbanan***).

D'rabbanan (pronounced d'-rah-bah-NAHN): Aramaic for "from our Rabbis," a category of mitzvah said to spring from rabbinic fiat, rather than directly from the Torah (see its opposite, ***d'ora'ita***).

Ein Keloheinu (pronounced ayn kay-loh-HAY-noo): Literally, "There is none like our God," a concluding prayer of the *Musaf* service.

El Adon (pronounced ayl ah-DOHN): An early medieval (or, perhaps, ancient) poem celebrating God as a king enthroned on high; it is arranged as an acrostic, that is, each line begins with a different letter of the alphabet. Nowadays, *El Adon* is a popular Sabbath morning hymn.

Gaon (pronounced gah-OHN; plural: *Geonim*, pronounced g'-oh-NEEM): Title for the leading Rabbis in Babylon (present-day Iraq) from about 750 to 1038. From a biblical word meaning "glory," which is equivalent in the title to saying "Your Excellence."

Genizah (pronounced g'-NEE-zah): A cache of documents, in particular the one discovered at the turn of the twentieth century in an old synagogue in Cairo; the source of our knowledge about how Jews prayed in the Land of Israel and vicinity prior to the twelfth century. From a word meaning "to store or hide away," "to archive."

Geonim: See ***Gaon***.

Gra (pronounced GRAH): Acronym for the *Gaon Rabbi Eliyah* (Eliyahu begins with an *alef*; hence the final "a" in the acronym), the Vilna Gaon, Elijah of Vilna, 1730–1797.

Haftarah (pronounced hahf-tah-RAH or, commonly, hahf-TOE-rah): The section of Scripture taken from the prophets and read publicly as part of Shabbat and holiday worship services. From a word meaning "to conclude," because it is the "concluding reading," that is, it follows a reading from the Torah (the Five Books of Moses).

Halakhah (pronounced hah-lah-KHAH or, commonly, hah-LAH-khah): The Hebrew word for "Jewish law." Also used as an anglicized adjective, halakhic (pronounced hah-LAH-khic), meaning "legal." From the Hebrew word meaning "to walk" or "to go," denoting the way in which a person should walk through life.

Hallel (pronounced hah-LAYL or, commonly, HAH-layl): A Hebrew word meaning "praise" and, by extension, the name given to sets of psalms that are recited liturgically in praise of God: Psalms 145–150, the Daily *Hallel*, are recited each morning; Psalm 136, the Great *Hallel*, is recited on Shabbat and holidays and is part of the Passover Seder. Psalms 113–118, the best-known *Hallel*, known more fully as the Egyptian *Hallel*, are recited on holidays and get their name from Psalm 114:1, which celebrates the moment "when Israel left Egypt."

Hallel Hagadol (pronounced hah-LAYL [or, commonly, HAH-layl] hah-gah-DOHL): Literally, "the Great *Hallel*." *Hallel* derives from the Hebrew word for "praise" and, by extension, comes to mean sets of psalms (or, sometimes, individual psalms) recited liturgically in praise of God. One particular *Hallel*, Psalm 136, called the Great *Hallel*, is recited in the synagogue on Shabbat and holidays, and at home as part of the Passover Seder.

Hat'fillah (pronounced hah-t'-fee-LAH): Literally, "the *T'fillah*," another name for the *Amidah*. See *T'fillah*.

Hoeche K'dushah (pronounced HAY-kh' k'-DOO-shah): A Yiddish term combining German and Hebrew and meaning, literally, "the High *K'dushah*." Refers to a way to shorten the time it takes to say the *Amidah* by avoiding the necessity of having the prayer leader repeat it all after it is said silently by the congregation.

Inclusio (pronounced in-CLOO-zee-oh): A rhetorical style common to biblical prayer, whereby the end of a composition reiterates the theme or words with which the composition began.

Kabbalah (pronounced kah-bah-LAH or, commonly, kah-BAH-lah): A general term for Jewish mysticism, but used properly for a specific mystical doctrine that began in western Europe in the eleventh or twelfth century; recorded in the *Zohar* (see *Zohar*) in the thirteenth century, and then further elaborated, especially in the Land of Israel (in Safed), in the sixteenth century. From a Hebrew word meaning "to receive" or "to welcome," and secondarily, "tradition," implying the receiving of tradition from one's past.

Kaddish (pronounced kah-DEESH or, more commonly, KAH-dish): One of several prayers from a Hebrew word meaning "holy," and therefore the name given to a prayer affirming God's holiness. This prayer was composed in the first century but later found its way into the service in several forms, including one known as the Mourner's *Kaddish.*

Kavod (pronounced kah-VOHD): Literally, "glory," but used philosophically and liturgically by the German pietists (see ***Chasidei Ashkenaz***) to refer to the manifest aspect of God, as opposed to the unknown and unknowable divine essence.

Kavvanah (pronounced kah-vah-NAH): From a word meaning "to direct," and therefore used technically to denote the state of directing one's words and thoughts sincerely to God, as opposed to the rote recitation of prayer.

K'dushah (pronounced k'-doo-SHAH or, commonly, k'-DOO-shah): From the Hebrew word meaning "holy," and therefore one of several prayers from the first or second century occurring in several places and versions, all of which have in common the citing of Isaiah 6:3—*Kadosh, kadosh, kadosh* …, "Holy, holy, holy is the Lord of hosts. The whole earth is full of his glory."

K'dushat Hashem (pronounced k'-doo-SHAHT hah-SHEM): Literally, "sanctification of the name [of God]," and the full name for the prayer that is generally called *K'dushah* (see ***K'dushah***). Best known as the third blessing in the *Amidah,* but found also prior to the morning *Sh'ma.* Used also in variant form *kiddush hashem* (pronounced kee-DOOSH hah-SHEM) as a term to describe dying for the sanctification of God's name, that is, martyrdom.

K'dushat Hayom (pronounced k'-doo-SHAHT hah-YOHM): Literally, "the holiness of the day," hence, the technical name of prayers that express the presence of a sacred day (Shabbat or holidays). There are three instances: the *Kiddush* that inaugurates the day either at the dinner table or at the opening evening *(Ma'ariv)* service; the fourth benediction of the Shabbat or holiday *Amidah*; and the final benediction after the *Haftarah* is recited.

K'dushta (pronounced k'-doosh-TAH or, commonly, k'-DOOSH-tah): The most famous genre of liturgical poem in antiquity. It had nine parts inserted throughout the first three blessings of the Shabbat or holiday *Amidah*; the last seven were placed within the third benediction, the *K'dushat Hashem,* allowing the poem to reach its climax there.

Korbanot (pronounced kohr-bah-NOHT; singular: *korban,* pronounced kohr-BAHN): Literally, "sacrifices," but used liturgically to denote passages from Torah and rabbinic literature that explain how sacrifices are to be offered. These are inserted especially in the *Birkhot Hashachar* and the *Musaf* service.

Ma'amad (pronounced mah-ah-MAHD): From the root "to stand," and designating a geographically representative group of laypeople who accompanied their priestly representatives to Jerusalem (see ***Mishmar***) when their turn came to oversee the public sacrifice; a parallel *ma'amad* group is described as remaining home and meeting liturgically at the time.

Ma'ariv (pronounced mah-ah-REEV or, commonly, MAH-ah-reev): From the Hebrew word *erev* (pronounced EH-rev), meaning "evening"; one of two titles used for the evening worship service (also called ***Arvit***).

Machzor Vitry (pronounced mahkh-ZOHR veet-REE or, commonly, MAHKH-zohr VEET-ree): Literally, the *machzor* (prayer book containing the annual cycle of liturgy) from Vitry (in France). The most significant early French commentary to the liturgy, composed in the tenth and/or eleventh century, primarily by Simchah of Vitry, a student of *Rashi*.

Maimonides, Moses (known also as *Rambam*, pronounced RAHM-bahm): Most important Jewish philosopher of all time; also a physician and very significant legal authority. Born in Spain, he moved to Egypt where he lived most of his life (1135–1204).

Merkavah (pronounced mehr-kah-VAH, but, commonly, mehr-KAH-vah): Literally "chariot"; hence, the name of a school of Jewish mysticism that pictured God seated in a throne-like chariot, surrounded by angels reciting, "Holy, holy, holy."

Mid'ora'ita (pronounced mee-d'-oh-RYE-tah): Strictly speaking, commandments derived directly from Torah, which are of a higher order than those rooted only in rabbinic ordinance (called ***mid'rabbanan***), but all are binding.

Mid'rabbanan (pronounced mee-d'-rah-bah-NAHN): Commandments rooted only in rabbinic ordinance. See ***Mid'ora'ita***.

Midrash (pronounced meed-RAHSH or, commonly, MID-rahsh): From a Hebrew word meaning "to ferret out the meaning of a text," and therefore a rabbinic interpretation of a biblical word or verse. By extension, a body of rabbinic literature that offers classical interpretations of the Bible.

Minchah (pronounced meen-KHAH or, more commonly, MIN-khah): Originally the name of a type of sacrifice, then the word for a sacrifice offered during the afternoon, and now the name for the afternoon synagogue service usually scheduled just before nightfall. *Minchah* means "afternoon."

Minhag (pronounced meen-HAHG or, commonly, MIN-hahg): The Hebrew word for custom and, therefore, used liturgically to describe the customary way that different groups of Jews pray. By extension, *minhag* means a "rite," as in *Minhag Ashkenaz*, meaning "the rite of prayer, or the customary way of prayer for Jews in *Ashkenaz*"— that is, northern and eastern Europe.

Mishmar (pronounced mish-MAHR): In Temple times, the population of the Land of Israel is said to have been divided into regions, each of which sent priests *(kohanim)* for roughly two weeks a year, to take a turn overseeing the Temple sacrifices. Each such geographically representative group was called a *mishmar* (from the root *sh.m.r*, "to watch over").

Mishnah (pronounced mish-NAH or, commonly, MISH-nah): The name of the definitive six-volume statement of Jewish law from the Land of Israel, c. 200 C.E., that culminates the era called tannaitic (after the title we give the Rabbis to that point; see **Tanna**, **Tannaim**). But equally, the name applied to any particular teaching in that statement, for which the plural, *mishnayot* (pronounced mish-nah-YOHT), exists also (more than one such teaching).

Mitzvah (pronounced meetz-VAH or, commonly, MITZ-vah; plural: *mitzvot*, pronounced meetz-VOTE): A Hebrew word used commonly to mean "good deed," but in the more technical sense, denoting any commandment from God and therefore, by extension, what God wants us to do. Reciting the *Sh'ma* morning and evening, for instance, is a *mitzvah*.

Musaf (pronounced moo-SAHF or, commonly, MOO-sahf): The Hebrew word meaning "extra" or "added," and, therefore, the title of the additional sacrifice that was offered in the Temple on Shabbat and holy days. It is now the name given to an additional service of worship appended to the morning service on those days.

Nishmat kol cha'i (pronounced neesh-MAHT kohl KHA'i): A blessing mentioned in the Talmud as one of two benedictions in use as the *Birkat Hashir* (see **Birkat Hashir**), the blessing that ends a psalm collection known as *Hallel* (see **Hallel**). Nowadays we use it (1) as part of a longer *Birkat Hashir*, after the Daily *Hallel*, that constitutes the central section of the *P'sukei D'zimrah* (see **P'sukei D'zimrah**) for Sabbaths and festivals; and (2) to conclude a similar *Hallel* in the Passover Haggadah.

Olah (pronounced oh-LAH): From the Hebrew word meaning "to go up," and, hence, the Temple offering consisting of an animal wholly offered up to God, because it was entirely consumed by sacrificial fire.

Olam haba (pronounced oh-LAHM hah-BAH, but, popularly, OH-lahm hah-BAH): Literally, "the world-to-come," a term for one of the three most common eschatological promises of rabbinic Judaism. The others are *Y'mot hamashi'ach* (pronounced y'MOHT hah-mah-SHEE-ahkh), "messianic days" (that is, the era after the coming of the messiah); and *T'chi'at hametim* (pronounced t'chee-YAHT hah-may-TEEM), "the resurrection of the dead."

Piyyut (pronounced pee-YOOT; plural: *piyyutim*, pronounced pee-yoo-TEEM): Literally, "a poem," but used technically to mean liturgical poems composed in classical and medieval times and inserted into the standard prayers on special occasions.

P'sukei D'zimrah (pronounced p'-soo-KAY d'-zim-RAH or, commonly, p'-SOO-kay d'-ZIM-rah): Literally, "verses of song," and therefore the title of a lengthy set of opening morning prayers that contain psalms and songs and serve as spiritual preparation prior to the official Call to Prayer.

Rashi (pronounced RAH-shee): Acronym for *Rabbi Shlomo* [Solomon] ben *Isaac*, French commentator on Bible and Talmud, 1040–1105; founder of school of Jewish thought and custom, whence various liturgical works came into being, among them *Machzor Vitry* and *Siddur Rashi*.

Rishonim (pronounced ree-shoh-NEEM, but popularly, ree-SHOH-nim): The name given to Jewish legal authorities from the completion of the Talmud to the middle of the sixteenth century. The word means, literally, "earlier ones," as opposed to the "later ones," authorities after that time who are held in lower regard and are called *Acharonim* (pronounced ah-khah-roh-NEEM or, commonly, akh-ROH-nim). Singular: *Rishon* (pronounced ree-SHOHN) and *Acharon* (pronounced ah-khah-ROHN).

R'ma (pronounced r'-MAH): An acronym for Rabbi Moses Isserles, sixteenth-century Poland, chief Ashkenazi commentator on the *Shulchan Arukh*, the sixteenth-century Sefardi code by Joseph Caro.

Rosh (pronounced ROHSH): The Rosh (1250–1328), otherwise known as Rabbeinu Asher, or Asher ben Yechiel, was a significant halakhic authority, first in Germany and later in Spain. His son, Jacob ben Asher, codified many of his father's views alongside his own in his influential law code, the *Tur*.

Rosh Chodesh (pronounced rohsh KHOH-desh): Literally, "the head of the month," and therefore the Hebrew name for the one- or two-day New Moon period with which lunar months begin. It is marked as a holiday in Jewish tradition, a period of new beginnings.

Rubric (pronounced ROO-brick): A technical term for any discrete section of liturgy, whether a prayer or a set of prayers. The *Sh'ma* and Its Blessings is one of several large rubrics in the service; within that large rubric, the *Sh'ma* or any one of its accompanying blessings may be called a rubric as well.

Seder Rav Amram (pronounced SAY-dehr rahv AHM-rahm): First known comprehensive Jewish prayer book, emanating from Rav Amram Gaon (c. 860 C.E.), a leading Jewish scholar and head of Sura, a famed academy in Babylonia (modern-day Iraq).

Sefardi (pronounced s'-fahr-DEE or, commonly, s'-FAHR-dee): From the Hebrew word *Safarad* (pronounced s'-fah-RAHD), meaning the geographic area of modern-day Spain and Portugal. Sefardi is the adjective, describing the liturgical rituals and customs that are derived from *Sefarad* prior to the expulsion of Jews from there at the end of the fifteenth century, as opposed to Ashkenazi (see *Ashkenazi*), meaning the liturgical rituals and customs common to northern and eastern Europe. Nowadays Sefardi refers also to the customs of Jews from North Africa and Arab lands, whose ancestors came from Spain.

Septuagint (pronounced sehp-TOO-a jint): Latin for "seventy," reflecting the myth that King Ptolemy of Egypt asked seventy-two Jews to translate the Torah into Greek; refers, therefore, to the first Greek translation of the Bible, begun (probably) in the third century B.C.E. The original Septuagint included only the Torah, but now we use the term to include also translations of other biblical books that were added to it.

Shabbat (pronounced shah-BAHT): The Hebrew word for "Sabbath," from a word meaning "to rest."

Shacharit (pronounced shah-khah-REET or, commonly, SHAH-khah-reet): The name given to the morning worship service; from the Hebrew word *shachar* (SHAH-khar), meaning "morning."

Sh'chitah (pronounced sh'-khee-TAH or, commonly sh'-KHEE-tah): Ritual slaughter, which requires a prior blessing affirming the commandment to slaughter animals only in a prescribed way.

Shir Hakavod (pronounced SHEER hah-kah-VOHD): Literally, "song of glory," a medieval Ashkenaz prayer reflecting the mystical doctrine of German pietists in the twelfth and thirteenth centuries, now used to conclude the *Musaf* service.

Sh'liach tsibbur (pronounced sh'-LEE-ahkh tsee-BOOR): Literally, the "agent of the congregation" and, therefore, the name given to the person who leads the prayer service.

Sh'ma (pronounced sh'-MAH): The central prayer in the first of the two main units in the worship service, the second being the *Amidah* (see *Amidah*). The *Sh'ma* comprises three citations from the Bible, and the larger unit in which it is embedded (called the *Sh'ma* and Its Blessings) is composed of a formal Call to Prayer (see *Bar'khu*) and a series of blessings on the theological themes that, together with the *Sh'ma*, constitute a liturgical creed of faith. *Sh'ma*, meaning "hear," is the first word of the first line of the first biblical citation, "Hear O Israel: Adonai is our God; Adonai is One," which is the paradigmatic statement of Jewish faith, the Jews' absolute commitment to the presence of a single and unique God in time and space.

Sh'moneh Esreh (pronounced sh'-moh-NEH ehs-RAY): A Hebrew word meaning "eighteen" and, therefore, a name given to the second of the two main units in the worship service that once had eighteen benedictions in it (it now has nineteen), known also as the *Amidah* (see **Amidah**).

Shulchan Arukh (pronounced shool-KHAN ah-ROOKH or, commonly, SHOOL-khan AH-rookh): The name given to the best-known code of Jewish law, compiled by Joseph Caro in the Land of Israel and published in 1565. *Shulchan Arukh* means "The Set Table" and refers to the ease with which the various laws are set forth—like a table prepared with food ready for consumption.

Siddur (pronounced see-DOOR or, commonly, SIH-d'r): From the Hebrew word *seder*, meaning "order," and therefore, by extension, the name given to the "order of prayers," or prayer book.

Siluk (pronounced see-LOOK or, commonly, SEE-look): The climactic and final part of the genre of liturgical poem known as *K'dushta* (see **K'dushta**), occurring in the *K'dushat Hashem*, the third benediction of the *Amidah*.

Song of Glory: See **Shir Hakavod**.

Tachanun (pronounced TAH-khah-noon): A Hebrew word meaning "supplications" and, by extension, the title of the large unit of prayer that follows the *Amidah*, which is largely supplicatory in character.

Talmud (pronounced tahl-MOOD or, more commonly, TAHL-m'd): The name given to each of two great compendia of Jewish law and lore compiled over several centuries and, ever since, the literary core of the rabbinic heritage. The Talmud Yerushalmi (pronounced y'-roo-SHAHL-mee), the "Jerusalem Talmud," is earlier, a product of the Land of Israel generally dated about 400 C.E. The better-known Talmud Bavli (pronounced BAHV-lee), or "Babylonian Talmud," took shape in Babylonia (present-day Iraq) and is traditionally dated about 550 C.E. When people say "the" Talmud without specifying which one they mean, they are referring to the Babylonian version. Talmud means "teaching."

Tamid (pronounced tah-MEED): From the Hebrew *tamid* meaning "always, regular"; hence, the "regular sacrifice" offered daily in the Temple, both morning and afternoon.

Tanna (pronounced TAH-nah): The title of authorities in the time of the Mishnah, that is, prior to the third century. Plural: *Tannaim* (pronounced tah-nah-EEM or, commonly, tah-NAH-yim).

T'chi'at hametim (pronounced t'chee-YAHT hah-may-TEEM): Literally, "the resurrection of the dead," a term for one of the three most common eschatological promises of rabbinic Judaism. The others are *Olam haba* (pronounced oh-LAHM hah-BAH, but, popularly, OH-lahm hah-BAH), "the world-to-come," and *Y'mot hamashi'ach* (pronounced y'MOHT hah-mah-SHEE-ahkh), "messianic days" (that is, the era after the coming of the messiah).

T'fillah (pronounced t'-fee-LAH or, commonly, t'-FEE-lah): A Hebrew word meaning "prayer" but used technically to mean a specific prayer, namely, the second of the two main units in the worship service. It is known also as the *Amidah* or the *Sh'moneh Esreh* (see **Amidah**). Also the title of the sixteenth blessing of the *Amidah*, a petition for God to accept our prayer.

Tosafot (pronounced toh-sah-FOHT or, popularly, TOH-sah-foht): Literally, "additional," referring to "additional" twelfth- to fourteenth-century Franco-German halakhists and commentators, the spiritual (and, to some extent, even familial) descendants of the French commentator *Rashi* (1040–1105).

Tur (pronounced TOOR): The shorthand title applied to a fourteenth-century code of Jewish law, compiled by Jacob ben Asher in Spain, and the source for much of our knowledge about medieval liturgical practice. *Tur* means "row" or "column." The full name of the code is *Arba'ah Turim* (pronounced ahr-bah-AH too-REEM), "The Four Rows," with each row (or *Tur*) being a separate section of law on a given broad tppic.

Un'taneh Tokef (pronounced oo-n'-TAH-neh TOH-kehf): A *piyyut* (liturgical poem) for the High Holy Days emphasizing the awesome nature of these days when we stand before God for judgment; but originally, the ninth part (see **Siluk**) of a longer poem for the *Amidah* called *K'dushta* (see **K'dushta**). Although widely connected with a legend of Jewish martyrdom in medieval Germany, the poem more likely derives from a Byzantine poet, circa sixth century. It is known for its conclusion: "Penitence, prayer, and charity avert a bad decree."

Vay'khulu (pronounced vah-y'-KHOO-loo): Literally, "they were finished," the beginning of Genesis 2:1–2, announcing the end of creation; hence, the introductory paragraph of the Friday evening *Kiddush*, and part of the Friday *Ma'ariv K'dushat Hayom* ("Sanctification of the Day," the all-important middle benediction in the Shabbat *Amidah*). See **K'dushat Hayom**.

YHVH: The ineffable (so, unpronounceable) four-letter name of God, referred to in English as "the tetragrammaton," and traditionally pronounced *Adonai*.

Yichud (pronounced yee-KHOOD): Literally, "unification"; in kabbalistic worship, prayers have esoteric significance, generally the unification of the letters that make up God's name, but standing also for the conjoining of God's masculine and feminine aspects and, deeper still, the coming together of the shattered universe in which we live.

Used also for the seclusion and (in late antiquity and into the Middle Ages) the actual physical union of a married couple at the end of their wedding service.

Yishtabach (pronounced yish-tah-BAKH): The first word and, therefore, the title of the blessing used as the *Birkat Hashir* for weekdays (see **Birkat Hashir**). On Sabbaths and festivals, it is expanded by the addition of *Nishmat kol cha'i* (pronounced neesh-MAHT kohl KHA'i), a blessing mentioned in the Talmud (see **Nishmat kol cha'i**).

Yom tov (pronounced yohm-TOHV): Literally, "good day," hence "festival, holiday."

Yotser (pronounced yoh-TSAYR or, commonly, YOH-tsayr): The Hebrew word meaning "creator" and, by extension, the title of the first blessing in the *Sh'ma* and Its Blessings, which is on the theme of God's creation of the universe.

Zohar (pronounced ZOH-hahr): A shorthand title for *Sefer Hazohar* (pronounced SAY-fer hah-ZOH-hahr), literally, "The Book of Splendor," which is the primary compendium of mystical thought in Judaism; written mostly by Moses de Leon in Spain near the end of the thirteenth century and, ever since, the chief source for the study of Kabbalah (see **Kabbalah**).

Notes

Notes

Notes

Notes

Notes

CPSIA information can be obtained
at www.ICGtesting.com
Printed in the USA
BVOW09s1218190417
481707BV00011B/372/P